Always Going Home

Always Going Home

Lauris and Frances Edmond:
A mother and daughter story

FRANCES EDMOND

OTAGO UNIVERSITY PRESS
Te Whare Tā o Te Wānanga o Ōtākou

For Fiona Kidman and Peter Wills

For the loving support and stories of my sisters
Stephanie and Katherine

For all my dear friends who have kept me going through
the writing process – you know who you are!

Contents

Preface

This is my personal narrative of my mother, poet Lauris Edmond. The idea for this book arose after Sue Fitchett and I edited *Night Burns with a White Fire: The essential Lauris Edmond*, which was published in 2017. Having collected the best of my mother's work, I found myself wanting to explore further the sources of her writing. And when in conversation with publisher Roger Steele I found myself remarking on who or what had prompted particular poems, he suggested that if I knew these things, I should write them down.

I had earlier declined a proposal to write a literary biography, as such a scholarly task felt beyond me. This suggestion, however, was different. More within my grasp. For the next six months I talked about it a lot, great enthusiasm overlaying trepidation. I consulted those of Lauris's literary friends and colleagues with whom I am in regular contact (especially Fiona Kidman, Fleur Adcock, Vincent O'Sullivan, Harry Ricketts, Riemke Ensing and Michael Harlow); her former publishers, Anne French and Elizabeth Caffin; and her friend Lynne Dovey, who had the unhappy experience of arriving for dinner with Lauris only to discover she had died. All endorsed the idea of some sort of personal biography.

Over the next few years I thought about Mum, visited the places we had lived as a family, made copious notes, sorted through

the letters she wrote me and those I'd written to her, which were
returned to me after her death. I went through her archive at the
Alexander Turnbull Library, and read the diaries of hers that are in
my possession.

But since Lauris had already written an autobiography (in three
volumes), and my brother, Martin, had written our father's story
and delved into family history in a number of his other books, what
could there possibly be left to say? Quite a lot, I came to realise. As
a frequent sounding board for Lauris throughout my adulthood, I
am privy to a lot about her life that has never been aired. There's
the obvious business of who she slept with, when and where, and
all that 'who said what about whom' kind of stuff. I also know
something about the wounds Lauris carried, and about her inability
to manage, or even greatly influence, the shifting tides of grief
and resentment within the Edmond family. Mum poured out her
troubles to me over the disintegration of her marriage and various
relationship breakdowns with my siblings.

As my mother's sole literary executor, there is much about her
writing career that only I know. I regularly gave her feedback, and
we collaborated not infrequently, from when I graduated from Toi
Whakaari/New Zealand Drama School in 1975 until her death in
2000. I performed her work, both live and on radio, with her and on
my own. She wrote a play for me. After her death, I put together the
text of her final book of poems, *Late Song*, as well as co-editing the
posthumous 'best of' already mentioned.

What I concluded I could do was tell a story – my story – of the
interweavings, the connections between my mother and me, the
journey of our lives and where they intersected. In her own work,
Mum omitted mention of a number of problematic aspects of her
marriage and family life in order to preserve/protect; I do not believe
such silence is any longer necessary. In this sense, I acknowledge that
I am writing not only about her, but also about family, friends and
colleagues in relation to her. This book takes a more intimate look at

some areas of Lauris's inner/private life than her autobiography or my brother Martin's writings about the family. I am a repository of sometimes uncomfortable insider knowledge, and there are stories I feel need telling.

I did not see any point in retelling the chronological story – that's been done. Rather, I have written chapters around her life experience and her interests, introducing poems associated with those times. The book is written in three parts. 'Origins' is about grandmothering, childhood, a bit of family history. 'Moving On' looks at the major crises in Lauris's life, her emergence as a writer and the themes and ideas that engrossed her. 'Realisation' looks at Lauris's life as she developed as a significant writer.

My first source for this account is memory. Then conversations with friends and colleagues and those who knew and loved Lauris. Her archive in the Alexander Turnbull Library unveiled many things I did not know or only half knew.

I found, in the writing process, that the personal story of my mother and myself, within the wider family context, refused to stay in the background. I succumbed, allowing it in, which changed the nature of the task I had embarked on, making it more intimate and personal. When I reread our correspondence and her diaries I realised I had a goldmine: between them, they comprehensively revealed her inner self, her personal processes, as well as unfolding the relationship between us – its blessings and its complications. I have thus reproduced here a lot of verbatim text.

Lauris is, to me, first and foremost, my mother. In the years I lived at home with her she wasn't a writer; her first book was published when I was in my mid-twenties. I cannot see her as a writer distinct from that relationship; she is always, and inescapably, my mother, who became a writer. My view of her writing is thus filtered through daughterly attitudes and perspectives, affected by the pleasures of the genuine intimacy and affection we shared, but also by the difficult times, the resentments and complications, the times we fell out.

It is, and has always been, a relatively uncomplicated process for me to admire Lauris for her skill as a writer, to love and respect the works she created, to honour her for them and them for her, even through, and despite, the ups and downs of our personal relationship. Her words speak to me, shape my experience, my view of the world; I would be infinitely poorer without them.

This, then, is a daughter writing about her beloved, complicated, difficult, compelling, impossible but greatly admired mother.

Editorial note

All unattributed quotes come from Lauris's diaries, letters, emails, conversations.

Acknowledgements

Many people have helped me pull this book together and I am grateful to them all. Sue Fitchett, my first reader and kaitiaki of the book, who has been unfailingly staunch and supportive. Fiona Kidman and Fleur Adcock, who were wonderful and engaging life-long friends to Lauris and now me. My oldest friend, Claudia, who came all the way from England for three months and whose help let me finish the book. Vincent O'Sullivan and Harry Ricketts, who gave over time to let me interview them. Anne French, Michael Harlow, Doug Anderson and Lauris's cousin, Val Powel, who gave invaluable first-hand information. Thanks to Riemke Ensing for conversations about Lauris, Dee O'Connor for memories and stories and my immediate Edmond whānau, especially my cousin Murray Edmond, for input and support. Thanks also to Christina Milligan, who gave feedback on early versions of some chapters. Creative New Zealand gave me a generous research grant and Audrey Waugh (now Stratford) at the Turnbull Library was thorough and unfailingly generous with her time and knowledge. Robert Cross, Stephen McCurdy, Stephanie McKee, Tim Steele, Jane Taylor and Max Oettli kindly provided photographs. The very dedicated Elizabeth Alley provided me with taped interviews she'd done with Lauris for National Radio. Jane Warren did a wonderful job editing the final draft. Thanks also to my publisher, Sue Wootton, who has been a dream to work with, along with the staff at Otago University Press, and copy editor, Rachel Scott, for their sterling work. Most of all, thanks to my partner, Peter, who has stood by me, tended to my needs, sourced and sorted the photographs and ensured this is the best book it could be.

PART I
Origins

1. Somewhere you are always going home

Somewhere you are always going home;
some shred of the rag of events
is forever being torn off and kept

Lauris was born in Dannevirke, in 1924, to Fanny and Lewis Scott, both the children of assisted immigrants who arrived from England in the late nineteenth century. Fanny had trained as a teacher, and Lewis acquired a variety of skills running small businesses. After a few peripatetic years, they moved to the Bay of Plenty, settling in a house owned by Lewis's parents in Osier Road, Greenmeadows, southwest of Napier. Lewis joined the family business of painting and paperhanging.

Osier Road was Lauris's first home, the house of her childhood, the house from which she left to embark on her adult life. From 'At Greenmeadows':

Old roads have a life they cannot lose
though every house that some time
toed their line is carried off
by progress or decay.

It is an evocative opening to a poem in which Lauris relishes childhood's 'confident innocence' and tricks of memory. Greenmeadows was rural in those days, the Osier Road house 'across the road from the Convent'.[1] Next to the house was a paddock where she played in the long grass and wrote childish poems and plays, and where Lewis sometimes grew vegetables to sell at the market. I have been unable to locate the house.[2] From 'Discovery':

> Home is where your life
> holds you in its hand and, when
> it is ready, puts you quietly down.

The first part of Lauris's adult life – or what she sometimes called 'life number one' – was as wife and mother, bringing up six children in small towns in the North Island of New Zealand, wherever Trevor – her husband, my father – worked as a high school teacher.

Even when she moved on from the immediacy of mothering and into the world of writing, family remained central to Lauris's being – her way of living. There are many poems dedicated to and/or about her children, her grandchildren, her family – the 'home' world she inhabited and loved, and that sustained her.

'The Names' is a much-loved and often-quoted hymn to her family. It's an early poem and one of the few that explicitly names us all; we are identified and listed sequentially, eldest to youngest:

> Your names have still their old power,
> they sing softly like voices across water.
> Virginia Frances Martin Rachel Stephanie
> Katherine – the sounds blend and chant
> in some closed chamber of the ear ...

From *Salt from the North*, Lauris's third collection, it's early enough in her career for the question of the appropriateness of using her children in her work not to have surfaced, for family attitudes to still be relatively neutral. As an evocation of motherhood, of maternal devotion, I find it sublime:

> the names will never leave me, I hear
> them calling like boatmen far over
> the harbour at first light. They will sound
> in the dreams of your children's children.

As well as writing about her children and grandchildren, she went back to her own childhood and to her life as a young woman and her experience of childbirth in 'Two Birth Poems: 1. A Shift of Emphasis; 2. Zero Population Growth':

> 1.
> Cradled in the world's lap lies instead
> a tiny grey-faced rag of flesh
> with a cry as thin as muslin,
> and all the power to possess the earth
> curled up behind the blindness of its eyes.
>
> 2.
> Later I noticed a small sardonic smile
> on the curtain, having a swing;
> it chirped 'You've done it.
> You clever thing.'

These are Ohakune poems, Burns Street poems, from her first collection, *In Middle Air*. Lauris and Trevor moved to Ohakune ('Kune, as we called it) in 1948 when my older sister, Virginia, was a baby; the remaining five of us were born there. In those days, once in labour, a woman went to hospital (in Lauris's case Raetihi). She was washed, given a pubic shave and, once the contractions had reached the critical stage – the cervix fully dilated, the baby head's crowning (the hard work, the painful bit) – she was sedated.[3] For the delivery of her first four children, this was Lauris's experience. After each birth, the baby was taken to the hygienic safety of the hospital nursery and the new mother confined to bed, required to rest after her ordeal – for up to 10 days. She was permitted to see her baby only at the designated four-hourly feeding times.

The revelation of actual childbirth came for Lauris with the arrival of her fifth child, who was born so precipitately there was no time for proper procedures. If Stephanie hadn't so spectacularly broken the rules, Lauris would not have had the ecstatic experience of the moment of birth, nor would there be these two delightful birth poems.

'Piano Practice' is another poem for the baby who rushed into the world in defiance of medical protocol:

> Child, creature, little anxious girl,
> your whole body frowns,
> your clambering hands
> grapple mountains. The rocky crotchets mass
> above you, and suspense hangs
> on quavering slopes
> past the next hard turning.

We all learned the piano, we girls, as part of 'female accomplishment'. It was a Scott family tradition; Lauris and her sister Lindsay both started at the age of seven, across the road at St Joseph's Convent. Lauris played rather well. My strongest memories of her playing are the Sunday night ritual of 'frog jumps'– a series of children's songs – Dad and us kids in a circle performing the actions (walking, jumping, rabbit hops, frog jumps).[4]

With an expanding family, it would have been miraculous if Lauris had found time to play, let alone practise the piano. What little time she did manage to hoard for herself was undoubtedly spent on writing, but it wasn't until I was in my second year at drama school that *In Middle Air* was published. It was 1975 and Lauris was 51. I was in Wellington, working as an actor, and as Lauris was travelling overseas at the time, I organised a lunchtime reading of her work at Circa Theatre – our first collaboration. I was thrilled by this opportunity to integrate my mother, the poet, into my own working life. This was a thing I, and no one else, could do.

Despite my associations with her work being intimate from the beginning, there was a day when I realised – in a sudden flowering of hurt and neglect – that while she had written poems for many of my siblings, Lauris had not written one for me. I was visiting her at Grass Street in Wellington when I broached the subject with what I hoped was a mature and nonchalant detachment. 'Learning to Ride' was the result, a poem that, if I'm unwary, can still produce

a tear, not merely because it evokes my long-ago childhood in
Ohakune and the horse-riding passion I shared with my older sister,
but because there's also a mother's wish that her children's lives be
forever uncomplicated by loss and hurt:

> Dear girl, when you ride again
> let it be over round hills,
> the cliffs not too close, let
> your hands lie easily now
> and under green willows
> catkins fall on your hair.

Lauris wrote:

> *This poem was written for and about Frances … She has always
> seemed to me to be a person who spoke with her whole body,
> not just her mouth or face, and I remembered how this showed
> when she was quite small and learning to ride her Pony Club
> nag. Then in my mind's eye, I saw other, later pictures of her,
> always with the speaking body doing its part. But I have to admit
> that the very last line slips into another gear, going right back
> to my own childhood. There was a big old willow where I often
> played. I loved its smell, its changes of season – and its little seed
> heads, the catkins; I even loved the word. So when it made its
> appearance, I let it stay.*

For many years Lauris wrestled with a dramatically overactive
imagination where her teenage children were concerned. If one of us
was late home, the cause was never the simple or obvious one. In her
mind it was 'cars in ditches, dead bodies strewn all over the road,
swimmers drowned, children lost or kidnapped or unaccountably
mutilated'. Calamitous social breakdown and personal mayhem
were far more likely than rebellious teenagers ignoring the wishes
of parents, succumbing to a desire to please themselves, reluctant to
curtail the luxury and privacy of being alone with a boy in a car.

Because Dad was deputy, then principal, of the local high school,
boys in cars tended to be rather more obedient about time and

expectations, in the interests of gaining and maintaining a place in the First XV or First XI.

Nevertheless, Lauris's intense anxiety was potent. In 'Thinking of Children' she approaches the anxious, almost overpowering concern she felt for her children's well-being, laying out the terrors that possessed her with unflinching honesty but also a wry assessment of her self-preoccupation:

> safe and alive is what you're muttering
> under your sun hat
> in the garden, please God that's all, they grow
> they recover when hurt
> come home at night, the cruel road
> allows them through, the hospital
> doesn't want them, magistrates don't know
> their names, their beautiful skin and
> hurtable bodies. I'm hateful ...
>
> never mind about anyone else,
> let mine be all right.[5]

Lauris's preoccupation with her children's safety had other manifestations. In the Greytown years (1962–66) swimming was my obsession; I spent a great deal of my leisure time down at the local baths training and then competing, both locally and nationally. Even when my dedication developed into a race-winning accomplishment, Lauris was not merely unsupportive, she opposed it. One reason, I think, was that in swimming togs, half my youthful body was exposed, and thus I was in danger of being prey to boys whose lusts might overcome them; or even that I might succumb to the temptations of sex. Little did she know how innocent my encounters with boys were; at most the occasional chaste pressing-together of lips.

Opposition was also based on her strong ideas about suitable activities. Approval ratings were high for reading the right books (not comics – they were trash), and in fact intellectual pursuits of all kinds, especially being top of the class – with the exception of science, the province of nerdy boys with damp hands and taxi door ears. Tennis was acceptable, as was phys ed at school. However, when I won a gold medal at the National Swimming Championships in 1965, her anxious prejudices were overwhelmed by maternal pride and suddenly swimming was acceptable.

On one occasion, however, Mum's fears turned out to be well grounded. One evening in Greytown, when I was 14 and biking home after swimming training, I encountered Dad in the family car, driving down dark, tree-lined Kuratawhiti Street on the lookout for me. Something dreadful had happened and, driving slowly behind my bike, he escorted me to the chemist shop in the main street, behind which were our crowded and unlovely living quarters (a house Lauris hated).

There, I learned of the appalling event: my younger sister Rachel had been sexually molested in the toilet block of the local primary school by a disturbed young man who had claimed to be a teacher. He had asked her to show him around and, being the child of a schoolteacher, she had obliged. That's as much as I was told at the time. Did we – did she – have no knowledge of what we now call 'stranger danger'? I don't recall being warned of such things, but we lived in small towns where most people knew each other, and as a teacher's children we were particularly visible.

I have a lingering sense of the secrecy, the family shame surrounding this terrible experience, but little sense that we came together as a family to protect vulnerable Rachel. That was Lauris's role: the full force of her passionate mothering went into 'helping' Rachel: attempting to explain the young man's 'awful necessity' (a phrase from Rachel's diary) and the randomness of her being the victim.

The rest of us were kept apart; encouraged to continue our lives as if nothing had happened. Were we requested not to talk about it? Some years before the sexual revolution, common decency ensured that people did not talk about 'that sort of thing'. I would not anyway have had the means – the language, and embarrassment is a very effective silencer.

I remember seeing Rachel's panties lying in a bucket beside the washing machine, saved as evidence. A small innocent rag of cotton infused with a confusion of fascination, disgust and horror. She was 10 at the time.

A girl in the neighbouring town of Carterton was attacked by the same young man, who was caught and charged. Rape is often portrayed as the victim's fault, but no-one could blame a child. Was Rachel raped? Yes. Was she taken by police to a line-up where possible suspects were paraded in front of her, a 10-year-old girl? Yes. At the time, I didn't know these things. What happened to Rachel was just that, something that happened to her.

For a time afterwards we exercised a careful reticence around Rachel, but as the actual event receded it was, if not exactly forgotten, pushed to the margins where painful events could be buried as tragic family secrets.

It goes without saying that Lauris's fear for the safety and well-being of her children intensified thereafter.[6]

In later life, Lauris expected that, her own years of intense mothering well over, she might feel a certain world-weariness towards being a grandmother. This was not so – she took to the role with a surprised and continuing delight, 'Grandmothering' becoming for her a cherished version of 'home' work.

> *... every new arrival confirms my conviction that there is, or can be, a special affinity between the very young and those beyond active parenthood. Parents see conscience-building as part of their job; grandparents have left this duty behind and can enjoy being as open to experience – as amoral? – as children themselves. My inclination is often to say, 'Why not?' when children want to experiment; as a mother I far more often said, 'Not just now' or 'Think of the effect on ...' or 'It's not your turn.'[7]*

As her family expanded and more and more grandchildren
arrived, it became a ritual for Lauris to write a poem, and/or
dedicate a book, to the latest addition. Her first grandchild, Ruth,
was born to Stephanie in 1977, while Lauris was travelling in
Czechoslovakia.[8] On her return to London she found a telegram
waiting for her at New Zealand House, and in *The Quick World*
(volume three of her autobiography), she comments on the birth:

> *The fact that my closest attention was every day fixed on my
> literary occupations, rather than my old domestic ones, was
> beside the point. Life, not art, would always sweep in and grab
> the prizes.*

This is a theme – a conflict – to which she would regularly return
and never completely resolve.

Naturally, there were poems about this first grandchild: 'Applied
Astronomy', 'Red Nightgown', 'Square Dance'. The latter two
expand the view into generations – grandmother, mother, daughter.
In 'Square Dance', from the vantage point of the 1990s, she looks
back (nigh on 100 years) to her grandmother, Clara Eliza Price
(1867–1921), imagining a pathway beyond the teeming present
when this first granddaughter, carrying the heritage of her forebears,
moves into a future none of us can yet imagine. It's a poem of
family; of history; of the labours, trials and rewards of motherhood,
of being women:

> ... Let me tell you
>
> of long-dead Clara, show you the silent peak
> of the mind on which I stand, looking back
>
> a whole century to her, forward to you,
> sweetly alive here, carrying like a lively germ
>
> the secrets of future time ...

'Tempo', a wonderfully ecstatic poem about giving birth to a
daughter, she wrote – completed, actually – for the birth of my first

child, Tess. Lauris didn't ever tell me this, but according to Fiona Kidman, 'Tempo' was begun when she was pregnant with me, a sweet generational link:

> My ace my adventure
> my sweet-smelling atom
> my planet, my grain of miraculous dust
> my green leaf, my feather
> my lily my lark
> look at her, angels –
> this is my daughter.

Lauris wrote about it:

> *This poem has a curious history. I began to write down its images, each a picture of the sensations of pregnancy, month by month, but for some reason didn't finish the piece – perhaps I had the baby and was then too busy. More surprising I forgot all about it. Then years later, my daughter was having her first baby, the poem came back into my mind and I finished it for her.*

One hospital birth was quite enough for me. I had my second child, George, at home, where the midwife ran me a bath and opened a bottle of champagne. 'Really' is the poem Lauris wrote for 'little George' (named after 'big George' Henare, an acting colleague and treasured friend): 'right now it fits you beautifully, your reality, / I like you in it; hello.'

For my third, Patrick, at home, with Lauris in attendance, it was she who opened the champagne, while I clutched my prize and rang family members and friends to tell them of my achievement. 'Midwife' is her affectionate depiction of the events of that December afternoon, dedicated to the midwife, Heather Waugh – 'we know a maestro when we see one'.

Although she was not present at the births of my two eldest children, Lauris visited soon after and was ever present in my family life – letters and visits, faxes and phone calls, books she made by hand for each of my children, rugs knitted for their beds, presents at Easters, birthdays, Christmases and other occasions when no festive excuse was in evidence, just a desire to connect, to be part of her extended family's daily round of sustaining activities.

And, of course, poems. I used to wonder when she found time to do any work with four daughters (two of them resident in Wellington) and an ever-increasing number of grandchildren, all of whom received her detailed and devoted grandmotherly attention.

In those early years I took the opportunity to drive down to Wellington from Auckland to visit her whenever I could. When the children were older, it became a regular event for one of them to fly to Wellington as a 'UM' (unaccompanied minor) to stay with her. They had fun times; Lauris was an endlessly inventive grandmother – things (possessions) were never 'out of bounds', they were to be used, not preserved. Not even delicate, bone-china teacups were off limits for childish play; nor did she notice when games or tea parties became a little boisterous and china became chipped or broken. After her death, when we cleaned out her china cabinet, there was barely a piece intact.

Indeed, there's a story that Fleur Adcock tells. Fleur was staying at Grass Street while Lauris was away and the house was burgled. Fleur couldn't tell if anything had been taken so she rang my sister, Stephanie, who replied blithely, 'Oh Lauris doesn't care about *things!*' It was true: for many years, despite repeated admonitions from her family, she refused to lock her house, leaving the front door open to whoever might wish to enter.

Was such casualness a hangover from more settled times? Our Burns Street family home in Ohakune was never locked either. One summer, an uncle and his family turned up to visit; they found the back door ajar, a mummified cat lying on the step and the vacuum cleaner in the middle of the kitchen floor. We were nowhere to be seen, having gone on our annual camping sojourn.

Lauris's willingness and pleasure in being an active, committed grandmother had another aspect. Her departure from her marriage and her pursuit of her own life were seen by some as adversely affecting her children, and the family's temptation to punish her by withdrawing all contact was not always resisted – I used to accuse her of treating my house like a hotel when she came to stay and spent the time gallivanting around Auckland. Undoubtedly her grandmotherly devotions and availability were genuine, but they also ensured her usefulness to her children, giving her a chance to rebuild and/or maintain some kind of contact when relationships were fractured.

Despite her busy, productive professional life, a persistent dichotomy continued to trouble her – the modern independent life versus the traditional one. She defended the boundary with a worthy assertion in her piece on grandmothering – 'for all that, when the chips are down, I would always put family first.'[9]

That was not always my experience, though with hindsight, I can see that this tension between her life and her art was a factor. She lived in Wellington, surrounded by immediate family, including two of my sisters, Virginia and Stephanie, while I lived in Auckland. There were times when I wanted help, respite, some time out, but a grandmotherly visit would take her out of her milieu. In Wellington she could blend, compromise, adjust, whereas coming to another city removed much of the elasticity between the demands of work and family.

Lauris described her life as divided into 'life number one' and 'life number two', but she would also declare that they were not sequential, continuing to cross over and sometimes blend. Her journey was drawn out, messy, agonising and, although she learned acceptance, there were unresolved knotty tangles in the shadows that could, and did at times, catch her unawares, trip her up and tumble her into a morass of grief and loss.

She marked a beginning of this journey in *Bonfires in the Rain*, when the family stayed at Kennedy Park motor camp in Napier:

> *One afternoon I sat in the tent alone and watched the family out on the grass playing cricket with their father. I often elected to stay in or about the tent instead of romping around with bats*

and balls because it was a chance to feed, even temporarily, my
permanently unsatisfied craving to read; it was also the only time
in the year when Trevor, a natural sportsman, was completely
at his children's disposal. All was well. I turned my pages
peacefully, then at a sudden shout looked up, and as I watched
a kind of somersault took place in my mind. The figures moving
about on that green background suddenly changed, took on a
new angle, almost a new dimension. I saw them as I never had
before – they were my dearest people in all the world, almost
everything I thought and did was directed towards their welfare,
their happiness and fulfilment. And I saw with blinding clarity
that not one of them thought there was a single thing to be done
for me, in my turn. I didn't have a turn. I didn't exist, except
as I helped them to exist. Without them I was nothing, and so
they perceived me – theirs, useful, indeed necessary, loved, of
course, depended upon; but as a person with possible separate
requirements of my own, not there. And nobody, not even I,
thought this unbalanced or wrong. I shook all over, that moment
in a hot afternoon.

And then there's a reference in 'Sunday Night', an early poem
from the collection *In Middle Air*: 'What is a woman that she /
should wake and sleep in other people's lives?'. What indeed?
Lauris's eloquent expression of her status in the family, of a woman's
– a mother's – status in the wider world, is both particular and
universal. Of course her epiphany in the tent at Kennedy Park went
unremarked by her children; her unerringly accurate assessment of
her place in the family scheme guaranteed there was nothing for us
to notice. What could she have said anyway that we would have
understood, recognised? 'I have needs and aspirations of my own. I
want my own life.' We would have looked at her blankly, wondered
what on earth she was talking about and carried on with our game
of cricket.

And what of Dad? Were we interested in him? Did we have
different, more open expectations? Yes. He knew about the world,
he knew about school, he was a teacher, he could explain things I

didn't understand. I remember standing beside his desk in the house in Burns Street, a frown of concentration on my face as he explained articles to me – the definite and the indefinite. The lesson at school had left me mystified, but Dad explained them in a way I completely understood. It was Dad, too, who taught me to tie my shoelaces. Being, like me, a natural left-hander, he was able to guide my fingers through the process. Dad's skills were demonstrably useful; Lauris provided the staples of home management, which could be taken for granted.

2. Hawke's Bay: The Price and Scott families

auris begins volume one of her autobiography, *Hot October*
(1989), with a captivating and colourful description of the
Napier earthquake of 1931. It was 3 February, the first day of
the school year, and the first day of school for her younger sister,
Lindsay. Fortuitously, the earthquake struck at 10.47am – playtime
– when most of the pupils at Greenmeadows Primary School were
outside as the brick edifice came crashing down with the force of the
quake. 'Earthquake Magic', from *In Middle Air*, commemorates the
event:

> Something flew at us out of the sky
> jumbled us bumbled us madly around,
> and the quick ground
> ran everywhere away from us,
> there was no catching it; the air,
> the sky, was full of things
> happening, and noises – wings
> monkeys trumpets engines
> houses falling down.
>
> Indeed the school – little, frowning,
> everlasting school – did fall
> or, rather, grew, and flew about us
> spreading a red enormous smoke;

some magic had it: six years old,
you know that anything can happen –
miracles, bricks blossoming
into clouds, walls holding
up their hands in great surprise,
a mat pulled mischievously
out from under everything.

But there was – perhaps there always is –
your little sister. Hold to her –
like you, she has not seen before
these conjuring tricks
with clouds and bricks:
they do not confound her. She was born
knowing how to manage earthquakes,
and that you cannot simply wonder
at the world's rocket going off;
she will always make it come
walking back and talking sense.
You need her. You are right to love her.

In the ensuing chaos and confusion, Fanny, the girls' mother,
arrives at the school clutching the lilac bush that had been growing
at the gate of their house – it had come out in her hand when she
grabbed at it as the shaking began. Clive, Lauris's older brother,
appears nonchalantly out of the dust and debris of the schoolhouse
and the whole family (Fanny and Lewis, their children, Clive, Lauris
and Lindsay) manage to discover each other and reassemble.[1]

In the afternoon, Lauris's family set off to drive to Napier to
find relations – aunts, cousins and a grandmother, Lewis's sisters,
their families and his mother. Everyone else in town is of a similar
mind, however; mayhem and damage to the roads, as well as fallen
bridges, turn them back.

Lauris wrote in *Hot October* of going in search of her father's
family but not her mother's. Why? Fanny's mother died in 1921 but
her father, William, had retired to Hastings in 1930 and, as they

were a farming family, it's probable that some of Fanny's numerous brothers were still in the district. Possibly, relations with Lewis's family were more substantial at the time. They were likely aware, also, that devastation in urban Napier would be greater than in the rolling pastoral lands of rural Hawke's Bay.

Nevertheless, this is 1930, and from Lauris's writing, one gets a very strong sense of family connection and intimacy fostered by her maternal grandmother, Clara, and handed down to Fanny, who in turn handed it down to Lauris. It may simply be that the trip to Napier in the car provided Lauris the writer with more dramatic descriptive opportunities.[2] The elusive scraps in her autobiography about Lewis's family are some of the few that are extant, whereas Fanny's family appear more regularly and more comprehensively in her writing, perhaps adding weight to my theory about dramatic opportunity.

Lauris was often vague about dates, times and geographical detail: 'Born in Dannevirke' is a typical piece of Lauris imprecision. It wasn't until after her death that I discovered that she, Clive and Lindsay were actually all born while Fanny and Lewis lived at Maharahara, some 16 kilometres southwest of Dannevirke, in southern Hawke's Bay. Lewis managed the post office store and had a small carrying business with a horse and gig. I knew nothing of Maharahara in Lauris's lifetime, though I knew of Osier Road, Greenmeadows. A casual mention by one of my Scott cousins when I was visiting Uncle Clive, some years after Lauris died, alerted me.

I went there for the first time in April 2017. Maharahara is no longer a settlement; it's farming country, and nothing remains of the store my grandfather operated. I found its probable location by knocking on the door of the former dairy co-op, now a house. The woman there sent me to talk to an ageing resident by the name of Peter Barrows, a nice if rather wandery man. He showed me a woodcut he'd made of early Maharahara; told me a chap called

Scott had helped his grandfather build a waterwheel. Given that Peter might be 10–15 years my senior, it could conceivably have been a young Lewis; the dates would work – sort of – but that's all I discovered.

Lauris's inaccuracies – incorrect arrival, birth and death dates – suggest a lack of interest in family history beyond what was required for whatever she was writing at any particular time – an article about Fanny; her own life story. But history, including family history fascinates me. It gives me a sense of my location in the world, both immediate and distant. Not exactly 'knowing one's place' in the social and economic hierarchies – though that's part of it – more one's heritage; a sense of belonging.

As a Pākehā New Zealander, I am aware of the nourishing and sustaining power of whakapapa, even a little envious of it. Does whakapapa matter? I think so, as a contribution to one's sense of identity. Age is a factor here too; as the road ahead shortens, the temptation to look back into infinite distance becomes more appealing and rewarding. And so, in 2004, I sent my mitochondrial DNA to Oxford Ancestors so they could trace our female line back through the generations.

Mitochondrial DNA passes directly from mother to child; thus it is my children's, mine, Lauris's, Fanny's, Clara's, Clara Emma's and so on, back through a thousand grandmothers and into the mists of time. I discovered a singular lack of diversity: my family was related to 45 per cent of Western Europeans and our collective mitochondrial DNA can be traced back 25,000 years to the south of France, any claim to racial uniqueness reduced to irrevocable absurdity.

The migrations from Britain to New Zealand of my father's family – Edmond/McLeod (paternal), Trevarthen/Harney (maternal) – have been recorded and written about by my historian cousin, Rod Edmond[3], though there's only sketchy information about Lauris's family – Scott/Seers (paternal), Price/Lister (maternal), or, further back, Stannet (paternal), Richlieu and Burrt (maternal). There's a family tree of the Price/Lister clan prepared by the youngest of Lauris's maternal uncles, Clive, though little is known before the first half of the nineteenth century. About the Scott/Seers, there are only a few notes.

The arrival here of the two families fits neatly into nineteenth-century tales of British migration to the colonies.[4] Both families came from areas of England that provided a significant proportion of New Zealand's nineteenth-century migrant population. Lauris's maternal grandmother, Clara Lister, hailed from Middlesex[5], while Lewis's parents came from the home counties of Berkshire and Buckinghamshire. William Price, Lauris's maternal grandfather, was the only northerner.[6] (See family tree on page 290.)

Lister/Price (Lauris's mother's family)

Albert and Harriet Lister's family sailed for New Zealand on 12 March 1874, on the *Halcione*. What was the trigger? How did they make the decision to abandon the life they knew for one they didn't? To take a family with four children ranging in age from seven years (Clara Eliza) down to George (a mere four months old) on a 15-week journey by sailing ship to the other side of the world speaks of what – courage? Foolhardiness? Deprivation? Desperation? A spirit of adventure? Possibly a little of each.

The only record I have is the Price family tree; the few sketchy stories that have been passed down relate to life here in New Zealand. There are no diaries I know of, and the few letters attached to the family tree were written by relatives left behind in Middlesex.

Life in the new country, in the colony, was tough. Doubtless it took all the resources of these resourceful people; the luxury of time to contemplate, evaluate and record remembrances in a diary not available in the daily struggle to survive.

One snippet: Clara Eliza's father, Albert, is on the passenger list as a wood turner, though, according to my great-uncle, Clive, he was in fact a steel plate engraver in the printing industry. Lauris claimed he was a printer who had thought he would get more work in New Zealand (not all trades were eligible for assisted passage, which might explain the alteration – or the subterfuge if that's what it was).

To add to the confusion, Albert is listed on his marriage certificate (to his first wife, Clara Emma) as a pianoforte maker. I understand the connection between wood turning and pianoforte making, but if there's also a connection with steel plate engraving it eludes me. Perhaps he was all of these at various times? This certainly speaks to a flexible disposition, a creative attitude to necessity – valuable qualities in a new and unformed land.

The *Halcione* docked at Napier on 4 July 1874, during the inhospitable New Zealand winter. At least two inauspicious events took place during this sailing. On the day of departure from Erith, the gangway caught in the water as it was being shipped and tossed the second officer, the carpenter and a seaman into the river. Another sailor dived in with a buoy. The second officer and the carpenter were saved; the seaman drowned.

Then on 31 May, Captain Bishop was found dead in bed from a sudden stroke. The first officer, Croker, took over command.

Purpose built for the New Zealand run, the *Halcione* made 26 trips in all, but only one to the port of Napier – the one on which my great-great-grandparents and their family arrived, along with 331 other migrants. What did they do, and where did they go when they disembarked? Did Albert have a job lined up or did he have to find one?

Clara Eliza Lister (Lauris's maternal grandmother)

Born: 27 October 1867
Birthplace: London
Father: Albert Lister
Mother: Clara Emma Lister (née Burrt, died 1869)
Stepmother: Harriet Lister
Full siblings: None
Half siblings: 3+

Lauris wrote that, 'In New Zealand the family lived together in
Hawke's Bay (on a farm out of Hastings) till Harriet, the stepmother,
died in 1880.' At that point Clara, who was 13, became the family
housekeeper, running the house and caring for the children until
her father married for a third time in 1883. In June of the following
year, at the tender age of 17, Clara married William Price. The only
other information about her is on her marriage certificate – before
her marriage she lived at Waipawa. At home with her family still?
Or employed in domestic service in someone else's household?

From 'Square Dance':

> You, Clara Eliza, five-foot legendary grandmother,
> battling wood fires in a freezing dawn,
>
> riding to town with an empty purse, the old man
> blank with booze – I can see you, moving about
>
> in the dim grey weather where history lodges,
> it whirls like fog over the Poukawa farm; now
>
> it clears, and you're there in the gig, reining in
> a bolting horse, three terrified children
>
> gripping your skirt ... I think I have always
> known you, from tales that had their first telling
>
> three years before I was born, when consumption
> at last devoured you. August little lady, you used
>
> every second of your dense half century creating
> a clan, taking for materials your doggedness,
>
> imagination, love. It's time, you know, that we met
> more exactly – if a generation's twenty years,
>
> three already lie between us. I step forward,
> take your small calloused hand: the skin's weathered,

quite dark, but your brown eyes are sharp and –
no one had told me this – glinting with laughter.

In this poem, Lauris describes her grandparents' farm at
Poukawa. Yet in other writings about her Hawke's Bay family, she
describes the farm as being at Raukawa – another fairly typical piece
of Lauris imprecision. Both are localities in rural Hawke's Bay. On
my journey of exploration in 2017 I visited not only Maharahara,
but Poukawa and Raukawa. Having assumed that my great-
grandfather owned his farm, I was mystified by the two locations
with similar names. The discovery that great-grandfather Price was a
farm *manager* rather than a farm owner explained the confusion: he
managed farms in both locations at different times in his life.

William Price (Lauris's maternal grandfather)

Born: 12 August 1864
Birthplace: Stockton-on-Tees, Yorkshire
Father: William Price (died in an accident, 1868)
Mother: Alice Price (née Richlieu)
Stepfather: John Brenkley
Full siblings: 2

Lauris writes that William was 'an intelligent, lively-minded, bossy
man, but for many years he was also an incorrigible drinker and
gambler'. As a young child he was sent out to work, carrying lunches
in a local brickyard – an indication, one presumes, of straightened
economic circumstances, most likely after the death of his father.

Like Clara's father, William's mother married again fairly
promptly. When one had a brood of children, remaining single was
not a viable option for women or men.

Despite the relative profitability of farming in Yorkshire at the
time, William's stepfather, John Brenkley (described in passenger
lists as a farm labourer), chose to emigrate with his family; William
– along with his two older sisters, and travelling under their

stepfather's name – sailed from London for New Zealand on the *Fernglen* on 9 December 1876, arriving in Napier on 20 March 1877.[7] Aside from time in the Veterinary Corps at Trentham in World War I, William was to spend the rest of his life in Hawke's Bay.

Along with other migrants, the Brenkleys were accommodated at military barracks until they moved on to prearranged destinations. William's first job was for a Mr Harding at Mt Vernon Station in Waipukurau. He was clearly an enterprising young man; by the time of his marriage to Clara, aged 20, he was running his own butchery in Ormondville. The other thing of note is that, although William arrived in New Zealand under his stepfather's name, by the time of his marriage he had reverted to his father's name of Price.

Clara and William married at St Mary's Church in Waipukurau on 8 June 1884. According to his son Clive, William 'spent the greater part of his life in farming pursuits'.[8] At Ormondville, William worked as a farm contractor, but also dealt in timber (for example, supplying, under contract, wooden sleepers for the Napier/Woodville railway). As a jobbing farmer without land, he worked at various locations around Hawke's Bay – as farm manager at Poukawa during World War I and then, until his retirement in 1930, at Waimotu on Raukawa Road.

Clive describes William as having 'a quite remarkable skill with animals' and 'being an acknowledged expert with horses'. Like many immigrants, he was largely self-taught. Although he developed an impressive skill with numbers, financial success eluded him. At various times in his early life he owned properties, but tough economic times and his profligacy with drink and money put paid to permanency. At the outbreak of World War I, however, he went on the wagon and remained sober until Clara's death in 1921. I wonder what family or economic crises (though they would be intimately connected) precipitated this radical change in behaviour?

Despite their peripatetic lifestyle, William and Clara set about making a family, a clan, in this raw, new land – constructing an inheritance to be passed down to future generations. Clara, 'a slender slip of a girl, barely five feet tall', somehow managed in those difficult pioneering conditions to raise a family of 12. Those conditions included cooking and washing outdoors, and it is testament to her dedication and skill that all Clara's children survived. Clive wrote: 'The children, on the whole, were healthy and happy, due to her efforts. An excellent housekeeper and devoted mother, she was dearly loved and completely trusted by all who knew her.' Behind Clive's words I sense a protectiveness of his mother and an implicit moral judgement of his father's debauched ways.

Clive, 12 years younger than his sister Fanny, describes his anxiety and apprehension at the frequent rows, Fanny standing up to their father when he attacked her for her 'superior ways and stiff-necked pride'. In many ways like William, 'Fanny was his most articulate and forthright opponent; they had a permanent furious quarrel'. Lauris wrote of Fanny in a similar vein, as not only particularly able but the one who often led family opposition to their father's behaviour. As Fanny got older, she felt increasing 'bitterness against "The Old Man" and along with it a strong and sometimes protective affection for her mother'.

Lauris's first cousin, Val Powell, enlightened me long after Lauris was dead about a probable cause for Fanny's bitterness towards her father. Chatting at a Powell family party, Val told me our great-grandfather, William Price, had sexually molested two of his daughters (Fanny, and Val's mother, Alice). I asked Val how she knew – she said her brother Garth had told her before he died. According to Val, neither Alice nor Fanny had ever talked about sex – it was a taboo subject. (Alice didn't even tell Val the 'facts of life'.) Alice, however, had told Val's father George, about the abuse; he in turn told Garth.

I asked Val if she knew what he did. Arriving home in the horse and trap, he would holler for his daughters to come and escort him across the paddock to the house – this much I had been told by Lauris. Did he kiss and fondle them as they walked him home,

or was it more than that? Did he rape them? Val didn't know. It
explains Fanny's anxiety about sex and drink though, and Lauris's,
too, in my early years.

Common sense would suggest that as Fanny matured and had
her own children, a fiercely protective impulse may well have
required her to confront, or at least acknowledge, William's drinking
and gambling and sexually predatory behaviour. Her bitterness
against 'the Old Man' surely contained a sense of outrage at the
violation she and her sister had been subjected to as girls.

Overall, the Price clan emerge as clever, strong-willed, hard-
working and adventurous – the women as well as the men. Alice,
for example, would assist her father when he was herding wild
horses, which he would subsequently break in and sell. The
brothers were authoritative and resourceful, the sisters dignified and
sometimes intimidating: a combination of William's wilfulness and
volatility and Clara's strength and dignity. A rather fixed worldview
pervaded, though; they were a self-righteous lot – no doubt as
a result of William's drinking and gambling. None of the rest of
the family drank except for son Tom, who inherited his father's
weakness for booze.

Lauris wrote of

> *the emotional intensity, irascible temper, and a saving sense
> of the absurd that were Price family characteristics ... They
> exhibited and passed on pioneer virtues of family loyalty,
> ambition for their children, independence of mind. They brought
> with them or developed (or both) a moral code that emphasised
> truthfulness, fair play and, perhaps most importantly, courage,
> 'facing up' to things.*

It is difficult for me to accommodate William's sexual predation
on his daughters into this pioneering moral code. Did Clara know,
or was sex such a taboo subject that it couldn't be talked of in any
context? Did notions of 'male entitlement' ensure that no one dared
question what William did? Was there a determined and wilful
blindness towards such disgraceful behaviour?

Clara was versatile and capable, making use of medicines she found in the bush, developing considerable skill with horses.[9] Lauris addressed Clara as Grandmamma, as we kids addressed Fanny. As a child, it seemed to me affected and artificial, but then 'homely' and 'motherly' are not words I would use to describe Grandmamma Fanny. From the descriptions I have of Great-Grandmamma Clara, they seem considerably more appropriate to her.

Clara died of consumption in May 1921, two months after Fanny married Lewis Scott and three years before Lauris was born. William died suddenly on 3 July 1944, when Lauris was 20 years old.

Fanny Price (Lauris's mother)
Dates: 23 October 1896–12 January 1967
Birthplace: Norsewood
Father: William Price
Mother: Clara Eliza (née Lister)
Full siblings: 11

Fanny would have been born at home, her mother attended by a midwife and/or other female family members, or neighbours with practical experience of childbirth, though by the time Clara was giving birth to her eighth child, she probably knew as much as or more than most about the process.

The youngest of Fanny's sisters, Dorothy (Dorrie or Dot), died of rheumatic fever in 1924, aged 23, less than two months after Lauris was born, and Lauris was given Dorothy as a second name. Lauris mistakenly recorded Dorrie's death as happening in 1921, thus giving that year added weight and significance: 'Grandmamma Clara died; Dorrie died; Fanny married Lewis; her sister, Alice, married George Powell.' In Lauris's world, emotional truth was always more vivid, more dramatically true, and thus carried more weight, than mere facts. Making a connection between Clara's and Dorrie's deaths and Fanny's marriage creates potency; an irresistibly charged atmosphere of loss and love around Fanny.

Scott/Seers (Lauris's father's family)

Lauris's paternal grandparents were Ada (née Seers) and Herbert Scott. Before I embarked on this book, I knew almost nothing about them. I have a few file boxes of material on Lindsay and Lauris's younger brother, John, which had been part of Lauris's personal papers when she died. I had already looked through them without finding anything useful. I searched again for something – anything – and this time I came across a handwritten description of their origins. It was exactly what I was looking for and had been sent to Lauris by a cousin, Cherry Swayn. Her letter, dated 14 April 1993, reads: 'I've given you the "bones" of the Scott/Seers and am quite prepared to expand it if you'd like.' She goes on to say, 'Perhaps Frances could write to me if she wants anything more extensive. Not that there is much but I could enlarge a bit.'

To help 'enlarge' my knowledge, I also ordered a copy of their son Lewis's birth certificate, which added some welcome details about places and dates. This is what I discovered:

Ada Emma Seers (Lauris's paternal grandmother)

Born: 30 October 1862
Birthplace: Dropmore, Buckinghamshire
Father: William Seers (born 1832, gamekeeper)
Mother: Emma Seers (née Scott, born 1835, died of appendicitis)
Lived at: Littleworth Common, Burnham, Buckinghamshire

Herbert Mortimer Scott (Lauris's paternal grandfather)

Dates: 1859–1930
Birthplace: Cookham Dean, Berkshire
Father: James Scott: 1827–1905
Mother: Sarah Scott (née Stannet, died giving birth to twins who also died)

Herbert and Ada married in London on 3 March 1883 and, according to cousin Cherry, came to New Zealand a couple of years after their marriage. There is no reference to the name of the ship they travelled on, but it might have been the *Laira*, which arrived at Napier in 1886. Ada and Herbert were first cousins (his father, James, and her mother, Emma, were brother and sister). Thus, rather than two family histories, there is but one. Herbert's sister Alice also came to New Zealand, perhaps at the same time. She had been married in England, to a man by the name of Hamblin.

The Scott family, like the Prices, were assisted immigrants, tradesmen and small businesspeople – keeping poultry, making and selling herbal ointment (extracted from rosemary), painting and paperhanging. Lauris's father, Lewis, was the third child. In Lauris's writings, Grandfather Herbert is a shadowy figure. He died when she was six years old so there were few memories. Her father Lewis is described as a mild, kindly man, content to leave the foreground to his elegant, dignified wife. Lauris wrote of her father: 'In his heart … an ancient tribal patriarch still, self-effacing and tentative though he might be when faced with the concentrated volubility of the crowd.' I like to think Lewis inherited those worthy qualities from Herbert.

Grandmother Ada was much more present in Lauris's life and known as 'a seer'. That, along with her interest in the occult and the fact that the Scotts made and sold herbal ointments, suggests that the alternative ('crackpot') thread in my family originated in the Seers/Scott branch, though readily adopted by Fanny. It appeals to me – I have definitely 'inherited' the 'crackpot' view of healing, as well as an affinity with the art of 'seeing', despite my rational mind raising doubts about its efficacy.

Lewis Herbert Scott (Lauris's father)
Dates: 11 May 1893–17 October 1953
Birthplace: Greenmeadows, Bay of Plenty
Father: Herbert Mortimer Scott (1859–1930)
Mother: Ada Emma Scott (née Seers)
Full siblings: 4

Lewis Scott married Fanny Price in Hastings on 26 March 1921. The two had much in common. Both were interested in a healthy diet, read occult literature, practised natural healing and were attracted to an alternative political theory – social credit.[10] Lewis did not believe in paying taxes. Instead, he rolled up bundles of money in oil cloth, stashed them in tins and buried them in the garden of the farmlet at Pyes Pa. HT (Hidden Treasure), we knew it as.

He left a map, so the family story goes: X marks the spot. After his death, my father and uncles, under cover of darkness, dug up the tins and retrieved the filthy lucre, which was apportioned among the families. There was intense discussion about the wisdom of banking the notes, as the numbers might be so old as to raise suspicion as to where they had been languishing all these years. I believe our portion bought Lauris a sewing machine and the Challen piano I played as a child.

Pyes Pa was the last residence Fanny and Lewis shared, the place where Lewis finally had the opportunity to build his utopia, his Eden – an idyllic farmlet with orchards and gardens producing abundantly, the realisation of what they had attempted at Osier Road in Greenmeadows, turning their passion for healthy food and natural living into a way of life. In those days, such preoccupations were the province of eccentrics and cranks, which my grandparents, with their blind faith in unorthodoxy, most certainly were. Soft-covered suitcases full of fruit – grapefruit, oranges, tree tomatoes (tamarillos) and Chinese gooseberries (kiwifruit) – would arrive for us at the Ohakune railway station.

Fanny Price was given a genteel Jane Austen name when she was born; my grandmother as namesake to the heroine of *Mansfield Park*. By the time she reached her middle years, however, she struggled with the name's less savoury associations – who wants to be named after a bum (in the US) or female genitalia (in the rest of the world)? In my late childhood, I recall her signing telegrams 'Eliza', though the affectation didn't last and she reverted to Fanny.

I have the misfortune of having inherited both her names: Frances

Elizabeth. I too have struggled with Frances, though no one has ever been permitted to call me Fanny – well, not to my face. When I was young, even Frances was problematic, a cross-gender name that was a source of constant embarrassment, continual misspelling (as Francis, the male spelling), teasing ('Frances is a sissy' after Francis of Assisi), which reduced me to tears, thus proving that I was.

I remember Fanny using a pendulum – a glass bead hanging from a piece of cotton which she kept in her spectacles case. She would hang it over food and the direction it swung would tell her whether or not that particular item was something she could eat that day. A tall, thin, severe and moralistic woman, to my childish sense it seemed that some days she would only eat cake and others only lettuce.

Despite their preoccupation with a healthy lifestyle and natural diet, there were unforeseen and tragic consequences for both Fanny and Lewis as a result of their resistance to orthodoxy and mainstream medical thinking. Fanny, like her mother, Clara, contracted consumption – known as tuberculosis (TB) by then – and though rushed to hospital after a lung haemorrhage, she refused to stay there and set about curing herself at home: a careful diet, rest and controlled exercise.

Even when new and efficacious drugs were developed in 1952 she refused to take them. It was only after the death of her husband that she eventually submitted to the treatment that cured her, but for the rest of her life her lungs were irrevocably impaired. In my last years at school, when we were living in Huntly, she could not climb the few stairs of our house without gasping.

For Lewis, the consequences were more devastating. When he became ill in 1951, his suspicion of orthodox medicine prevented an early diagnosis of the bowel cancer that killed him two years later.

'The Sums' and 'Eden Cultivated' were poems Lauris wrote for her mother. The latter evokes fruitfulness and female work, embracing the smells of summer, of childhood, of home, with a hint – a threat – of the unexpected in the last line:

> – for how do you know, this time,
> if she will offer you one apple
> or many, or possibly none at all?

Most likely a Hawke's Bay poem, though it could be set at Pyes Pa,
it's a fine example of bringing women's work out of silence and into
public view. Late summer heat, horticultural abundance and it's
time for Fanny to get out the preserving pan for the annual ritual of
bottling and preserving fruit and vegetables to be consumed in the
dark, infertile days of winter.

I remember Pyes Pa – in Lauris's words 'the best place to go for a
holiday' – though I would have been a small child when it was sold
after Lewis died. I have an image of a low-slung, elegant house with
wide wooden verandahs, expansive lawns and a line of trees along
the grassy margin. Memory conjures me wandering under the trees,
exploring, finding myself on the edge of a steep drop, a bank, falling
into a gully below. It's the sense of danger in my child's mind that
sustains the recollection.

I have looked for this house, as I have looked for the one in
Greenmeadows. Pyes Pa is suburban now, with no trace left of the
orchards and small farmlets from my grandparents' days. I asked
Cousin Val, but her only recollection was that it was nearer the town
end of Pyes Pa Road. She remembers the gully as I do.

While there are a number of poems about Hawke's Bay and
the farming world of Lauris's uncles, there's only one about her
father. 'At Pyes Pa', from *The Pear Tree*, records Lauris's inarticulate
grief and Lewis's disappointment as he lies on the verandah facing
imminent death, voicing his concern for his children and his trees:

> My father, a mild and unheroic man,
> died bravely; shrunken by disease
> and disappointment he lay on the verandah
> he had built, seeing across his partly
> planted orchard a blue shimmer of sea
> and mountain in a country rich, he had
> supposed, in continuity.

After the Napier earthquake, Grandma Ada moved with Aunty Grace (Lewis's sister), Uncle Will and their family to Greenmeadows, near Fanny and Lewis. It must have felt like a kind of homecoming for Grandma Ada since the house that Lewis and Fanny lived in had been the family home until Lewis bought it when Herbert died in 1930.

Lauris wrote of biking around to Aunty Grace's, taking the family darning and mending to Grandma Ada, she of the long grey plait, funny dry voice and cackling laugh, smoking thin roll-your-owns in a tortoiseshell cigarette holder, laughing at her own wickedness which, she claimed, would send her to hell when she died, while telling Lauris she was clever and must have a career – be a headmistress.

She must have been a tippler, hence the odour of Christmas cake and port, of staleness, old clothes, the past. Ada died on 10 September 1948 in Napier Public Hospital, from carcinoma of the stomach and senility. She had reached the grand age of 85; the last of Lauris's grandparents. It was Grandma Ada and the aunts (Grace and Sibyl) that Lauris's family set off to find the afternoon of the Napier earthquake.

So here they all are, in shadowy outline but in outline nonetheless: Clara Eliza and William Price, Ada Emma and Herbert Mortimer Scott, and their children, Fanny Price and Lewis Scott. Lauris's parents and grandparents, my grandparents and great-grandparents, those nineteenth-century adventurers who sailed across the world to begin a new life in the raw colony of New Zealand, and who bequeathed to their descendants not only their DNA but their hardiness of spirit, their aspirations, eccentricities and dreams.

3. Ohakune: Old roads have a life they cannot lose

The top photo on page IV shows the Edmond family in the garden of the house in Burns Street, before the two youngest were born. Lauris would have been about 32. We are a model 1950s family except that the girls outnumber the boys – a model family would have had two of each. Worse was to come – the last two were also girls.[1]

Lauris looks tired, wistful. It is possible that she is in the early stages of the first of her 'accidental' pregnancies. We elder four were all 'planned', born as close as possible to the school holidays (December, February, the next two in January). This ensured Dad would be home and able to assist in running the household. A combination of carelessness, an unconscious desire to have more children, a healthy sex drive and abundant fertility led to our family being the size normally reserved for Catholics (whose job was to provide the fodder for God's world domination).

Lauris would look at this photo and see golden years – a busy, active, happy, young family with no hint of future calamities. Cares certainly – never quite enough money; the recent tragic loss of her brother John to suicide; the death of her father, Lewis, a couple of years earlier; the struggles of her mother, Fanny, to make a new life for herself. Although Lauris was young enough to still believe that love came down as reliably as rain, the loss of her brother and father brought mortality, the fragile unreliability of life, close, and it never left her.

I know that feeling – my sister Rachel committed suicide when I was even younger, 25. Grief at the death of one so young penetrates your inner being, takes up residence and never leaves. You learn to live with it but it lurks and can creep up on you unheralded, waves of loss washing over you: a memory, a poem, talking about her can find me overcome with tears.

Lauris had a powerful sense of 'home', of attachment to the physical places in which she lived. It wasn't merely the physical of course – the psychic and emotional blend and bleed into it. For her, the 'homes' were Osier Road, Burns Street and ultimately Grass Street.

The house in Burns Street, an old kauri villa enveloped by beautiful trees, expansive lawns and gardens, lies poised where farm and town co-mingle – only Mrs Aubrey and the Jamesons beyond. Behind the house, built in the early twentieth century, runs the Mangawhero River, whose beginnings lie up on Mt Ruapehu's southwestern slopes and whose waters drain into another river of my childhood, the Whangaehu.[2] This was the river of the Tangiwai disaster on Christmas Eve 1953, its sulphurous waters disturbing my nights with images of a tumbling train and floating bodies.

I can still recall the ghostly whisper of the Mangawhero skimming the enormous silence as I lay awake in the bedroom at the end of the verandah, tormented by the mysterious threat of the darkness. The river was believed a watery danger, out of bounds without parental supervision, though at times I disobeyed, climbed through the dilapidated wire and batten fence and, standing next to a big old pine tree, stared fascinated into rocky rushing waters.

The Mangateitei Stream was also close by, joining the Mangawhero a hundred or so metres up the road. We didn't swim in the Mangawhero but we used to take our horses into the Mangateitei by the bridge. There was an easement, a rough track of sorts, that took you down to a narrow stony beach, and from there into a pool deep enough to swim in, though not over any childish head. Virginia and I would ride our horses into the river until the day Lauris saw a human turd floating in its full glory down the river. She ordered us out of the water and forbade us ever to take ourselves or our horses in again.

Our household water came from corrugated iron tanks on a stand outside the washhouse window, and in summer there was always the danger of running dry. An abiding image is of Dad tapping a stick on the tanks to measure the water level by the sound.

Although Burns Street was the home of my childhood, I was born at 77 Arawa Street, a school-house that, from the outside, still looked in 2017 much as it must have in 1948 when Lauris and Trevor moved to Ohakune: 'A neat undistinguished three-bedroomed wooden bungalow, probably built to an Education Department plan and much the same as thousands of other school-houses,' is how Lauris described it.

They bought the Burns Street house in 1955 – a commitment to small-town life. A family friend and the art teacher at Ruapehu College, Stan Frost, helped us move in. One of my memories is watching with curiosity as he put together our children's beds in the front bedroom, transforming a stack of wooden ends and wirewoves into things to sleep on.

This was the house in which my siblings and I played out the delights and agonies of a small-town childhood, as the offspring of educated, aspiring parents. In this house, this childhood world, Lauris is unequivocally the centre, the perennial certainty and comfort, 'the disfigured legs that with a stolid / magnificence used to hold up the world' ('The Sums').[3]

She was an industrious mother and home-keeper and she passed it on, teaching us – her daughters, that is – to sew and cook and wash and clean. Throughout our childhood she bottled and preserved, the top shelves in the walk-in pantry at Burns Street lined with jars of peaches and plums, tomatoes, beetroot and beans. In my images of her she is inside the house, while Trevor I connect more readily with the outdoors (though Lauris maintained the flower gardens – women's work).

Dad leaves every weekday morning to work at Ruapehu College. At home in the evenings, he sits at a desk in the corner of the small sitting room we called the 'verandah room', marking, preparing lessons, or endlessly writing his MA thesis, occasionally raising his voice in an authoritative 'Be quiet!' at noisy children.[4] At the weekend he coaches sports teams and grows vegetables in the not insubstantial garden.

Mum is in the kitchen – at the sink, by the stove, at the table, a sewing machine set up in front of her as she stitches dresses and pants, skirts and blouses, coats for her ever-expanding family.

The washhouse conjures another set of familiar images: our clothes agitating in greyish water in the green machine or being caught in wet bundles on the end of a stick and shoved through the ringer, flopping down flattened into the cold rinsing water in the concrete tubs on the other side. Above the tubs, a small, dirty, four-paned window lets in a bit of light and offers a glimpse of Mt Ruapehu.

Beneath the stone tubs lived a mysterious tin bucket oozing a strange smell, a fetid earthy reek of blood and secret desires. A curious child, I once lifted the lid, discovered rags, bits of old towels, floating in pinkish water. I had no idea what they were, though instinct told me they were forbidden territory. In the corner of the washhouse stood an enormous old copper, though without fire in its belly – there was electricity by the time we lived in the house.

On Sundays, when the fire was lit in the front living room, Lauris would be sitting by it or playing the piano for the ritual 'frog jumps', always finishing with 'Here we go round the mulberry bush', which in our house concluded with 'This is the way we run to bed, run to bed, run to bed, this is the way we run to bed on a cold and frosty morning'. We probably chanted 'evening', not 'morning', though 'cold and frosty' would often have been the case. And if we were not quick enough, the reward would be 'kick and thump', though in my memory it remains a threat only – we were always too quick to discover whether it would actually happen.

We went blackberrying too, out by Horopito with other families
– the Watsons in particular. Murray Watson taught with Dad; his
wife, Margaret, was a warm and companionable friend of Lauris's,
the two of them discreetly sharing a lack of interest in the regular
Friday night drinking sessions at the Sunbeam Club where their
husbands and other teachers indulged in 'school talk'.

Blackberrying was a memorable outing amid great rolling
tangles of blackberry bushes in rough, tussocky paddocks. We were
expected to pick the black sticky masses of fruit until prickles and
boredom got the better of us. Presenting the meagre contents of
my bowl to Lauris, I would say, 'Is that enough? Can I go and play
now?'

Once, while the others kept picking, my brother and I found
a creek, tree-lined and sunk below the level of the paddock, an
arcane fairytale world of water gurgling over moss-covered rocks
into limpid pools, ferns brushing the dark water with their delicate
green fronds, and over all, tutu or toot waving its lethal arms.[5] We
splashed in the creek, over and around the mossy rocks, oblivious
of wet shoes and clothes, locked into a sense of childish wonder at
this magical place. At the end of such a day, back home at the house
in Burns Street, Lauris would make blackberry and apple pie with
cream for pudding.

My first experience of the magic of the circus was in Ohakune, when
Bullens toured small town New Zealand, delighting both children
and adults with their wild animals and antics. But the magic became
tragic. Summer, December 1957, and the 'Big Top' was set up in the
paddock behind Railway Row at the Junction. Of an afternoon,
Lauris took us to visit. I remember the musky smell of hay, shit and
danger emanating from the cages. The creatures smelled as if they
would eat you.

I don't remember seeing an actual circus performance, but
Mollie, the elephant, a prized creature who could stand on her

front legs and wave her back legs in the air, ate toot growing on the banks of the Mangawhero and died a gruesome, agonised death, all attempts to save her in vain.

I can still recall the enormity, the strangeness of her death; the image of Mollie's grave, a huge mound of fresh red earth, remains. I biked the 3.5 kilometres to the Junction without asking permission in order to see it, to see if what I had been told was true. I was afraid to get too close in case she wasn't really dead – in case she woke up, rose spectre-like from the earth, looked me balefully in the eye as the mound moved to swallow me up and these fateful words reverberated across the sunny afternoon: 'You have been a naughty girl!'[6]

As was traditional, Lauris was the 'hands on' parent, tending wounded knees and feelings. It was she who read stories, listened as I learned to read – I remember a Janet and John book, the image on the last page indelibly fixed: Janet, freckly, gingery, skin 'English' pallid, stands timidly next to a swing. She looks weak, too scared to swing high. Playing outside, climbing trees, throwing myself around, knees covered in grass stains, dresses ripped around the waistband was more my style.

The bedroom we four children first shared in the Burns Street house was opposite the front living room. Waking in the darkness one night, I crept down the long hallway, past the hallway's tall red curtains, in search of parental comfort. I arrived at the kitchen door to find it closed, faint voices beyond it, Dad's a murmur, Mum's raised in tearful anxiety – something about money. Paralysed by a sense of doom, of the end of the world as I knew it, I was unable either to open the door (and risk parental reproval) or to return to bed on my own initiative. I don't remember the resolution. Perhaps with a nervous shuffling and whimpering I eventually slipped into the room, or maybe a maternal sixth sense picked up my presence and I was whisked away, sent back to bed, told: 'There's nothing to be afraid of!'

Oh, but there was! There was *Abou Ben Adhem*, the poem having entered my consciousness with its celestial visitations and pious morality and its 'angel writing in a book of gold … "The names of those who love the Lord".'[7] When I woke at night with the moon shining through the window, terror possessed me in case there was indeed an angel. It had nothing to do with whether or not I wanted, or feared, my name being added to the angel's book, not a whit. I knew nothing of God, religion not being part of our family culture. I can still quote the first few lines, though its worthy sanctimony leaves me cold.

What terrified me was that if angels were real, then so were ghosts, devils, monsters and all the other strange creatures whose disembodied noises inhabited the night, including possums, whose claws, scratching across the corrugated iron roof made a fearful screeching. Even after I had learned the source of the noise from my fearlessly impatient older sister Virginia, it was still capable of disturbing my nights.[8]

After my two sisters and I had moved to the 'outside bedroom' – accessed from the 'verandah room' – whenever I awoke and found myself in the clutches of the fearful dark, terrified of the threats that inhabited it, I was unable to get out of bed and go in search of Mum. The house was never locked – neither our bedroom nor the verandah room door – but going 'outside' into the dark and creeping along the few steps was not an option for me: I was quite simply frozen with fear. I would lie in bed and cry, 'Mummy, Mummy, Mummy, *MUMMY!*', desperation and hysteria mounting until she appeared, struggling out of sleep, to comfort me and soothe my unreasonable night terrors.

Lauris's parenting style did not include all of the rigours Fanny had imposed. Fanny was very fixed in her views, particularly over politics and health. I did not know, however, until Val Powell enlightened me, in tones of mildly bewildered censure, that Fanny sent her children outside to run barefoot on frosty ground – scourging the body, expunging self-indulgence – with the certain expectation that there would be similar benefits to the psyche. Fanny wished to instil in her children the kind of exacting self-discipline of mind and body that her father, with his weakness for drink, gambling and inappropriate sexual behaviour, had so blatantly and embarrassingly lacked.

Lauris was more liberal and the privations of her childhood were not repeated in ours – there was no ordering us outside in freezing Ohakune winters to toughen our feet and our minds! Nevertheless, I can see the legacy of such moral and physical strictures in her lack of tolerance of ailments and weaknesses. 'You're not sick, certainly not sick enough to stay home from school. Come on, get up and get dressed.'

Telling the truth was an inviolable absolute. When I was about seven, a broken 78 gramophone record was found under my bed. I was ordered by Lauris to confess to having broken the record and hidden it there. I denied doing so but, as I was considered to be less than particular with the truth, I was not believed. Lauris continued to insist that I admit to my crime, which I continued to deny. I was right and knew I was right. The battle of wills continued, my self-righteousness and self-pity growing in stature the more she insisted, until it reached a point where I was quite simply an exhausted wreck. She eventually gave up and no one ever confessed. Goodness knows which of my venal siblings committed the crime and then slipped the guilty evidence under my bed, hoping my parents would assume I was the perpetrator.

As an adult, Lauris admitted to me that the 'broken record' episode had been a salutary experience for her. She believed she was doing the 'right thing' in forcing me to own up: it would be a useful lesson, 'character-building'. However, when her persistence did not result in the anticipated outcome, she saw that not only were her methods unsuccessful but the consequences hurtful and destructive.

As a child, I wasn't aware that Lauris's codes of 'proper behaviour' were particularly strict – that was just the way it was. It came home to me when I became a parent. A complaining child who claimed to be ailing but didn't appear to have much the matter with them would receive scant sympathy from me, until bewildered distress propelled me into examining the origin of my response. Remembering my own hurt and humiliation at Lauris's insistence on weathering vicissitudes without complaint mortified me into a change of heart and habit. I decided to be a softer, more indulgent mother.

One of the few poems that directly references Burns Street and Ohakune, is 'August, Ohakune', an early poem that evokes the strangeness and gothic potency of the town and the mountain whose presence not only overshadowed the skyline and the psyche of the town, but left its indelible mark on us all:

> All night in winter the dogs howled
> up the hill in the mad woman's house –
> she had forty living inside ...

It was true. The house across the road was occupied by a Miss Seth-Smith. The road frontage, dense with trees, undergrowth spilling onto the margins of the gravel road, concealed a driveway that disappeared into bushy darkness as it climbed the hill. Leaving the road, entering that forbidding gloom, creeping up that drive induced a palpitating heart, ears and eyes on high alert, legs atremble and geared for instant flight. The house, an imposing old villa whose high frontage loomed over the bush, with steep steps up to a verandah, emanated a sinister Wuthering Heights-like aura that both fascinated and terrified.

The story we knew was that Miss Seth-Smith's father had been a 'remittance man'.[9] We knew nothing of the character of Mr Seth-Smith because he was dead. There was a farm, how substantial I've no idea, though I do remember my father proclaiming that its management was quite beyond Miss Seth-Smith. She had the dogs, though. Forty may be an exaggeration, but there was a great pack of them, yapping and dancing around her. They slept in her bed with her, or so we believed.

For extended periods she wasn't in residence – we knew they had taken her away to the 'mad house' in Porirua. At times when she was, she had boarders. Lauris describes her as appearing occasionally, 'walking down the road, or calling to see me, dirty, derelict, half mad, but bearing herself with a dignity that had a touch of grandeur about it'.

Once, when I was eight or nine, I went inside Miss Seth-Smith's house with the son and daughter of the current boarders. Unusually, I had walked home from school with them; I was seized by embarrassment and secret admiration when he had danced along the footpath lifting his leg and farting gleefully – nothing like that happened in our family! Wide-eyed with wonder and trepidation, I followed them up the steps, through the front door and into a substantial hallway.

At the far end, my wild imagination saw the most enormous trolley – the kind that is trundled out laden with cakes for afternoon tea in respectable sitting rooms, only this one, in dark-stained wood, towered over us, the upper layer reaching all the way to the ceiling. The only other inhabitant hung on the wall, 'an ancient stag, /eyeless, ghastly holes gouged / by rats, above the blackened door'.

Nothing remains in my memory beyond these two images. I suspect that the gouged, rat-eaten eyes come from a later time when Miss Seth-Smith had permanently disappeared, the front verandah had tumbled down and the house was rapidly descending into dereliction.

A couple of doors down from us lived a large Catholic family, the Jamesons. They went to the convent school, so we didn't really know them. They were liars and skites, boasting that they were related to Johnny Devlin, New Zealand's answer to Elvis Presley. Creatures such as Johnny Devlin and Elvis Presley were despised in our household – ignorant uncultivated louts who sang stupid mooning songs about 'lerve' (Dad's word).[10] However, Devlin was born in Raetihi and lived in Ohakune for a while before his family settled in Whanganui. It might've been true after all.

I was scared of the Jamesons. They used to gang up with the Berridges, a family of boys who lived up the road and over the bridge in Bracken Street. A favourite pastime of theirs was to torment sissies like me on their way home from school – name-calling, threats of what they might do if they caught me. Out of this arose The Wednesday War: Edmonds versus Jamesons and Berridges (realistically it was probably only Martin and me, Virginia being older and morally superior, the others too young). We, unpractised in the arts of fighting and scragging (Lauris would never have approved), hurled insults from behind our gate, on either side of which was a large, unruly hedge. In retaliation, they threw balls of mud at our house. It was terrifying and terrifically exciting both, especially as we were securely on our own property with the house as ultimate retreat. When explanation was demanded over the state of the front of the house, what could we possibly say? We knew nothing.

Years later, when I met Billy Berridge at a school reunion, he was mortified; he had no recollection of the childhood misery he had inflicted.

Next to the Jamesons' house was the stone crusher – a monster machine that chewed rocks into gravel to be spread on local roads – while beyond were paddocks, farmland, trees and scrub along the banks of the Mangawhero River. When our horses had performed one of their regular escapes, they could usually be found further down the road, munching on wild grasses growing on the verge near the river. On occasion, they found their way across the Mangawhero and into the 'Māori Bush', as we called it, where they were much more difficult to find.

Lauris described the memorable night Virginia, searching for them in the Māori Bush as darkness descended, did not return home. Lauris panicked; Trevor rang the local police declaring her lost; the rest of us sat around the fire in the sitting room in a state of desperate tension. Eventually, casually, Virginia arrived home, the horses in tow, wondering what all the fuss was about. It had taken her time to get to the horses, as much of the ground in the bush was soft and swampy. This was an early example of Lauris's anxiety over her children's safety.

Our horses were but one manifestation of wandering stock in Burns Street – there was also Miss Seth-Smith's bull, which didn't seem to have a home paddock. Its sinister presence was regularly encountered as it wandered the neighbourhood, finding its way down driveways and, to the chagrin of gardeners, into vegetable gardens where it helped itself.

One fateful Friday afternoon, Lauris discovered the large brute munching happily in our garden. Bulls being unpredictable, shooing it out was not an option. She rang Trevor at school, and he rang the local policeman, who hopped on his bicycle and pedalled over. Over his shoulder he carried a rifle and, exercising his discretion as the local law enforcement officer, he unceremoniously shot the beast stone dead. This was not quite what had been expected, although no one, bar Miss Seth-Smith, was greatly disturbed. I tiptoed past the gruesome mound of animal flesh that lay in our garden, afraid that it might not really be dead, that it might rise up, look balefully at me, lower its head and charge.

So what on earth was to happen to the great dead thing? A few nights later, after dark, there was a knock on the back door. Dad opened it to find Miss Seth-Smith, wearing a dripping oilskin and clutching a large carving knife in her hand. 'I've come to get my bull,' she said. She carved great chunks off it and took them home to feed her 'half starved, truculent, snarling' dogs. To be honest I don't remember them snarling; it's the bull, the beast, I remember – alive and dead. Another gothic Ohakune image.

'Over all was the mountain, Snow Queen / of an old tale, brilliant and deadly'. Lauris says the image comes from a story she remembers from her childhood about a queen with splinters of ice in her heart. Such dramatic tales were not unfamiliar; drama was part of our childhood. Lauris and Trevor had both been involved in drama at teachers' training college and university, though at that time there was no such thing as 'professional theatre' in New Zealand. We had a black and white photo of Dad as Henry Higgins lounging in a chair in a Dunedin Teachers' College production of *Pygmalion*; others of Lauris in a play with Bruce Mason at Wellington Teachers' College. During my childhood, they wrote (probably Lauris wrote) and performed plays, while Dad directed Gilbert and Sullivan operas at the high schools where he taught.

There's an irony in the fact that I always attributed my interest in theatre, my acting heritage, to my father. Even after Lauris had 'come out' as a writer I continued to do so – after all, she was a poet, not a dramatist or an actor. Yet it was Lauris and her family who had been actively engaged in drama, Fanny, for example, wrote plays for the local drama club in Greenmeadows. Lauris's description of writing and directing a sketch at training college, and her secret delight in playing 'the frantic producer', are testament to her experience and commitment. My father's family were businesspeople and not engaged in the arts. Nevertheless, it was his involvement in *Pygmalion* that I took as my 'acting heritage'.[11] It's another example of female invisibility – how I learned that my mother's activities were marginal while my father's took centre stage.

I remember one play Lauris wrote for Ken Lawn's birthday.[12] It was a thinly disguised portrayal of their group of friends and the thrills and absurdities of their lives in a small town. I remember a sense of excitement surrounding the important pieces of paper covered with Lauris's spidery handwriting; the tissue of carbon paper rustling beneath the top copy; the character names down the side of the page; the dialogue beside those names. Songbooks were spread over the table in the front room in the search for tunes for the lyrics Lauris had scrawled.

I recall costumes, too, though the image I have of pink silky satin spilling out of Lauris's sewing machine I think belongs to preparations for a New Year's Eve 1920s party: champagne and the Charleston. There were rehearsals – the muffled sound of the piano, voices swirling behind the closed door of the big front room. A line (and the tune) from one of the songs has stayed with me: 'My name is Flan I am your man, a problem does delight me.' Flan was Stan Frost, bed-assembler, Englishman, 'bachelor'.[13]

Just inside and behind the front door of the Burns Street house was the 'toy cupboard', a large wooden chest, painted cream, with three pale green cupboards beneath three pale green drawers. Inside was a jumbled mess of card games and board games, balls and knucklebones, a Viewmaster with its circular cards of transparencies that revealed vivid photographs of exotic landscapes and wild animals.

Next to the cupboard was the door to the front bedroom, and opposite was the door to the living room. Immediately beyond these doors was an archway with floor-to-ceiling red curtains, marking out a perfect stage area, with entrances either side.

Inspired by parental example, I decided I too would make a play. I persuaded my most obliging sister, Rachel, into this escapade and we spent a long morning behind the curtains, whispering intently, looking in the toy cupboard for 'props' and deciding what we would do. It being my venture, I did most of the planning, describing to Rachel what the play was about and what we would do.

We were ready to begin; the red curtains were ceremoniously opened to reveal Mum and selected siblings seated on children's chairs facing us, Rachel and me, the performers, expectancy in their gaze. Sudden bewilderment – what were we actually going to do? Bemused, uncertain, I began to talk about what we were going to do, then stopped as the realisation sank in that this was not the way plays happened.

Standing in front of my mother, feeling stupid, I realised instantly that knowing and doing were not the same thing, and that we didn't actually have a play. I'd talked about one, but I hadn't constructed one. The turbulent chaos of my imagination had not been translated or ordered into something coherent and presentable. It was my first and most fundamental lesson about drama; one I have never forgotten. Drama is action: performance requires preparation, writing and rehearsal.

Lauris was kind and encouraging over the non-event of my play and did not seek to improve or educate me. Perhaps she saw that I already understood.

Lauris and Trevor became involved with the Community Arts Service (CAS), established by the government in 1947 with the mission to bring performing arts – opera, ballet and theatre – to small-town North Island New Zealand. My first experience of live performance was seeing Puccini's *The Barber of Seville* in the rat-infested Ohakune Junction Hall (made possible by CAS), with Mary O'Brien, dressed in a rather dull dress sitting downstage left, singing her heart out. I can still see her, recapture the sense of wonder, the magic of real people up on a stage in front of an audience.

The ballet came to 'Kune too – Poul Gnatt's production of *Petrouchka*, the performers billeted with hospitable locals, including, naturally, Lauris and Trevor. Dorothea Franchi, the pianist who accompanied the ballet – and who reputedly carried a set of screwdrivers to fix dilapidated pianos in rural halls – stayed with us. A fierce woman, she spent her time in our front room practising on our Challen piano. Unaware of the sacredness of 'practice', I had the temerity at one point to enter the room, only to be severely reprimanded for 'interrupting' and sent packing. The sharpness of her voice, the sting of dismissal, are still present in my memory.

I didn't aspire to being an opera singer, though the possibility arose that I might be a concert pianist. After seeing the ballet, though, I wanted to be a dancer, with a graceful speaking body like those I had witnessed on stage. I begged Lauris to let me go to ballet but I was not allowed – 'too tall' was the reason given, though there may have been more compelling reasons like cost, and a reluctance to become involved in 'ballet culture'. We already had 'horse culture'; we did not need another all-consuming and expensive childhood obsession.

Mt Ruapehu is an abiding image of Ohakune. You could see it from the bathroom window at Burns Street; indeed, everywhere you went, there was the mountain, shining with snow, shrouded in cloud or bare and blue in summer. As a child I had no consciousness of it – it was just there, in the same way that we lived in Ohakune just because we did. The idea that we might live in another town without a mountain was inconceivable. It wasn't until Mum and Dad announced we were moving, and a rush of incomprehension, of dispossession swept over me, that I understood that this was where I belonged, where I would always belong. I was 11 years old.

It's still true. Burns Street shimmers in ghostly outline behind every house I have lived in, in substance, memory and imagination. I have spent my adult life recreating that magical haven, the alchemy not merely physical but a sanctuary of parental omniscience, the eternity of the early world where the greatest disasters are broken skin or a broken limb.

Whose dream, whose fantasy fulfilled was Burns Street? My guess is Lauris's, inherited from her parents. Trevor, a pragmatic man, would have appreciated the aesthetic of Burns Street – the substantial, graceful house, the long-established, beautifully maintained gardens – but he would also have been acutely aware on a practical level of how much maintenance it required. Maintenance meant money, and money caused him anxiety. Their overdraft, despite regular attention, never seemed to reduce itself to a non-worrying level.[14]

All my life I have gone back to 'Kune, the rough wild landscape that was imprinted on my psyche as a child stirring me in ways no other place ever has or can. What is it? Childhood? Time of innocence? Before I learned of the world's indifferent cruelties? Before multiple tragedies engulfed my family? All of those, but something else as well. The enormous silence, the great emptiness of the tussock plateau, the dark brooding of the immemorial bush, the thin high-country air where sound travels like thistledown, an echo across a fathomless ravine – that is what I remember, that is what stirs and contracts my heart every time I visit the town and commune with the mountain and the floating remnants of my childhood. I have taken thousands of photographs in a vain attempt to give substance to a yearning for what is irretrievably passed.

And Lauris? She felt something of the same attachment, not so much to Ohakune as a town, a place, a landscape, but more for what it represented in her life – rich years spent nurturing a growing and lively family, years when there was an expanding sense of future promise.

Only a couple of years after we left Ohakune, signs of fracturing in the façade of the idyll began to appear – Trevor's first mental breakdown; Rachel's rape in Greytown. And Lauris went back to university, reading feminist thought, beginning to understand that there were more options than she had hitherto considered, that the inner malaise she felt was not personal but a state recognised and experienced by women the world over. Perhaps there's a hint of this in the final line of 'August, Ohakune'– 'brooding / on the fate of frozen villages', and Lauris certainly captures the feeling of the town's gothic isolation:

> the river,
> intermittently tapping its menacing morse
> and the morepork call through the dark;
> at last the frost hunted us in
> to take shelter in a cold uneasy sleep.

On a recent journey I passed through Ohakune and stopped for a night. I walked down to the Burns Street house and discovered it was for sale. As I lingered, indulging in the pleasurable ache of memory, a family arrived who were thinking of buying it; a real estate agent was on the way. When they learned I had lived there as a child they asked if I would like to look through it with them. Would I ever!

The trees and gardens are long gone, the large, graceful section subdivided and built on – chalets, houses for winter skiers and the like. From the road, the house looks much as it always did, though a little worse for wear – the roof needs repair and it could do with a paint job. The front door still has the same frosted glass. Inside, the house is both acutely familiar and dislocatingly unrecognisable. The generous front room, where the piano stood against the interior wall, is now a bedroom, though the marvellously elaborate embossed ceiling and the fireplace with its kauri mantelpiece are still there.

The original children's bedroom opposite the living room is still a bedroom. In fact, most of the rooms are bedrooms; the house appears to be a winter lodge for mountain and snow adventurers, while the back part of the house has been so completely reconstructed as to be unrecognisable. Gone is the kitchen with its long walk-in pantry, the flour and sugar bins, eggs preserved in jelly, jars of dried fruit and nuts, biscuit and cake tins out of reach on the top shelf along with Lauris's preserves. Gone are the washhouse, the back porch, the bathroom next to Mum and Dad's bedroom. Instead, there's a wide back verandah with more bedrooms off it, and a sort of rumpus room where our kitchen used to be.

It feels neither right nor familiar, and I know with an absolute knowing that this old house lives and breathes in my memory rather than in its current rather tatty reality. Any attempt to lay its unprepossessing present over my vivid and engrossing recollections is not only futile, but actively destructive. I thank the family – who decide against buying it (too much work) – and leave.

4. Dark days: 1975

The night burns with a white fire
and the moths move silently
among the moon flowers; I see her
in the garden standing quite still
beyond the blurred darkness of the fig tree
smiling a little, her pale face
familiar but smaller than I remember it.
I cannot go to her; the Acheron,
river of sorrow, lies between us,
and the moon flowers' unearthly forebodings.

This poem is about my sister Rachel, dead in 1975 by her own hand at the age of 21, after several unsuccessful attempts and some years of struggling with mental illness. Sometime in 1973 I stood with Lauris by a bed in Auckland Hospital, watching as Rachel came to, after taking an overdose. I can still see her eyes flickering as they opened, the sigh of hurt breath, the frown of sadness creasing her young face as she turned away from us, murmuring the despairing words, 'I don't want to be here.'

At 23, I don't think I had any concept of the dark places to which she could and often did go. Did Lauris? Probably. 'A Note from Auckland', from *Salt from the North*, doesn't directly mention Rachel, but records Lauris's experience of visiting her in Ward 10:

Over the hill
the hospital is full of the hurt
of people holding tightly to
being alive, and some who must
drink the black juices of death.

'The Night Burns with a White Fire' is one of many, many poems Lauris wrote over the next 25 years as she attempted to understand, to be reconciled with, Rachel's suicide. She had watched a similar process happen with her younger brother, John, who took his own life in July 1955. Death, the final fullstop, is never in the frame until it has actually occurred. We could neither know nor believe that Rachel would eventually take that devastating path. In the last couple of years of her life, I remember an aura of anxiety – panic is not too strong a word – that clung to Mum where Rachel was concerned. What could she – what could we – do that might help, make a difference? Earlier in 1975, when Rachel had come back home to the house in Fergusson Drive, Heretaunga, after another suicide attempt, I remember Lauris telling me of a night when Rachel, possessed by inner terrors, cowered in her and Trevor's bed. Lying between them, they held her as she desperately and vainly tried to 'expel the demons'.

There's an earlier story. When still a teenager living at home in Heretaunga, Rachel had a dream: it was night and she was going out with friends in a car. As it turned off Hutt Road onto Haywards Hill Road another car, its headlights off, came hurtling down the hill and crashed into the car Rachel was in. I don't know the outcome in Rachel's dream but this sequence of events did subsequently take place, though fortunately, in the material world, the quick driver of the vehicle Rachel was in took evasive action and a collision was avoided. With hindsight, the dream contained, if not exactly a premonition of her own death, at least a sense that the grim reaper was close at hand.

Another story about Rachel comes from our Ohakune childhood and became a recurring nightmare of mine. Occasionally we would go on outings with other families, particularly the Lawns, whose house was located in a landscape of ragged hills. A track – more a stock route, though wide enough for a vehicle – cuts into the side of a conical hill as it carves its way up a near-vertical cliff, rivulets of murky water drizzling down into oily pools at the base, the corrugated hillside falling steeply to a narrow gully floor where a stream trickles.

This particular Sunday afternoon a dozen or so people, adults and children, straggle along the track avoiding cowpats, an after-lunch activity to occupy restless children. A sudden cry heralds an abrupt shift in energy and focus as Rachel trips and falls over the edge, rolling awkwardly down the corrugated hill like a rag doll, turning over and over. Dad strides crablike after her. I stare, my breath held as I will him to catch her, to save her from falling all the way to the bottom. After a few steps he does; he lifts her and carries her back to the safety of the track. My breath releases.

My dream ends differently: Rachel falls, tumbling, rolling over and over down the hillside, bumping over little ridges, down and down and down, her long black hair swirling and tangling about her. Dad goes after her but he is slow – painfully, incompetently slow. 'Hurry,' I silently beg him. 'HURRY!' But Rachel falls. Just before she reaches the trickle of water in the gully at the bottom, where I know she will lie face down in the water, I wake in a panic, hot and distressed. The dream is always the same: Rachel falls, Dad cannot catch her and I wake just before she lands in the gully. My sister falling forever into everlasting darkness, madness and death – eternity. I dream this dream over and over and over throughout my childhood and into my teenage years. Another premonition?

It is 1975, my second year at drama school. Late one winter afternoon, Wednesday 25 June, Mum rings to say Rachel has disappeared. A cold kept her home from work, but it's more than that. Mum has spent the day trying to draw her out of a 'pale, hollow-eyed silence'. In a moment of respite, Mum falls asleep and Rachel slips out of the house.

I get in my car and when I arrive at Fergusson Drive there's an ambulance in the driveway. Rachel has been found, wandering cold and distracted around the local park, and brought home. I stand with Mum as Rachel is helped into the ambulance, taken to Hutt Hospital.

Those of us in Wellington visit her the next night. Rachel is wan, ethereal, half out of this world, gentle and sad. She's taken weedkiller, paraquat – it's cheap and readily available. In a few days at most, it will cause her organs to fail: kidneys, liver, heart, lungs. There's no known remedy, the doctors tell us. There's nothing anyone can do for her now. Rachel knows, accepts. None of us is capable of saying words that acknowledge or even imply, however indirectly, that she will die. It's as if silence can obliterate this terrifying truth.

Saturday morning, 28 June. The paraquat has done its lethal, paralysing work and Rachel is now on life support. Mum, Katherine and I go to the hospital where Rachel lies unconscious, breathing with an oxygen mask. There's nothing for us to do. In the waiting room next door we sit, wordless, numb, possessed by dread. After a while, a doctor tells us the time has come to take her off life support. Helplessly, we pace the waiting room while in the next room Rachel slowly dies.

The police come; suicide is a crime and her body has to be identified. Mum, benumbed by shock and grief, asks me to do it. The policeman opens the door to the room where Rachel lies on her side facing the wall, her long black hair falling down her back. I stay by the door, paralysed in the presence of her death. I can barely see – the enormity of what is before me clouds my vision – nevertheless, the image is imprinted. It is still with me. 'Is that your sister?' the policeman asks, kindly enough. Yes, I nod.

Of what we do next, I have no recollection. I presume we went home to the house at Fergusson Drive and made tea. At Rachel's private funeral (we are unable face the world, its questions and judgements) I watch Lauris struggling to find the courage to bend over her open coffin, over her immobile face with its death mask of pancake makeup she would never have worn in life. I watch our mother tenderly touch her frozen face, brush her lips across the forehead of her dead daughter.

In her diary entry for that day, Lauris wrote:

When I looked at her dead face I was not afraid – though I did suddenly recognise the suffering which had never appeared in any living expression: it was there in the last look her living self had left, an imprint on her dead face, to remain now until everything vanishes but her bones. A look of age and suffering comprehension of far more than any young girl should know or have to know. So that was Rachel, I thought quickly – that was how it felt! And then I had that other quick sense that she must not be wished back. I touched her face, and it was colder than anything in the world – not like a person, and that was reassurance of a kind. There was no expecting life back there either.

It's a cold windy day at Akatārawa Cemetery when we bury her, our words whipped by the wind, tossed like rags into a torn-off corner of the sky. I read the song from *Cymbeline*, Act IV Scene II, a piece I learned at drama school.[1] Martin reads a piece from the New Testament, Hebrews 6:7–10.[2] A moment before he says the words 'But, beloved, we are persuaded better things of you', the wind dies and those few forgiving words stand clear of the tempest that has surrounded us since her death, a sign perhaps that she, at least, at last, is at peace.

In the aftermath we are kind, forgiving. Lauris writes in her diary of 'Frances ringing up every day, being tender and watchful to us all', and regularly comes to visit me where I live at Owhiro Bay, on Wellington's south coast:

I am at Frances's house and the sea in a southerly wind is all high green hills rolling over. A wonderful place – rocks like black cities, a sky full of storms. And this little warm shabby house, with its fierce little gas fire, and things hanging everywhere – the old brown brocade on the table, an orange rug over a squab-settee, Frances's Indian floral cotton on the couch, coats in a far corner. A little winter house, full of kindness and security and the wild weather everywhere around it.

Some months later, Lauris and I are required to attend the Coroner's Court. Neither of us knows what to expect, but what we do know is that reliving those terrible days is almost more than we can bear. We weep helplessly, profusely, as we mumble incoherent answers to the coroner's questions. He is kind, does not keep us long.

It's years before any of us can relive those days with even a modicum of equanimity. Indeed, in my forties, lying on my bed in the home I share with my partner and three children, I am overcome not only with grief and the loss of her but with regret and shame – why did we not sit with her, hold her, comfort her (and ourselves) as she died? We didn't know how: 'I cannot go to her: the Acheron, / river of sorrow, lies between us.'

After Rachel died it was impossible not to speculate on whether her dreadful violation at the age of 10 had contributed to the mental disarray to which she eventually succumbed. I didn't ever talk to her about it. Even in my twenties I wouldn't have known how to ask such private, transgressive questions. If she didn't talk about it, how could I risk distressing her, opening old wounds?

I would now, but she has been dead for over 45 years, more than twice as long as her lifetime. In Lauris's diaries, Rachel's death is only referred to in passing and her autobiography doesn't mention it in any detail either. Why not? It's a potent psychic event in the family. Shame? The stigma attached to a perceived failure of parental care? A lingering residue of her strongly moral and moralistic upbringing? Perhaps a sense also that this symptom of the chaos that was beginning to penetrate the heart of Lauris's large unruly family was better left undisturbed and unexamined.

Lauris's first grandchild, Ruth, was born slightly less than two years after Rachel's death. To Lauris, it felt as though the family was beginning to recover, to expand again after the terrible contraction of death and grief. There's no pathway back to life after a young and tragic death but all of the first-born daughters of Lauris's daughters have Rachel as their middle name, a quiet gentle breath to keep her memory alive and present in our lives and those of the next generation.

When in Wellington, if at all possible, I visit her grave in
Akatārawa – and Lauris's too. Although I miss my mother, visiting
her grave, standing or kneeling by her headstone, remembering her,
does not arouse the same grief as I feel about Rachel. Even after
more than 45 years, the feeling of terrible loss still regularly assails
me. More often than not I shed tears – for her, for the loss of her, for
her loss of a life so young, so vulnerable, and for the bewildering and
incomprehensible vacuum her suicide still represents in our family.

In 1975, disaster beset Trevor. After a number of nervous
breakdowns, he was forced to relinquish his headmaster's job at
Heretaunga College and go to work at the Correspondence School
in Wellington. He regarded this as a failure, to which he could never
be reconciled.

Two years earlier, Easter 1973, at a loose end after an intense
summer touring New Zealand with The Living Troupe,[3] I went
home for a visit. Dad had also come home – from Ashburn Hall in
Dunedin, a privately run residential psychiatric facility, where he was
recovering from an earlier breakdown. Shock treatment was one of
the therapies used, though no ameliorating effect was in evidence. He
spent the whole of Easter in his pyjamas, pacing the marital bedroom
in a state of acute distress, always a glass of something in his hand.
He was desperate and so was Lauris – who was this stranger in
the house, this person so reduced and raw that we did not want to
believe it to be husband or father? His distress was ours also.

He resisted returning to Ashburn Hall, though it was obvious
to all that he could not go back to work. None of us could provide
the care he needed; he had to go back there, offering respite for him
and some peace and sanity for the household. If he didn't, how were
we – how was Lauris – going to cope? But she could not or would
not take him. Or perhaps he refused to go with her? Whatever the
reason, it was decided I would accompany my father to Dunedin.
Lauris drove us to Wellington Airport.

Dad was subdued on the flight; on the half-hour taxi trip from Dunedin Airport to Ashburn Hall he became increasingly withdrawn, and by the time we arrived it seemed he no longer recognised the outer world or the daughter at his side. I escorted him up the steps and a nurse came to greet him. 'How are you, Trevor?' 'Not too good,' he replied, and sought the solidity of a wall. The nurse took him gently by the arm. Unable to abandon the safety of the wall, he slid his back along its surface, lengthening the distance between us until eventually they turned a corner, disappeared from sight. He did not look back. He did not say goodbye. How could this be my father?

My task was done but what on earth was I to do now? Lauris and I had not planned any further ahead and my return flight was not until tomorrow morning. Where was I to stay? I walked out the door, came to an aimless halt at the top of the steps. Fortunately, the taxi was still there. At my request, the driver took me somewhere spartan and cheap. I was awoken next morning by the mournful sounds of The Last Post – it was Anzac Day, the irony of losing my father the day before not lost on me. I shed bitter tears – for him, for myself. Never again would I be able to see him as a grownup authority; our roles had been irreversibly reversed.

By this time Lauris was working in Wellington, editing the *PPTA Journal* for the Post Primary Teachers' Association. Returning to Wellington, to the place where she began her adult life some 30-odd years earlier, was a homecoming and a new beginning, the first steps along a pathway she would follow for the rest of her life.

1975 was International Women's Year, an auspicious year to publish her first volume of poetry. *In Middle Air* went on to win the PEN Best First Book of the Year Award. Six weeks before Rachel's death, Lauris wrote to me of the manuscript being accepted for publication:

The publisher has accepted my book, but is pretty slow about getting going on it – I had to ring him up to get him to say yes or no, and now I think he's said enough to keep me quiet for a while. I am terribly delighted of course, but won't quite believe it until it happens. Write to me again dearest Frances; I miss you and will be very glad when you come back to my town again. You're a dear dear girl, and I hope that being too busy is still doing you good.

Later that year, the lovely house at 401 Fergusson Drive, now blighted by tragedy, was put on the market. Lauris and Trevor moved to Wellington to a house at 22 Grass Street, halfway down a hillside walkway in Oriental Bay. Grass Street would become Lauris's house, chosen after the death of Rachel, and Trevor's loss of his headmaster's job, propelled the family out of Upper Hutt. It was not just her home, it became her anchorage, her centre, the place where she was to construct and realise her identity as a writer, as an independent woman on her own terms – as a grandmother too, since the first of 15 grandchildren was born after she and Trevor moved there.

Of course, at the time she could not 'know' this future, or that she was beginning her second life, forging an identity as a writer, or that Grass Street would become a kind of 'literary salon'. She would live there for the rest of her life and die there.

PART II

Moving on

5. The Edmond family

The extreme lows of 1975 were counterpointed by the publication of Lauris's successful first book of poems the same year. Such uncomfortable conjunctions were repeated through my mother's literary life over the next 25 years. Evolving family opposition to her use of family in her writing was a further complicating factor.

Roger Robinson wrote in *Te Ara: Dictionary of New Zealand Biography*:

> *Lauris Edmond was 51 when she began to publish poetry, and quickly won attention as a voice that was both mature and fresh. Identified at first with the 1970s upsurge of poetry by women, she was later recognised for her breadth of appeal and ability to reach people who otherwise read little poetry, as well as earning high honours in the literary and academic worlds. She is now recognised as one of the best New Zealand poets of the late twentieth century, a compelling voice for women, an exquisite poet of the epiphanic moment, and a writer who left Wellington some of its most distinctive verbal evocations.*

This 'public' view of Lauris is in abrupt contrast to the 'private' view of some family members. While much of the opposition took place inside the family there was the notable occasion when my sisters Virginia and Stephanie wrote a disclaiming letter to a Wellington newspaper, questioning the 'truth' of what Lauris had written in the second volume of her autobiography, *Bonfires in the Rain* (1991), and dissociating themselves from her version. Yet, for Lauris, family was of fundamental importance and, given that making and nurturing a family is a profoundly creative act in itself, it's no surprise she wove it into in her writing.

Lauris and Trevor were modern, unconventional, educated and liberal – politically and socially. Both had flirted with communism in the 1940s, both rejected old-fashioned disciplinarian ideas of child-rearing in favour of more flexible, humanitarian ones. When we were young children, we addressed our parents as Lauris and Trevor. I remember when that changed. I would have been in my first years at primary school and at the school gate my addressing Lauris by her name raised small-town eyebrows. Conventional modes of address won the day and they became Mum and Dad.

As the years passed, they seemed to subscribe more to the 'natural order' of 1950s New Zealand: Dad operated out in the world of men and money; Mum was the homemaker – managing the expanding household.[1] Money was often tight, and although Lauris never had a job outside the home, bits and pieces of extra work were welcome when they could be found. Reporting on Ohakune events for the *Wanganui Chronicle* was one such venture they both took on, freelance work that could mostly be done at home.

Dad was a charming, good-humoured, successful teacher, involved in extra-curricular activities as well. He carried a natural authority about him both in the classroom and out of it, and pupils liked, admired and respected him. At home, in a house where women predominated six to two, he was an outsider; going out into the world he would take my only brother with him – to football and cricket games – while we girls stayed and played at home.

At the dinner table, especially when we older ones were teenagers and attending the school where Dad taught – by this time Kuranui College in Greytown – conversations focused on the life of the school, events and activities. It was not only his focus, but ours. Lauris, attempting to participate in such dinner-table talk, would be roundly rebuked by us, her children, with 'Shut up, Mum, you don't know what you're talking about.'

What on earth could she know, she who spent all day at home, looking after the house, servicing us and our needs? Did we take our cue from Dad? In some inchoate way we must have. Certainly, he did not admonish us. I think of this with shame: not one of us defended her, thought her interesting, saw anything wrong with such belittling. We took for granted that she – a woman and a mother – was boring; her place was in the background while Dad was the interesting, informed, intelligent parent. Nor, ironically, did I perceive in our treatment of her, our implicit assumptions, any implications for myself or my own future. She was not, could not be my role model.

After Trevor had his first breakdown, when I was 14, family dynamics entered a sustained period of gradual irrevocable change. Lauris devoted enormous thought and energy to Trevor's rehabilitation, while for us children he became increasingly absent and unavailable. He recovered for a time, got a new job as a headmaster and became involved in education politics as national president of the PPTA. After the move to Heretaunga there were more breakdowns and, although there were periods of respite there was no long-term recovery. My father's mental wellbeing was in a protracted decline, while Lauris began to discover (or perhaps rediscover) herself as a working woman and subsequently as a successful writer.

At a recent family birthday party, a journalist friend asked me if I thought Lauris's rise to significance as a writer and independent woman and Dad's decline into obscurity and illness were directly connected. It's an unfortunately simplistic idea, implicitly laying the blame for Dad's decline at Lauris's feet. As if there's a limited capacity in any relationship for public achievement and recognition, meaning that if one party is on the rise the other must, of necessity, be in decline.

Lauris caught the second wave of the feminist zeitgeist and rode it poetically and personally to distinction and acclaim, while Trevor lost himself, lost his path, and retreated into the shadows of an awkward, troubled, solitary existence. One was not, however, the direct cause of the other. The 'causes', if one can use such a blunt term, lie in their personalities and the tumultuous times in which they lived.

Dad would not, could not, did not know how to change, to adjust to new and often uncomfortable circumstances. Although he did not remain trapped in the kind of generational thinking that saw marriage as two halves with clearly defined roles that together made a whole, it was not in his nature to be adaptable in personal and domestic ways. He had no training at it, whereas Lauris, as a woman, had a lifetime's experience – training, if you like – in the art of adapting, fitting her needs and desires around the demands of others. She saw possibilities, explored and devoured them, cantered into an exciting and explorative future.

In a primordial sense, however, I have come to the conclusion that there's an Edmond family 'collective unconscious' – perhaps even a semi-conscious – that is seduced by the idea that Lauris's 'abandonment' was a significant contributor to Dad's breakdowns, his mental collapse, his decline into alcoholism and despair. Had she remained the dutiful loving wife, stood by him as loyal companion and helpmate, he could have been the man he should have been. It's a stultifyingly conventional idea, but the Edmond family culture is a mix of entrenched conservatism and liberating iconoclasm. The concept of a genuine role reversal in which Dad admired her efforts to recreate her life, supported her, allowed her to take centre stage while he took a back seat – has no substance. It's an empty fantasy. He felt betrayed, fought her and blamed her. That culture of blame is a hoary thread that still runs through the family.

Lauris as 'neglectful mother' is another trope: controlling, interfering, abandoning, manipulative. At times she was all of these things – a flawed human being like the rest of us – but she was loving, devoted, wise, generous, fun. In my childhood she was a conscientious, devoted mother – at times too much so: unwilling to let us out of her clutches, afraid of the dangerous world, a smothering moralistic parent. For my younger siblings, the roaring excitement of her own life left her much less time – or inclination, probably – to be the hands-on, totally engaged parent she had been for us older children. Trevor, defeated and self-absorbed, was even less competent or interested in parenting by then.

In the Edmond family parenting analysis, the failures – the 'crimes' – are attributed to them both, though Lauris, as mother, was the more culpable, as the parent who was ever present, dispensing judgements and determining behaviour. However, both were potent personalities. Culturally, and in a familial context, Dad, 'poor man', is easy to forgive: defeated, impotent, sad. Lauris – independent, successful, breaking the rules and embracing herself on her own terms while neglecting her 'proper role' – is an easy target.[2]

Lauris's ultimate maternal 'crime', though, was that she overshadowed us all – in the wider world she was more notable, more significant than any of us, her children or her husband. She did not 'know her place', refused to know it, refused to fit into the received definition of who she should be, how she should behave. It's still the case that for a woman to grasp opportunity is exceptional – to be remarked upon, analysed, evaluated as appropriate or not. In Lauris's day it was even tougher, which makes her ability to step outside convention and her resilience once having done so even more remarkable. My father's surprised response at Lauris wanting to do something for herself was, 'But your happiness is in my success.'

What would Lauris make of my analysis of the toxic miasma of Edmond family dynamics? Would it bear her scrutiny? She and I spent many hours discussing such things, but she's been dead for 20 years and my thinking has evolved in that time. I know she would agree that part of the price she paid for choosing her own path was the loss of family support and approval, a rejection of her work and even of her right to write. And any scrutiny would be tempered by

love and concern for her children; by a conflicting desire to protect
not only us, but her memories of what she dreamed for us all and
for herself; and by an unwillingness to apportion blame.

Loss is chameleon, opportunist, not merely grief, but longing for
what has irretrievably passed and gone. We want to relive our
experience, for it to last beyond momentary recollection when of
course it doesn't – that is the ache of longing. Living with this sense
of loss is part of the human condition, though it becomes more
particular and acute as we age. This is true whether our lives move
at a steady pace, drift or hurtle along. Lauris had a particularly
potent dose of it.

One particular aspect of loss that obsessed her was that of family
cohesion. Early in her writing life, in some notes for a proposed
interview with Riemke Ensing around 1977, she drew a parallel
between poetry-making and parenting:

> *These two impulses, the search for order and the capacity to live
> beyond it, are central to any creative experience. Considering
> them in the light of my own history I have come to the
> somewhat curious conclusion that there are more similarities
> between poetry-making and the other kind of parenthood than I
> had supposed.*

I recognise Lauris's desire for order in her parenting style; she
expected – nay, demanded – that we (her 'poems') be beautiful and
suitable, live up to her standards and aspirations.

In Ohakune, when we were young children and lived on the
fringes of town on a large, tree-lined section with neighbours some
distance away, achieving such standards was possible. When we
moved to Greytown and lived behind and above the chemist shop
on the main street, familial privacy and the pretence of perfection
were much harder to maintain (though even in Greytown we could
still be lined up and admired as a remarkably handsome family – not
an ugly dud among us).

In Greytown it was no longer possible for my teenage turbulence not to spill out of the house and become public knowledge. Lauris's attempts to keep me in order (forbidding me to get into cars with boys; insisting I stay home when I wanted to go out, read the 'right' books, wear the 'right' clothes, have the 'right' friends) led to endless trouble.

Once, in the kitchen, in a furious rage, I pushed her; she tripped backwards and fell to the floor in an ungainly heap. I had the decency to be shocked and mortified at my own force. It might even have given brief pause to my teenage tantrums but if so, it didn't last. I regularly shouted, flounced, raced stomping up the stairs, slamming the door to the bedroom I shared with well-behaved Rachel. So often and so loudly did I pound the stairs that the poor chemist in his shop below had to ask my parents if it would be possible to not have his custom disturbed by furious teenage feet.

I can't honestly say I experienced Lauris's parenting style as 'poetry-making', not even with hindsight. Tumult and pandemonium were common in our large and disparate household, conflicts between siblings rising like tidal waves roaring in and falling away just as quickly. When we were young, such phenomena could be dismissed as freedom of expression, but as the family grew up and the conflicts persisted, such lawlessness led to major, and in some cases permanent, ruptures.

In *The Quick World* Lauris wrote of 'dark passages of family conflict'. They mortified her, yet she was often self-justifying and chronically unable to leave well enough alone. Consequently, on occasion, various of her children withdrew, which was the most hurtful, the most effective punishment that could be inflicted on her. Then in the late 1980s:

> *Two (family) members suddenly – and then persistently – expressed such violent rage towards me that it took me a long time to grasp the fact that it was happening and longer still to understand the reasons for it.*

Some of these conflicts remained unresolved when she died, and indeed appear metaphorically epigenetic, passed down into the next generation, though it's too soon to know whether or for how long they will persist. My children and some of my nieces and nephews have become impatient with their parents' tortured family feuds, maintaining instead an affectionate distance.

As a family we had little or no experience of successful conflict resolution. Essentially, we learned that the outcome of any conflict could not be about getting what one wanted – that was unspeakably selfish. Even having the temerity to ask for what one wanted or needed was a travesty of good manners.[3] Being forbidden to assert what one wanted meant conflict could degenerate into preventing the other person getting what *they* wanted. Afterwards, the version of events that prevailed depended on the most persuasive occupation of the moral high ground. Resolution of the original conflict was never on the agenda. Once harsh words had been spoken, anger had dissipated, frayed tempers had settled and silence had gone on long enough, communication would be restored. The pattern would repeat itself over and over and wearyingly over again.[4]

Conflict turned up elsewhere, too. Lauris didn't like to be asked for help; she preferred to offer. Being asked had overtones of being taken for granted, as if her children only appreciated her for what she could do for them, and assumptions were being made about her willingness and availability. She was also wary of the sting of being cast in conventional roles.

During her year in Menton, France, in 1981 she travelled with Virginia and her family.[5] In her diary, Lauris wrote about the experience with some bitterness:

> *[I have] the feeling that I've been hired to be useful. And useful I am but it would be tactful of them occasionally to treat me as an independent individual who has chosen to come with them and who exists apart from their claim … they make me act an ungraceful role and do not even see that I am full of conflict about it. Her only personal approaches are about the wrongness*

of my clothes, or my hair or my habits … Her whole attitude to me is one of suspicion. I am to be cut down to size and kept that way. I couldn't bear it for long – the week is half over, just as well.

Moreover, I live, if I live with other people, by talking with them. There is virtually no conversation … and all attempts are interrupted by the children anyway.

A memorable breakdown between Lauris and me occurred over the possibility of her babysitting my children for a weekend so their father and I could go away. When it came to the crunch none of the possible weekends suited her. I, gripped with a sense of injustice, shouted at her. She justified herself; I rejected her justifications. Impasse! The energy ran out eventually; there was the predictable silence (quite a long one in this case) and eventual re-engagement.

One strand that runs through Edmond troubles arises, I think, from Lauris's habits of intense intimacy and how tightly she bound us together. She took for granted the primacy of the familial bond, and assumed that, as she didn't question it, nor would we. Wanting us to love each other (and her), she willed us to get along, to engage with each other, by using such dubious techniques as telling each of us what other family members thought and said about us, presumably hoping her 'advice' would encourage us to question our behaviours and 'improve'. Predictably, it only bred more conflict.

This desire for a strong familial bond can, I think, be traced back to her mother's family, the Prices, whose very survival, like that of all immigrant families of the time, depended on working together while aspiring to a better life. But we do not 'need' each other as the Prices did. These days, there is no longer any imperative to engage with members of one's family if there is no affinity, no attraction, no real liking.

By the 1990s, when her children were moving into their middle years, with their own families and busy lives, Lauris became preoccupied by the seemingly insoluble family rifts. After publication of the final volume of her autobiography, she finally had time to reflect on her parenting style and the origins of the animosity from various family members, particularly Virginia and Martin, who most steadfastly opposed her.

It was within this frame that her early confessions to me about her marital troubles were replaced by confessions of her struggles with family rifts. She would come to stay, or there would be letters or phone calls, where she would go over and over the territory, ask me what I thought, what she should do. For a good few years I listened, made suggestions, offered advice. Eventually I began to feel made use of. She was in my house with my family and yet all conversation, all attention, was on my older sister.

My frustration was partly that, despite all my careful listening and suggestions of possible pathways to a resolution, nothing changed; the problem remained intractable. When I reached my limit and asked her to stop going on and on about her broken relationship with Virginia, Lauris famously said to me, 'But how can we be friends if I can't talk to you about my problems?' To which some possible replies might be: 'You are my mother, not my friend, and she is my sister'; 'It's called "cross-generational bonding"'; 'Go and get some counselling'; 'What about talking to me about my family for a change?'. She did try. In an unsent letter to me dated January 1988, which I found among her papers, she wrote:

> *I thought yesterday that I wouldn't be able to come to stay with you (you would be kind about the family wars, I would cry and be feeble, I'd want to talk and talk about it – and none of it would be fair). The immediate reason was that I was right about Martin and I had a letter from him yesterday that still makes me reel from its viciousness; what I've decided to do is write this letter to you, getting some things off my chest, and then there is a good chance that I will be able to come, and not talk about it while I'm there.*

The letter continues about the hostility of Virginia and Trevor, and now Martin, and her pessimism at the possibility of any improvement. She concludes:

I know you said I'm not to 'know' these things, but actually at the moment I have to convince myself that there is no hope of anything better; otherwise I don't know how to survive it. There now, I hope that will stop me being obsessive when I see you. It's a couple of weeks away anyway, I must have got my house in order a bit by then.

In July 1992 she wrote in her diary:

I've fully admitted my moralistic cramping of [Virginia's] individuality when she was young. I see it only too clearly – absolutely, profoundly and in great anguish I see that with her, with Martin, with Rachel I didn't even begin to say as I should have 'You are wonderful as you are'. What I said was 'I love you but I want you to be better'. Worse, I think now that like all the legions of mothers without power or opportunity for separate development, I thought their 'being better' was part of me. So there was a fundamental unwillingness, incapacity to let go. That's the worst thing – in all my years of agonising about Rachel, and about the painfulness of everyone's breaking away, only now have I reached this ground base.

Dear Mum, you wore it so hard. I wish I had been more understanding, more comforting, not quite so caught up in my own stuff. But, you know, there's a point when what you did as a parent, with the best of intentions, simply has to be lived with; blame is pointless and destructive.

I didn't escape the 'moralistic cramping' any more than my siblings, though it took a different form, beginning earlier and lasting longer. Sloughing off this punitive baggage has been an essential part of my growing up – and eventually Lauris's too, though my journey out of the dark cave of Edmond family morality and into the light of liberation began earlier than hers. Part of it was my place in the family – middle child of the elder three, between the 'Princess' and the 'Golden Boy'. They were the ones who were imbued with Lauris's aspirations, while I was more problematic, 'difficult'. She is known to have said of me, 'Frances was never there when the moral lessons of the family were being instilled.'

It's my great good fortune, if not to my credit, that I was absent, that I missed out on such a dreary education. I was – metaphorically speaking – 'down the river with John Birch', a notorious teenage escapade where I got into a car with some local boys and they drove down to the Waiohine River. Nothing happened; it was merely that I had committed the unthinkable – deputy principal's wayward daughter caught with local boys in car!

Even as a child I often felt I didn't belong, that I was the 'black sheep', the 'adopted one'. Being 'not there', going away, was as much as anything a protective mechanism – finding people, places and things to do where I could be part of the action rather than the 'outsider'. Having a flexible approach to morality – being labelled as a liar – was, in this context, probably an asset, a bonus even.

Despite intermittent ruptures (hers and mine), thorny, complex relationships – both in and out of the family – were a continuing discussion we shared. Lauris's diary, 25 February 1995:

> *Frances said something very succinct and clear about this, one day in her garden when we talked on my January visit. I asked her why she thought it had taken such a staggeringly long and painful time for each person in the family (but especially the older ones) to grow away from their first family and into their own second, real one. She said I made it impossible – I wanted to be inside each person's life with them, and the rewards for letting me in were very great but in the end the penalties were terrible. The impossibility of shaping their independent selves in their own way, not mine. Of course I know this, but it was somehow clear and fair to hear her say it so simply. It made me think of Fanny – this is how I grew up, and eventually away, and this is exactly the reason it took me too so long to do so.*

And in late July of that year, she wrote:

I thought tonight that by taking so long to grow up and into myself that I had sold my children short. What I am now, this person who has learnt to give proper value to myself, and how to be tolerant and compassionate towards them, to leave them to learn for themselves (but in an atmosphere of shaped approval), I wish they'd had. They didn't because it wasn't there – all the best things in myself I kept a secret, held them in so they couldn't grow and become strong. And what values did I adopt instead? Trevor's – Trevor's timorous yet bossy dominance was what I allowed and took for myself. When it got too strong, too limiting, I didn't leave, I stayed there for years and years not using my own courage, and not letting my children have its benefits either – so nobody breathed really deeply in those years, as I do now in a world that is a million times larger than the one I allowed myself, or my children, when we lived with Trevor. Is this self-admiring, unjust to him? Or simply, sadly true?

Hindsight is an illuminating gift. What parent has not, in these terms, 'sold their children short'? And, given our patriarchal heritage, how many women can claim, with total honesty, never to have been subjected to the dominance of such ways of thinking or, in more intimate terms, the dominance of a man? It's also true that Lauris's understanding of the truth outstripped her ability to enact it. In the heat of the moment such reflective wisdom could not hold its ground.

In 1996, after a breakdown between my brother and me, which, naturally enough, I discussed with Lauris, she wrote to me:

I know I said quite a lot about my sense that, with Virginia, he was given too much of the wrong kind of power in the family. Mulling this over, I want to add something else. I've been pondering, for one thing, that our family made these late and painful discoveries when it was already moving apart anyway, as the new young families took over in importance. At that point we were all establishing differences that in an ideal family we would no doubt have recognised and respected much earlier.

This prompts me to raise another piece of heritage I think is relevant. When I left home to go to university, Lauris's style of intense and overpowering intimacy was what I thought of as the norm in relationships, what I expected and indeed wanted. Discovering that it wasn't, that such levels of intimacy were simply unsustainable, was an often painful, sometimes humiliating and occasionally ludicrous process of readjustment. I struggled, resisted, hoped; was disappointed, laughed at, withdrawn from as 'too much'; and often found myself turning to her in bewilderment, though as she was still firmly inside the walled garden of her marriage and the strict moral codes she had grown up with, her explanations were often, at that stage of my life anyway, unsatisfactory.

As I grew into adulthood, though there would always be a part of me that wanted intense intimacy, still sought it out in relationships, I came to understand that I would seldom find it, except in her. Thus, letting go of the ties that bound me to her was never going to be a simple process.

That evolved, of course. As the distance between us expanded, and I had my own family, what I wanted became more practical, less intimately and intensely emotional. Grandmotherly help and companionship were welcome, but I became increasingly resistant to 'advice'. Long periods of harmony and goodwill were interspersed with ungraceful and sometimes explosive tussles. I would throw her out of my life – though never permanently – while she would refuse to see the nature and consequences of what I described as her unwelcome meddling.

Nor was the letting go straightforward for her. The enforced slackening of the mother/child bonds created an emotional vacuum that, for someone like Lauris was unsustainable.

She began to shift her focus from the failing individual relationships to examination of the collective one – the family as a unit and her place in it. In her autobiography, this question – this search for a perspective on herself – was a fundamental and earnest consideration. But within the family, she struggled to integrate any insights into her behaviour. She wasn't malign, cruel or controlling in her intentions, and as she aged she came to a much better understanding of mistakes she had made – her moralistic generation had made – in parenting. Perhaps her major flaw was to be so very effective.

For a number of years, Raetihi was my and my children's summer holiday destination of choice – a version for me, and I hope eventually for them, of 'somewhere you are always going home'.

In the summer of 1996 Lauris joined us for a few days. One of the outings we took was a drive to Ohakune, to the Burns Street house. Nothing much happened – the car rolled past, we looked at it, she and I engaged within by personal recollections. For the rest of the afternoon, she was in an impossible mood, 'martyrising herself' as I called it. She was clearly distressed but when questioned, insisted there was nothing wrong, she was fine. Yet she sat in the front passenger seat melodramatically turned away, gazing silently out the car window, surreptitiously wiping away leaking tears. How could we not notice? Her gloomy presence infected us all.

Much later, she admitted she had indeed been pining for all that had been lost: home, an intact happy family, her third daughter, a loving relationship, unlimited possibilities, a future. Why didn't she say so at the time? I would have understood, my kids would have been kind and sympathetic. Some twist of personal drama, a desire to experience fully what she was feeling, coupled with some absurd notion of not 'imposing'; manners requiring her to keep her thoughts and feelings to herself? Yet pretending to an equilibrium she obviously didn't possess was a far greater imposition.

As the 1990s progressed and my life became more complicated, the stark realities of impending choices propelled me into more independent thinking. My fallings out with my mother became increasingly fraught and hurtful as a result, especially during 1997. These breakdowns were compounded by Lauris being unable to leave the restoration of equilibrium to time.

There were the letters that became famous within the family in which she persisted in explaining, justifying, moralising. Fiona Kidman told me that Lauris would show her drafts of letters before she sent them. Fiona read the drafts and invariably advised Lauris not to send them, Lauris invariably sent them, they invariably caused trouble:

> *Thank you for your letter. It is clear and straightforward, and I listen to what you say and respect your position. Thinking about it, I realise that the idea I had about you for so long was not really appropriate. That you were 'different' in the family – more tolerant, kinder, less aggressive than others in the family who were establishing their separate identity in a much fiercer way. No doubt you do have all those qualities, I believe you do, but I think I misunderstood the fact that I must not use them for myself. I should always have looked for comfort and advice to my own generation – and I enormously regret (because of the effects on you) that I did not.*
>
> *I didn't see, or fully understand, that you too were separating yourself, as everyone should and must, it was just that your style was different. You didn't have any responsibility for my problems about Virginia, or anyone else, and I should never have thought of you as a sort of family counsellor. Regret now is useless of course, it was a part of my own immaturity at the time and I could do no better ... However, when parents say they did their best, and didn't realise their own mistakes at the time – which is always true, it certainly is for me – I think this doesn't make the person in the younger generation feel any better. It's to do with the big shift in responsibility I suppose.*

To put our conflicts in context, though, the ones between Lauris and me were relatively minor compared with the major breakdowns between Lauris and Virginia, and Lauris and Martin, which lasted years.

At the end of 1997, when my own family disintegrated, the dynamic between us took another and much more benign and productive pathway. As I struggled through separation, Lauris was staunchly on my side: generous, thoughtful, loving and hugely supportive.

Another aspect of the disintegration of family cohesion that deeply troubled Lauris was the more broadly festering social problem of male aggression, particularly abusive behaviour towards women. Though it seldom found its way directly into her writing, one example is her last, unfinished project, which I worked on with her – the story of Pauline Brown, who shot her violent husband and was incarcerated in Arohata Women's Prison.

There was also a personal aspect to this issue. In Lauris's last few years, one of my sisters and I took out protection orders against abusive partners, struggling through the Family Court to find workable solutions that protected us and our children. Lauris found the fact of domestic violence in her close family network deeply distressing and did as much as she could to help my sister and me establish new and independent lives.

It caused her to reflect on her own experience of marriage and Trevor's angry ill-treatment of her, examining the power dynamic that played out within our formative family experience and how it had contributed to two of her daughters entering abusive, controlling relationships.

Abusive behaviour by men is only obliquely referred to in her writing ('Towards the Planet', 'Latter Day Lysistrata', 'A Desirable Property on an Elevated Section') while family conflict – the ruptures, the agonies – is territory she did not enter into. Presumably it was too raw and she couldn't find the words, a way in.

There's never a single cause; rather, a complex of factors that offer some insight. Obviously, there's the wider social context – the almost universal historical assumption that men are 'in charge', women are secondary. The underlying legacy from the monotheistic religions (and Greek thinking) is that a woman is a man's property, his chattel. The unequal power dynamic between Lauris and Trevor was a contributor. As Trevor came under stress in his job and their relationship foundered, he scoffed at her, belittled and demeaned her. As far as I am aware, he didn't stand over her, intimidate her, beat her up – as was done to me by my partner – but he was certainly capable of venomous verbal abuse. And, as already described, as a teenager I had been party to dismissing her, telling her to 'shut up', and not being called on it by him or anyone else.

In her diary Lauris wondered

> *how much those years when Trevor treated me as a boring and irritating sort of servant have implanted in her (V) – and Martin too – their present habit of treating me so scornfully. Probably it's got quite a lot to do with it. The sins of the fathers – of mothers; because my weakness was as much a part of the degrading business as his desire (or need) to use me as a butt. I had ceased to be anything at all for Trevor except what he needed, or what he was denied – nothing in myself at all.*

When we were young we did not question this second-class status of women – 'the weaker sex'. The attitude was pervasive and assumed to be the natural order of things, until second-wave feminism turned the spotlight on it. Thus, the example she set us – of accepting being on the receiving end of disparaging behaviour and not demanding respectful treatment – was not questioned either. Moreover, it's difficult to imagine how she might have done it without drawing down more contempt.

Conversely, there was her potency as parent and person, as psychological and moral force. To oppose her was futile. In her last years she explained to me that she had learned in her teacher training that it was her responsibility to be strong and authoritative, to give certainty – in other words to be 'right'.

After the publication of her autobiography, she wondered in her diary whether she should write something more:

… perhaps not for publication – more of the real truth of the terrible hatred Trevor turned on me, the bursts of venom, the contempt.[6] *Nobody knows of this because I of course kept it out of the story, and the children don't know and should not have to know. Perhaps Margaret [Scott], to whom I talked through all those years, is the only person who does – and she says, now, that other people as well (a few anyway) read my story as a declaration of self-interest – 'if only they knew what it was really like to be treated as you were by Trevor'. Of course, I long ago made up my mind that I could have saved my own skin if I'd cut all contact with him – and I couldn't seem to do it. Just let it go now, I suppose that's best; after all who in the world – and their own family – really understood the true nature of the hell people live in. This was, or is mine. There are many others.*

Dear Mum, I wish I had known more. Now I can see the patterns, know the truth of what you say. In all probability I wasn't ready, and the world at the time had not opened its eyes to the appalling treatment of women in our society, or the abuse of the vulnerable in our public institutions and churches.

I take issue with 'the children don't know and should not have to know'. Children are aware, even if not consciously; you cannot protect them from its effects. My children were profoundly affected by the dynamic between me and their father, just as I (we) were affected and influenced by that between Lauris and Trevor. To not be told anything is to be denied any opportunity to understand. But I know why she didn't tell us – the same reason I didn't tell my children: I didn't want to put them in the position of having to juggle conflicting parental versions of the relationship breakdown, perhaps forcing them to choose sides. I didn't think I had that right and I did not want to compete.

Looking back, I can see that within the Edmond family, Lauris and Trevor, as their relationship imploded, received typically unequal, gendered treatment. He attracted sympathy – his decline, his failures were met with tolerance and forgiveness, while she was maligned and criticised by many for her successful endeavours.

6. Daughter to mother: The wheel turns

A mother's love is bred into the bone.
A daughter wants her life to be her own.

It's a delight, this poem, this villanelle, this ironic riff on the evolving nature of the mother/daughter relationship, from its passionate beginnings and sacrifices to its sobering, hard-won self-knowledge. A mother of five daughters, Lauris wrote from experience. This second line rings particularly true for her daughters because of the intense intimacies she established and wished to sustain.

Here is Lauris describing me as a small child:

She ate everything in sight but seemed scarcely to sleep at all; when she was displeased she made the most dramatic scenes I had ever witnessed, throwing herself about with an abandonment that looked like flying. When she cried hard she went down and down the scale till she lost her breath, went deadly pale and actually became unconscious for a moment before she took an instinctive breath and began to revive.

She quite rends my heart at times, she is such a radiant little creature when happy and yet so many things seem to cause her frustration and dissatisfaction and give her that bewildered wistful air that is so pathetic.

Dearest Mother, there are so many things I wish I had said to you before you died, but you left so suddenly. At the time my own life was in such disarray as to leave little room for contemplation of either past or future; the present was furious enough. So this will have to do, though it's a great sadness that I will never receive a reply; of necessity, this is a one-sided conversation. I will try to imagine how you might respond, how you might share in my reminiscences, give your perspective, your version of events.

I find to my surprise that there are still some tender places, wounds that have not quite healed. Mostly they come from my childhood and teenage years and I wonder if that is because when you died, I had not yet begun to look back that far. They are hanging threads, things we did not talk about or resolve.

Bill Sellars, Fanny's 'boyfriend' after her husband died, is one of them. I still carry a sense of injustice even though, looking back to my childhood in the 1950s, I recognise that predatory sexual behaviour by men was undoubtedly pretty common and not something that was or could be easily challenged. There was no mechanism, no pathway, for a woman to complain. As with domestic violence, what a man did within four walls was his business.

Here is your version from *Bonfires in the Rain*:

> *And then they (Fanny and Bill) came to stay and he destroyed our tree – got up one morning and cut nearly all the branches off the dark amethyst conifer that spread most beautifully over the lawn. What on earth would have happened if we'd known then that he also used to corner Frances when no one was about and try to kiss her? Nobody did know till after he died …*

In fact, it wasn't 'a dark amethyst conifer' but a pair of tall, graceful, ivy-covered tī kōuka cabbage trees on the driveway – marvellous trees to climb. He didn't just cut off branches either; he felled them. And you *did* know he used to get me alone and kiss me. Virginia told you of the occasion when he sent her out of the room to be 'alone' with me. Apparently you replied, 'Don't leave her alone with him.' A pretty casual response. I wonder why you didn't ever say anything to me, offer comfort or some kind of explanation.

Then, while they were staying with us, he dropped dead in the street in Whanganui – a heart attack – and I felt terrible guilt, as if my hatred, my wishing him dead, had caused it. I think now you would apologise for the failure of care, but back then it was buried. Why? Too difficult to broach? Better to leave well alone?

The idea that you might challenge your mother's boyfriend was unimaginable and raising it with Fanny far too complicated. If Fanny had been able to take it in, it might have destroyed her, her relationship with Bill and possibly even hers with you. Fanny needed him, you knew that, and above all she had to be protected. Well-oiled female silence in smooth working order.

There's something else here too – when cousin Val told me of Grandfather William's sexual predations on his daughters, I suddenly understood your and Fanny's moral panic about sex and the impossibility of discussing it. I can only conclude that the account of this in *Bonfires in the Rain* was purposeful obfuscation – poetic licence – rather than memory lapse.

Your panic continued all through my teenage years. Another tender spot for me was your finding and reading my diary when I was about 14. It contained trivial bits of private information about boys and kissing, that sort of stuff. I remember a sense of helpless outrage that my privacy had been violated and I was powerless to do anything about it. I can still see your look of anxiety and outraged disappointment. I know you would say in your defence that you came from a family whose understanding or respect for personal privacy was negligible or possibly altogether absent, a family in which it was considered normal, for example, to open and read personal letters addressed to another family member. But still …

There's also the occasion when you called me 'used goods', informing me that 'no one will marry you now'. At the time I was mortified, though in the light of both our subsequent experience it's so absurd as to be hilarious.

This was in Huntly and they were not happy years. You hated the place; your marriage was in trouble. I also struggled, missing the group of friends I'd had at Kuranui College. Despite your heroic efforts to give me a thoroughly proper, strait-laced upbringing, I failed to maintain the family honour and at the age of 16 became a 'nice' girl rather than a 'good' girl – 'lost my cherry' as the saying goes.

The notion that I had let down myself and the family honour drove me to confess. Why? Was I seeking understanding, sympathy, absolution? You were absolutely petrified, forbidding me to see Ron ever again. There seemed to be an idea that if I stopped handing out sexual favours something of my virginity might remain intact – or even be restored? Or perhaps if no one knew, then something of my (or your) reputation might survive? Overriding all was the appalling prospect that I might become pregnant, which I didn't, though more by good fortune than good management. We'd have a good laugh over it now, although the 'used goods' damnation must have had some efficacy – I have never married.

The other piece of unfinished business from my teenage years has a little more substance. As the eldest daughter at home, it fell to me to be your confidante. I was 17 and ill-equipped for this role. After school I would resist coming home, lingering at the corner talking to Ron in case you were 'in a state' and wanting to pour it out all over me. I dreaded such encounters. Your problems with Dad could not be my concern and I didn't want to know. But I had no power to say 'no', and in any case you were not a woman who readily took 'no' for an answer. I know you would understand now how inappropriate, how damaging it was.

When I left home at the beginning of 1968 to go to 'varsity', as we called it then, I was shy and unformed and part of me didn't want to go. I'd had enough of school, I wanted life, but varsity was a huge step. Yet you were always there in the background, offering support and sustenance. The threads attaching me to home were strong, and for many years you were the person I most relied on: phone calls, visits home in holidays, and of course countless letters.

Nobody writes letters anymore but I have boxes and boxes of yours and you kept mine – as Fanny kept yours: inheritance of a habit. Mine are outpourings of angst and excitement, embarrassment and joie de vivre, the agonies and delights of young love, new ideas and ways of thinking and being. Incredibly, I told you absolutely everything. Here's one from when I was 20:

> *Firstly, a special birthday happiness to Steph. I have sent her a telegram and I will send a little something when my finances are in a more healthy state. At present, I have 50c in the bank, $3 in my purse and no pay for two more weeks. Anyway, how are all my dear family? I really loved being home. I only wish I could have stayed longer. Actually, I hate to have to confess this but I haven't done any real work yet. So much has happened in these last ten days – it is almost unbelievable. When I got back Sunday morning, I felt pretty miserable. Our little house was sour and dreary and nobody was there. So, I rang Bruce and he came over and I stayed at Sentinel Rd for several days. The weather was beautiful and perfectly clear, like summer except the air was chilly – a high, clear, blue sky and sunshine all day.*

Dramas with ex-boyfriend Kerry occupy the next section of the letter, concluding with:

> *Anyway, we parted on not particularly good terms. That night … Ian and Morgan and I went to the pub and I got the drunkest I've been for a long time and then we all went back to Sentinel Rd. Ian and Morgan had a fight and she tried to slash her wrists while Ian went home to his parents' place. Kerry had come to Sentinel Rd anyway to see Bruce (that's why I had gone out) but he hadn't left by the time I got back which I thought he would have. Of course when he was there and I was very drunk we had another long trauma – not as bad because we were not horrible to each other. I can't remember how it happened or what we*

*even said but he ended up staying the night with me which I
suppose was a mistake.*

*Friday night was again terrible. Kevin took me to dinner
at the Troika Restaurant and when I got home, my flatmates
(Graeme and Sandra) were fucking in my bed. I had left them
that evening being nasty to each other and I got home to find
them like that. I got a real shock especially since they were in
my bed (I bought a double bed last week – I know you'll think
I'm terrible but really, I had to buy a bed because I didn't have
one so I thought a double one would be more use to me than
a single one). Anyway, I was a bit drunk and a sort of insanity
took hold of me. I felt that my room was my home where I
lived and they didn't even care. I felt excluded and lost and with
nowhere to go. I couldn't bear the thought of sleeping in either
of their beds so I jumped in Graeme's car and took off. I didn't
even know where I was going. I drove the car like a maniac and
coming along Valley Rd put it in a spin and ended up on the
footpath facing the way I'd come. It didn't even give me much of
a fright. I was so upset and drunk I suppose. On my way back,
I met Bruce in his car – taking Kerry and Tom home – and they
stopped and took me back to Sentinel Rd. God it was terrible.
I felt humiliated by the whole performance and yet I hadn't
even really realised what I was doing. I told Graeme and Sandra
that I was really pissed off and they'd better not do it again and
of course that created tensions in our little flat and we are all
leaving. The affair between them has put me on the outer of
course. They are going to live together at Wood St; Sandra is
never going back to Piers (her husband) and she and Graeme
are talking of marriage. It is always amazing to find how little
people really care about you, how easily they can move on and
forget you exist.*

*I, from lack of anywhere else to go, am going back to
Sentinel Road where I can have Geordie's room. She and Jason
are taking a horse and cart and tent and going off to the country
to write fairy stories. So, that is the story of my first week
back in Auckland. Your faith in my ability to cope is not really
justified, is it?*

I had a really good talk to Lester yesterday. He is writing to you to see if you want his records. Up till a day or so ago he was very poor. He isn't now because Piers sent out 2lbs of grass from Thailand which he bought there for $5 and which has been sold here (1 and ¹/2lbs of it) for $700. You may think this is highly immoral and it probably is ... but so what?

Anyway I have done no work and I feel a little lifeless after all this hectic activity. We've all been stoned the last two nights on some of the grass Piers sent so I suppose that is part of it. Tomorrow, Ian, Tom, Kerry and I are going to Hatfields Beach where Bruce is staying so that should be pleasant. Very much love to you all dear family.

Frances

PS I left a big beautiful pink towel at home and a blue and white checked flannel. Could you send them back?

I look back with some surprise at the sheer chaos of my student life, though I admire my matter-of-factness: the ending is sheer pragmatism. It's addressed to all the family, but I'm certain you would not have placed such graphic outpourings in front of the eyes of my younger sisters – aged 16, 13 and 11. We'd read it now with bemused astonishment, but this was the level of honesty between us. You were galvanised with missionary zeal. I found this in your diary:

Frances has written rather a shocking letter, all about her emotional floods and storms, her violence under the stress of drink and disappointment, the futility of her days, sodden with great wet waves of feeling and lacking the shape and firmness of any systematic work – or indeed any work at all, it seems. I rang her up, quite alarmed and have sent her the train fare for her to come home for a few days this week. Some unpleasant things need to be said and I don't like putting them on paper and not knowing the moment of their arrival.

So far – Thursday of the next week – she hasn't come, though she's rung up to enquire fairly casually what the fuss is about. She can't come in the weekend – no reason but of course it is because that is when the really vital events occur, outings, men, crises. She acts as though a love affair is a fulltime occupation – and with her it seems to be specially when it's collapsing as hers with Kerry seems to continue to do, long after it's over it keeps coming back and staging another exit.

A bit sanctimonious, Mum, pulling me back into line – albeit in a poetic fashion. I'm not going to resist reminding you that when your own love affairs began you found them just as engrossing, indeed all-consuming, using your diaries (and letters to me), to relieve the turmoil, to order the mind and the emotions so as to be able to function in the quotidian world. No matter one's age, falling in love involves regressing to teenager!

This was in Heretaunga. I know the marital disruptions you had so brutally made me aware of in Huntly, rather than settling, had intensified. You were 26 years older than I, yet your life was in a similar state of turbulence. I also know that the freedoms of mine struck home, though you hadn't yet found a pathway to a life of your own; that came later.

I don't think I was aware how wretched you were; I suppose because my own young life was compelling enough. I'd left home and thus was no longer available as confidante. Martin was the eldest one left at home but the idea of confiding in a young man was inconceivable; he had more important things to do. When I found this in your diary, I understood how agonising it had been:

I am well aware that much of my present pain comes from the 'desolation of reality' in which I live with T, rather than the loss of something deeply comforting which I could have had and yet at the moment was not ready to take. In fact how much can one suffer from the loss of something one has never had? How much in any case does a single experience remain isolated from the other dreams and visions that surround and succeed it? A merging must happen; this makes it more unreal or less? Certainly more rich – though it can never be an imaginary substitute for the second chance I will almost certainly never get.

> *I have neither happiness nor a sense of value in myself. I am cast adrift between what I want and can't have and what I could have and can't bear.*

You sound so desolate, so defeated. It was Arthur Sewell you wanted but your terrors had driven you to reject his offer of intimacy.[1] And yet despite your private agonies you continued to involve yourself in mine. You welcomed my friends into the house, though privately you had to overcome reservations:

> *Frances left home at 8am today to join her dubious looking friends. In fact they were pleasant serious intelligent young men, the two I talked to – Kerry and Ian – but they looked rather alarmingly bearded and unkempt. Tonight Frances rang, late, to say they had met 'a guy in a pub' who had asked them to a party and there they were. While we talked someone else wanted the phone and she called 'Just a minute darling'. Who's that I said? 'Oh I don't know – just a guy …' The new love without possession. It occurs to me that this is something it has taken me most of my life to comprehend – and even now it does me no good.*

I have to laugh at 'alarming friends'. Our appearance was a statement; we were 'alternative' – long hair, dressing in rags, taking drugs, sleeping around, breaking the rules. You managed to accept them on the terms in which they presented themselves, engaged them in conversations about the state of the world without demanding they adhere to stuffy, conventional norms (you were also learning to allow me at least some of the same freedoms). And apparently, according to Bruce (who told me over a recent dinner), you flirted with him! Tut, tut, Mum!

But … I was proud of you. Many of my friends were ashamed of their parents but you were different – unusual, engaged. This continued through my early twenties when I was in the Living

Theatre Troupe, beginning my career as an actor. And then, in 1974, I came to Wellington to attend drama school and the nature and context of our interactions changed. Do you remember when I lived at home for a few months, daily travelling into Wellington to drama school from Heretaunga until I found a flat in Mt Victoria? You were valiantly trying to keep it all together but it was not a happy household. Those years were tumultuous ones – Rachel died; our family, as a unit, struggled in its death throes; while you and I embarked on our careers.

I remember going with you to book launches and other literary events while you were in the audience at whatever shows I was in. Our lives had taken very different paths yet there were patterns in common, and sympathies. You were a beacon, a role model to me and others of my generation as you threw off the yoke of expectation and created your own path into the world of writing. I loved and admired you for all of that – my mother, the poet; my mother reinventing her life on her own terms.

You weren't perfect. There were regular furious rows. One occurred when you interfered in my relationship. You said to me, 'I don't think you treat your partner very well' when you were under the impression he was having an affair. If he was, then who was treating whom 'not very well'? Still, a woman's job is to 'manage her man', eh? Where were your feminist principles, Mum, when I needed them?

The Wellington years came to an end when we both left in 1981 – you for Menton, me for Auckland and subsequently Australia. I know you always loved Wellington but six years there was quite enough for me; I found it a claustrophobic town, the high hills standing in judgement as they looked down into the dark heart of the city. When I left, I missed some of the intense intimacies, but Auckland's marvellous geographical sprawl and mellow climate allow a kind of privacy I never found in Wellington. It was also a relief to get away from my intrusive family; to live somewhere where my behaviour was not under your constant scrutiny. We never lived in the same town again, although our conversations about life and art and human behaviour continued.

While I was in Australia setting myself up for a professional working life, you were in Menton and exploring the cultural glories of Europe with W.H. (Bill) Oliver, Margaret Scott and others. We both missed the 1981 Springbok tour ructions, though I had been on protest marches, one with Dad in Wellington just before I left for Australia. From our separate locations we watched with a kind of disbelieving anger and grief as our country ripped itself apart over rugby and racism.

Later that year we each returned to New Zealand – you in October, bringing your expanded horizons and new perspectives on yourself and your writing, while I came back unexpectedly in December when my partner, who had returned to New Zealand for a job, suffered a brief but intense mental breakdown. You and Dad set aside your personal differences and came together as my parents. You were wonderfully supportive, considerate, kind – daily phone calls, thoughtful letters, offering the wisdom you had gleaned through Dad's numerous breakdowns. I felt blessed.

During the early 1980s, while you were publishing more books (including your selection of *The Letters of A.R.D. Fairburn*), and your reputation was growing, I was in the company at the Mercury Theatre: busy, productive years with plenty of good work coming my way.

Change was in the wind, though. In the middle of 1984, at the age of 34, I fell pregnant; another prospect opened up in my life and our relationship entered a new and dramatically different phase. You were delighted, while I wanted not just the baby but the whole caboodle – house, mortgage, garden, settled life. It was time to claw my way back into the middle classes.

Like you, I developed into my own independence late. It was a fierce struggle to get 'out from under' – you had to be forced to let go. Partly it was your personality – you could be stubborn, moralistic, insensitive, sometimes heartless and lacking in empathy.

Sometimes I thought I had 'escaped', only to find I was caught in your web by another sticky thread. You continued to complain that your children and grandchildren did not pay you enough attention, were not interested enough in you (a good dose of Fanny in here).

Yes, this is picking over the past, and yes, I agree it's pointless: it cannot be reinvented. I have said enough. I don't blame you – you loved me, you were the parent you were and much of what you bequeathed is wonderful, to be admired and respected. And if not, then coped with or repaired (if possible). Moreover, nothing can obliterate your literary achievements, or your powerful, creative, ingenious love and endeavour on behalf of your friends and especially your children and grandchildren.

I remember the years of grandbabies being born, sometimes several in one year; families with young children visiting, gathering at yours and each other's houses for festivities – Christmases, birthdays, school holidays, sometimes just for the sake of being together – a large, vital family enjoying and loving its abundance.

There were occasional tensions between maternally protective sisters, and there were the larger family conflicts that so distressed you, but still they were good years. You died before it all came to an end. As the children grew, they inevitably lost interest in family, decided there were cousins they didn't particularly want to play with, preferring the company of their friends. For us, the mothers, as children grew, the world of paid work became more insistent.

The current family situation would grieve you. Without your compelling presence and determination to maintain familial connections, distances have extended, relationships have collapsed and restoration of any sense of a collective is beyond any horizon I can see. None of us has your willpower or compulsion.

If you were still here, doubtless you and I would have continued to pursue an understanding of the weight of unresolved tensions and the apparent inability to compromise or forgive. We would agree that those things were always there, that the other side of 'intense intimacy' was an absence of necessity for politeness and manners. As a family, we had a layer missing – the skin of civility, the requirement to be courteous and get along simply because we were family.

'A mother's love is bred into the bone. / A daughter wants her life to be her own.' Yes, certainly, a daughter wants her life to be her own. But a daughter's love for her mother is also bred into the bone and you left long before I was ready for you to go. I still want to talk to you, read some poems with you, unpick family dynamics, laugh with you over human foibles – our own as well as other people's, drink a glass of wine (or several) with you. I wish you were here.

Lauris with Frances's children, Tess and George, at Oriental Bay, 1990. *Author collection*

II

Above: Fanny and Lewis in the garden at their Pyes Pa house, about 1942. *Author collection*

Opposite, top: Fanny, seated right in the front row, with eight of her 11 siblings, about 1950. *Author collection*

Opposite: Clara Eliza Lister, about 1885. *Author collection*

Above: The Edmond family, Ohakune, 1956. Lauris and Trevor with Virginia and Frances standing, Rachel and Martin seated. *Clive Scott*

Left: Rachel at her flat in Jervois Road, Ponsonby, 1973.

Max Oettli, Alexander Turnbull Library, Wellington, 107151

The former
Edmond family
home at Burns
Street, Ohakune,
2017. *Frances Edmond*

The Edmond family in Greytown, 1964. Back row: Rachel, Virginia,
Frances, Martin. Front row: Katherine, Trevor, Lauris, Stephanie.

Clive Scott

Frances and Lauris at Ewen Alison Avenue, Devonport,
November 1973. *Stephanie McKee*

Opposite: Lauris with Frances, 1950. *Author collection*

Lauris and Trevor's wedding, 16 May 1945. *Author collection*

Right: Lauris while at Wellington Teachers' Training College, 1942. *Author collection*

Below: Lauris at Grass Street, Oriental Bay, 1984. *Robert Cross*

Above: Lauris, Frances and Tess camping at Hawke's Bay, Christmas 1986. *Stephen McCurdy*

Opposite, top: Frances and Lauris at Riversdale Road, Avondale, summer 1987/8. *Stephen McCurdy*

Opposite: Lauris at Grass Street, Oriental Bay, 1988.

Image copyright Tim Steele

Lauris aged 73, two years before she died. *Jane Taylor*

7. Love's green darkness

I do not dream that you, young again,
might come to me darkly in love's green darkness.

Although this reference in 'The Waterfall' is to a lover – in this case Clarence Beeby (Beeb) – Lauris was intrigued by relationships of all kinds. She wrote many poems about romantic love, its powerful drive, its enchantments and complications, its failures, follies and disappointments, but this was not her only focus. She wrote about love in its many manifestations – the bonds between parents, parents and children and grandchildren, friends and wider whānau; love of art, books, music, theatre, film, laughter and wit, conversation, places and things, memories and experiences, travel, landscapes and the natural world.

Her upbringing, reinforced by her gender, instilled in her the belief that relationships are the bedrock, the foundation, on which a life is built – family first always. As her children matured, left home, moved into their own independent futures and she into hers, her world opened to include lovers and friends. Lauris loved to discuss the interior workings of relationships in contrast and alongside the exterior ones, examining the motivation behind the ordinary activities that occupy our days – the promptings, shameful and glorious; the boastful self-justifications and venal excuses; the selfless sacrifices and benevolent liberality that drive people to great generosity, manipulative control or downright meanness. All intrigued her.

Her friendships were diverse. Indeed, at her death, some were surprised to see how many people there were with whom she had had an intimate relationship. I used to wonder how she found time for all she crammed into her busy life. It's a thread in a tightly woven fabric, I think. She was a late starter, discovering herself anew at the beginning of her fifties, and there was an enormous amount of everything that simply couldn't wait, could not be put off for another day. There's a delightful poem from *Wellington Letter*, written about her first grandchild at two, that could as equally well have been penned about Lauris at 50:

> More and more she cries, at two years
> old, and more again – more plums more
> trees more nests and eggs (and squawking
> hens) more pips and melons dribbling
> from more lips, more dancing on the roof
> more night more day, sun splintering
> through cracks of early morning doors,
> more floors, more bare feet curling on
> their woody sheen, more arms and elbows
> toes and breasts, more white and smooth
> more round and small, more slips of
> grassy tips and petal shine, more
> gold and black and rosy, smell of feathers
> warm, wet, more scrape of gravel, kiss
> of dust, more soft sour sharp-sweet,
> more shooting stars more midnights,
> milk and apples, mountains, cats' miaows
> and mornings – more, she says. And now.

Lauris was 21 when she married Trevor on 16 May 1945, in the garden of Lewis and Fanny's farmlet at Pyes Pa.

She told me as an adult that after her first sexual encounter, on their honeymoon, she was disappointed – it had been painful, not pleasurable, and she thought, 'Is that what all the fuss is about?' She described having entered her marriage 'lightly enough', thinking, 'Oh well, if it doesn't work out, I'll get a divorce.' I was a little disconcerted by her casualness. Was her marriage merely a convenient arrangement, the automatic next step in a young woman's life? Is that all there is? Where was love?

For me and many of my generation, it was inconceivable that we would enter into a formal commitment without first exploring sexual compatibility, meaning such wedding-night disappointments were largely avoided.

When I was 19, Lester Calder proposed to me under one of the Morton Bay fig trees in Albert Park. I was struck dumb. I didn't know how to say 'no' to such a momentous question; hurting someone's feelings was not acceptable and in some part of my terrified mind I knew the offer was supposed to be an honour. Eventually I managed to squeak a 'yes' that was entirely lacking in conviction. Later, I understood that it was a version of what Lauris had gone through. At that time, a proposal was a means of introducing the possibility of sex: 'Will you marry me?' pretty much meant 'Can I go to bed with you?' Lester and I did the latter, and the marriage question evaporated. No such option was available to Lauris. She married my father and they embarked on the journey of marriage and making a family.

My parents' marriage remained relatively settled and constant for almost 20 years – quite a bounty in the scheme of things – and my childhood was a largely happy one. Parental tensions, if there were any, were managed discreetly. The disturbances in my childhood centred on my own fears, alienations, misapprehensions and mistakes – telling lies, charging up lollies on the account at the grocer's on the way home from school (until he reported to my mother); spending the change from buying Fanny's biscuits in the belief that she wouldn't notice (she did, and I was reprimanded as a sneak and a thief); being scared of the dark, of the bush; throwing tantrums; running away from home; imitating Dad's signature to get out of running in the school cross-country and being found out. Thus did I discover the word forgery, and that it was a crime.

There was the disruption of Trevor's first breakdown in Greytown in 1964, when I was 14. That something was amiss with Dad was abundantly apparent, but I was not drawn into the causes or the management of his collapse; that came later. The explanation I remember eventually being given was that it had something to do with his problematic relationship with his father, and the difficulties he had with the thought of handling the authority that went with the first headmaster's job he was offered, and which he eventually turned down. It might have been taken as a warning that his ambition for the top job should be considered with caution; that it wasn't a wise move to head down such a pathway.

Dad eventually did begin working as a principal in 1966 at Huntly College, where Mum was to teach a few hours a week also. While in Huntly she finally completed the BA in English she had begun before her marriage. She also met Arthur Sewell there. When she graduated, there was a photo in the *Waikato Times* with the caption 'Mother of six doffs the tea towel and dons a gown'. As well as working part time at Huntly College she taught young mothers in Playcentres. She was beginning to step beyond the role of wife and mother and into a life outside the family home – and to write poems.

Winds of social change were blowing across the Pacific from California where the young, strolling along Haight-Ashbury in extravagant motley, were taking psychedelic drugs, breaking old codes of accepted behaviour about sex and gender roles, protesting against the war in Vietnam. The intimations of change fed into a sense in Lauris, as in me, that there was a whole world out there that bore little or no resemblance to old-fashioned, mind-numbing and (to me) idiotic restrictions she was obliged to administer, and I had to live under. We were only in Huntly for three years, but it signalled the beginning of the misery, the gloom of defeat and despair that eventually overwhelmed Lauris and Trevor's marriage and the family.

At Fergusson Drive, Heretaunga – the most elegant, graceful, beautiful and 'middle class' house they lived in – the worst years continued. It was there that the family suffered its greatest defeats.

With her teaching experience and the completion of an MA in English Literature at Victoria University in 1972, Lauris was well qualified to take on the editorship of the *PPTA Journal*. She was 50 years old and saw this job as a significant and irrevocable step outside the world of her family and teaching into that of journalists and writers: a free-thinking milieu utterly unlike the stuffy conventions of school staffrooms. With the job came a new community, new friendships, new ways of looking at the world.

After Rachel's death and Dad's move to the Correspondence School in Wellington, there was nothing to keep them in the Hutt Valley, and plenty of hard memories to encourage them to leave. They returned to Wellington where, some 30 years earlier, they had begun their married life. They bought the house at 22 Grass Street.

A good many of her poems reflect on the breakdown of Lauris's marriage, on her grief at the loss, on learning about the implacable heartlessness of change, even when you seek it. Each draws its essence from a different location – places where we lived or visited as a family. 'Late Starling' is set in the lovely house in Fergusson Drive, with the pear tree and the dead pine. 'The Mountain' and 'The Ghost Moth' reference Ohakune – the mountain, the bush, the isolation, a watchful darkness, an evocation of the natural world as timeless, ancient, impenetrable. 'Camping', 'A Reckoning' and 'Signs' are less specifically located but their genesis is the inner workings of a family, its reliable habits and interdependencies and regret for their loss.

Still the marriage lumbered on – an old boot stuck on the foot that no amount of pulling could ease off. How do you let go when you don't know what is beyond? When my own domestic life was in freefall, a counsellor friend commented, 'It's hardest to give up the dream.' Lauris talked of 'the defeat of faith' – another way of saying the same thing. 'I wanted my new self, but could not bear to leave the old ...' Perhaps a profoundly flawed present was preferable to an imagined isolated future? She had a powerful fear of being alone.

Separation and divorce were socially frowned upon, and as we know, Lauris had a deep-seated sense of duty and responsibility towards family. She was determined to preserve something of what she and Trevor had created together. They fought, exchanging angry words, blaming each other for failing to be what the other expected, wanted or any longer felt an affinity with. Trevor drank. At a dinner party held for visiting American poet Robert Creeley, Trevor became so drunk and abusive to Lauris, she had to apologise and take him home.

She continued to manage the household they shared, however uncomfortable and ill-fitting it was. During her first venture into the wide world in 1977, it was I who went home to 'look after' my father; as a man he was assumed (correctly) to be incapable of doing it himself. It's an odd thing to write from the perspective of the twenty-first century, but Dad could not cook, or shop, or iron shirts, or operate a washing machine – all such 'women's work' had always be done for him. Slowly, patiently, probably reluctantly, he set about learning a few of these basic skills, since I could not be available at all times.

In early September 1978, in one of the first steps in Lauris and Trevor's lengthy journey towards separate lives, Trevor shifted downstairs at Grass Street, where a number of us had helped build separate habitable living quarters. My one and only experience of using a kanga hammer was driving the noisy vibrating machine into the hard clay under the house, carving out a space that my father eventually inhabited – beneath Lauris (an irresistible or perhaps convenient metaphorical interpretation). I helped Trevor paint the walls primrose yellow; he, absently and with a total lack of commitment, slapping his brush ineffectually at the same spot over and over again while I bit my tongue in frustration and painted the rest of the wall.

By 1981, Lauris's year in Menton, the marriage was well and truly over for her but she still harboured regrets, especially when there were difficulties in her own life and loneliness and sadness overwhelmed her:

> *Trevor never has intuitions, but he sees the stuff of his life. If only his sturdy matter-of-factness could have joined with my love of essence, so we had confluence and fertilising, instead of boredom and dislike. I can't write of this, it makes me cry. I am weak and sad altogether; these last few days I've been tired yet restless, inclined to wander from myself like a broken needle in a compass, losing the north.*

When Trevor shifted over the Remutaka Hill to Greytown in late 1981 he was returning to a place, a small town, where he had been successful and well respected. One of the catalysts had been Lauris's series of lovers in the bedroom above at Grass Street, but there were other contributing factors. Could he have had lovers of his own there? In his Greytown years there were women who would gladly have entered into intimacy with him, had he been willing, but he couldn't. It was not in his nature.

Now living separately, they kept in regular contact – they would ring each other to talk about family matters, she would visit him, he her when he came to Wellington. Their houses – Grass Street and Greytown – were understood as shared establishments. She, for example, continued to regard herself as having 'right of access' into Trevor's houses, entering without knocking. Perhaps he liked the familiarity, the continuity of her proprietorial ways. Meeting at a book launch in Unity Books, they retreated into a corner for 20 minutes of intense conversation. At family Christmases they would both be there, often irascible with each other but preserving, as well as they could, a shared notion of family.

Despite conflict between them, and Trevor's ill-treatment of her, I can still find some admiration for the continuity of contact they maintained over the years. I knew of no other families where this was the case. On one level they needed each other; Trevor learning how to run his own household asked the obvious person for advice: Lauris. She, with her notions of family as central to existence, believed that their shared history, their children, still bound them in some form of relationship. They maintained 'form' as our parents, so we were still – theoretically – a family.

Over one Christmas I inadvertently became caught in the crossfire. I'd been out with my kids and arrived back at Grass Street to find Dad sitting at the table writing. When I asked what, he growled, 'I'm just telling that bitch what I think of her.' Something in me snapped, some sense of outrage and injustice took over. 'Don't you dare talk about her like that. She's been kind and hospitable to you while you have taken almost no part in anything, you've just sat in a corner and poured your own drinks and ignored everyone.' Whereupon something in Dad snapped and he whacked me hard across the shoulders before withdrawing into angry silence.

I was shocked, and after dinner demanded an apology, not just for hitting me, but for his nastiness to Lauris and his rude behaviour over the whole of Christmas, which had been dreadful for everyone. Typically, accusations flowed – now with much shouting and blaming – but there was no resolution. Dad drank sullenly for the rest of evening and in the morning stormed off to catch his bus, brushing off proffered help with bags. It was awful, degrading – for him, for Lauris, for me.

Then there was the aftermath, which was dreadful in a different way. Lauris was full of tearful gratitude to me: 'No one has ever stood up for me before.' I was mortified. I had taken sides, unintentionally broken my own rule of remaining staunchly neutral. Despite the justice of my reprimand, and my sense that she did not deserve the treatment she had received from him (and nor did I), I could not allow myself to be perceived as aligned – that ground was far too treacherous. Was that fair? Not to her, but I had had enough experience of being embroiled in irreconcilable conflict to feel an imperative to avoid being seen to take a side.

Many family Christmases were marred by such conflict between them so why did we persist? After each one we would swear it was the last; then by the middle of the year we would relent, begin to hope, trust that it wouldn't happen again. There's a darker side to the continuity of the conflict: in an immutable way they remained bound to each other. Lauris never let go of the guilt at having abandoned her proper wifely role and by persisting with a connection to Trevor, not letting him go, she was able give herself a kind of absolution. It wasn't merely that she felt responsible for him, she could not 'let go the dream', the all-encompassing intertwining and taking for granted of two lives bound by love, connection, mutual interests, children. Had she met someone else, found something like the relationship she had initially enjoyed with Trevor, she might have let him go, but she didn't – though not for want of searching. For years she continued to fall in and out of love, hoping for a replacement. In her loneliness, and the drama of never-ending family conflict, she still had Trevor to turn to, to talk to, someone who had been a part of her whole adult life and who understood the dynamics. When a friend suggested she might divorce him her instant reply was, 'Oh no, I couldn't do that.' Somewhere in the recesses of her psychic cupboard, she couldn't or wouldn't let go. Nor could he – they never divorced.

For Trevor, despite her lovers, the bitterness, ill-will, arguing and trouble, Lauris remained 'the only one for me'. Perhaps never letting go absolved him of any need, or even inclination, to form another relationship. I was 40 when he died in 1990. I loved him as my father but I don't think I knew him well, not in the way that I knew and understood Lauris. He was a man and thus his thinking was less accessible.

It was more than that, though; after having our roles reversed when I delivered him to Ashburn Hall. it was no longer possible for me to see him as parent. He occupied the space but he didn't inhabit it; he was illustration, outline – to me, anyway. I don't mean he wasn't a three-dimensional human being – he was. But after his breakdowns, shock treatment and the loss of his career he was enormously and continuously preoccupied with himself and his failure, with 'if onlys': if only I hadn't lost my job; if I only I could have continued as a headmaster; if only I hadn't had to go to the Correspondence School.

He struggled with accepting what had happened and moving on. He talked endlessly of what others had done to him, or should have done, but seldom did he seem to recognise his own contribution to his predicament. Perhaps that was the real tragedy. He got stuck somewhere in the quicksand of marriage and career failure and it sucked him down, enclosed him, leaving no means of escape. Except in the company of Lauris – when he could be nasty, aggressive and judgemental – he was generally a benign, kindly, rather wistful, old-fashioned man.

A surprising new glimpse of Lauris was offered to me in recent years by one of her lovers, Günther Warner, now in his late eighties and suffering from Parkinson's Disease. Cigarette in one hand, glass of white wine in the other, making their unreliable dance to his mouth, he commented on his affair with Lauris in the 1970s when she edited the *PPTA Journal*. Wryly, he remarked that he had felt rather compromised because he had been a PPTA colleague of my father's and at the time Trevor was in a state of crisis. 'What could I do?' he asked with sheepish self-justification. 'Your mother was very persistent in the pursuit of her desires.'

Part of me thought 'Good for her', as I laughed at his story, though conjuring images of my mother being 'persistent in the pursuit of her desires' proved elusive. What had she done? Lured him into her office and taken her clothes off?

My experience as a mother reinforces the notion (if it needed reinforcement) that one's sexually aware teenage children are appalled, disgusted, at the idea of parental sex. In my teenage years I became conscious of my father as 'other' – a man – but with Lauris there was no such awareness. Even when I was in my thirties, I had no sense of Lauris as a sexual being. She was female, obviously, of the same essence as I, but she had no sexual aspect, with her wrinkled stomach and sagging, shrunken breasts. Was I wilfully oblivious, lucky, or just well-trained within the shielded feminine sphere? Probably all apply. Thinking in those terms, even considering the possibility of my mother as a sexual being, or my parents having an active sex life, was not a territory into which I ever ventured. I think too Lauris's sexuality was shrouded, confined by notions of propriety instilled in her by Fanny and the prim New Zealand culture of the 1920s and 1930s – one did not talk about sex, and one certainly did not display it.

In her autobiography Lauris described her initial terror at the prospect of 'extra-marital sex', of 'infidelity' – her initial inability to accept Arthur Sewell's proposition – and her subsequent coming to terms with it, her 'liberation'. She outlined her significant relationships (Arthur Sewell, Clarence Beeby, Bill (W.H.) Oliver and Hubert Witheford), while being more discreet about others, including Hone Tuwhare, Günther Warner, Denis Glover and Alan Wild. But there's something very proper in her writing about such matters – even given the zeitgeist of 'free love' she was carefully matter-of-fact, keeping within safe societal norms.

With me, however, Lauris was relatively open about matters to do with sex, often telling me stories about her sexual encounters. During her first overseas adventure in 1977 she wrote me letters full of her emotional agonies over her relatively new relationship with Bill Oliver. The letters were sent care of Ian McLymont, a friend, rather than to the house where Trevor might see them. She described falling asleep beneath Hubert as he ground away, taking forever to climax; she told me of making love with an academic from Waikato University on a berm somewhere in the posh Auckland suburb of Remuera at 3am (I confess to being impressed at the audacity).

Confidences went both ways: mine included the news that I was having an intense and illicit relationship with a woman; Lauris offered a bewildered confession that when another woman had kissed her, implicitly offering greater intimacy, Lauris had recoiled, repelled by the prospect. This was repeated to me later by her friend Fleur Adcock. I'd love to have been a witness to their conversation: two women poets in intimate discussion about sex and desire.

I have found out much more about Lauris's sexual adventuring from friends and from her diary since her death. I cannot help wondering why she was willing to be open in private and yet was so circumspect in public. And, perhaps more pointedly, why am I writing about her in this vein when she didn't? Am I merely snooping through bedroom doors and windows, indulging in salacious literary gossip?

Once she had discovered her sexuality, Lauris saw it as an essential part of her makeup, the 'charge' of it carrying over into her writing – each was resource, food for the other. Partly it was the times, the prevailing culture of sexual liberation, of opportunity to be grasped and experienced throughout the 1970s and 1980s until the Aids epidemic brought such licentiousness to a halt.

I think there's something else, though: a dichotomy that lies at the heart of what she inherited from Fanny. On the one hand, there were the strict moral codes of what a girl may or may not do, and on the other, there was the overpowering intimacy and lack of privacy practised by the Scott family. When Lauris abandoned the former, the latter had free rein. Inevitably there were some terrible consequences. She made some unforgivable mistakes, ones she regretted for the rest of her life.

One of her lovers would ring her, she would turn up at his house in the middle of the night, he would leave open a window through which she would climb and they would have sex while his wife was asleep upstairs. On one occasion she went to bed with an ex-boyfriend of one of her daughters. It's unsurprising that such episodes are not mentioned in her public writings.

In writing her life story, perhaps the failure to explicitly mention her exuberant sex life was an attempt to protect others as well as herself, but I think the omission is as much a comment on our prudish society as it is on her. It was 'unseemly' for a woman to be as sexually active as Lauris was in the 1980s and 90s. The idea of the sexually experienced woman as 'whore' still had currency, a hangover from pre-pill times. A woman with a past was not entitled to respect, she was easy game. She cannot have been unaware that public revelation would shock and possibly offend a significant proportion of her (mostly female) readership. Even within her own writing community there were people – mostly men, though some women as well – who were uncomfortable with her sexual activity. A male poet described Lauris as having an 'anthology of lovers', the tone disparaging.

My generation, on the other hand, was impatient with the concealment, the compromises, the sheer lies our parents' generation appeared at ease with. For students like me, the counterculture movement, of which the sexual revolution was but one manifestation, was *the* driving force. The late 1960s and into the 1970s in New Zealand, indeed all over the Western world, was a time of radical social change, a fracturing of old certainties in every imaginable way: political, social, sexual, religious, racial, educational. Even punctuation was questioned – capital letters were discarded as irrelevant – a form of literary (and therefore social) control.

Unpredictable times, unsettling, astonishingly exciting. We asked fundamental questions: what, if any, responsibility did we have to the society we lived in, most of whose values we rejected as repressive? Those values were obstacles to 'living', to being truly 'alive', in contrast to the deadliness inhabited, seemingly contentedly, by our parents and theirs before them. We were different, special, a new generation; it was our right, our responsibility, our mission to tell the truth as we saw it, to challenge everything, disturb reality, shake it, break it, reform it into something wild, exotic, iridescently beautiful.

My letters to Lauris from that time are full of such ardent, extravagant ideas and my passionate commitment to personal, political and sexual freedom. In response, she wrote in *Bonfires in the Rain*:

> *Frances asks me to understand all she means by her own declaration of faith, which means she asks me to feel as she does. She sees the organised materially comfortable but spiritually impoverished life of older people like ourselves as death to all she hopes for from life – freedom to be honest and spontaneous, opportunity to follow the calls of emotion and friendship, time to experience the living world of real feelings. How could I not understand, and agree – such desires are of the greatest possible importance. What I can't do is feel this as she does.*

For her generation it was different. The 'sexual revolution' overlaid but did not delete our Judaeo/Christian heritage with its tortuous efforts at controlling sexual desire and, when that failed, endlessly moralising about it.

Clearing a pathway through that baggage meant her journey out of her marriage was much more complicated, requiring convoluted shifts in thinking and constrained by stricter codes of behaviour than my rather simpler one: I went from being 'used goods' to being a woman on the pill with the freedom – and lack of guilt – to choose with whom and how she expressed her sexuality.

Despite Lauris's apparent liberation, there was a dark alcove in her psyche where she struggled to escape the idea that sex is the weapon of ultimate betrayal in any relationship. Sex as celebration, sex as manifestation of life force, sex as sacrament are ideas largely absent from Western culture. Sex as a rite is honoured only within strict social limits. But the discoveries I have made about my mother lead me to speculate that she did in fact have an intuitive sense of sex as celebration, as sacrament, as creative force, despite it not being a commonly held perspective.

For Lauris there was her age, too, which fuelled her desire to cram in as much of everything as she possibly could in her last couple of decades. In my generation we slept with our friends, changed partners frequently, indulged in one-night stands. I recall there was one university friend with whom I hadn't been to bed.

One night, finding ourselves together, he and I decided that, since we never had, it was time we did.

Lauris in her fifties and sixties would have been much more harshly judged for that kind of behaviour, yet part of me can't resist surmising that she behaved pretty much as I did. Acceptable in the young but undignified in the mature? For one with so little sense of personal boundaries within the family, this was one area of her life Lauris did try to keep separate, if somewhat inconsistently. Though she could not/would not talk about her sex life publicly, she was more forthcoming in correspondence with close friends. Fiona Kidman told me that Lauris had a constant string of lovers but they are not in the autobiography because she wanted to be seen as a 'nice' person.

Lauris's archive in the Alexander Turnbull Library contains numerous folders of letters from various adoring lovers, many of them explicitly, as well as implicitly, sexual. In wanting to be liked, admired, seen in her best light, she was as vain as the rest of us. While I understand her reasons, I cannot help thinking it a pity that she chose to conceal this aspect of herself. As her daughter, I admire her capacity for sex, delight in her energy and her exuberant lust for life, for adventure, for experience.

Lauris wrote many poems that have their source in her love affairs, though there's only one (that I am aware of) about Arthur, and it's about his funeral.[1] That was her first relationship post-Trevor, so perhaps she was still 'inside' her marriage and the conventions surrounding it.

There are a good many about her next lover, Beeb. He was the second of her 'grand old men', as I came to think of them – older, well-placed men who admired, patronised and nurtured her career. (After Arthur and Beeb, the other was Denis Glover.) Lauris and Beeb met when she was at the PPTA and he was director emeritus of the New Zealand Council for Educational Research (NZCER).

He was also on the executive of PEN (the New Zealand Society of Authors), an organisation in which Lauris rose to a position of some significance.

She interviewed Beeb for the *Journal* and he subsequently invited her to his office for a drink (his building was around the corner from hers). Beeb, like Arthur before him, was 20 years older than Lauris, likewise with a considerable reputation as a scholar and public figure.

Having lived in the shadowy world of domesticity and motherhood for so many years, Lauris felt lacking in public credibility; she hoped some of the substance and intellectual status of these 'grand old men' might be conferred on her, giving her validity in the new and risky world outside her marriage. She wrote of Beeb, 'Perhaps the very fact of his immense assurance was comforting to me; lacking my own, I was glad to "borrow" his.'

'Love Poem', 'Waterfall', 'The Condition' and 'The Third Person' are four poems that have their genesis in her relationship with Beeb.[2] About 'The Third Person' she said she 'truly didn't know what she would find' when she wrote it, yet it 'so authoritatively wrote itself'. Despite their long friendship, Lauris continued to feel 'a certain awe of Beeb', which finds its way into the poem:

> I do not know how to describe the third person but
> on days when the doves came hurtling over the city
> flung upwards in great purring armfuls outside your
>   window
> and fell, piling like black hail on ledges of buildings
> across the street, he came in, he was there – let us
> call him a man. He preened his purple feathers.

In the years I lived in Wellington I sometimes met up with the two of them, and during the year I spent in Auckland in the soap opera *Radio Waves* Lauris wrote regularly to me, and I to her.

Frances Edmond (FE) to Lauris Edmond (LE), 5 May 1978:

I love your letters – they are always amusing and full of interesting things about your life. So you are in love with Beeb again because he is a success. What a disgraceful confession to make!!!

LE to FE, 24 May 1978:

I am in a good deal of a mess – not the sort that shows on the outside, and indeed the outside (if you can call it that) is going smoothly now, or soon, because I am writing to you while waiting for Beeb to come to lunch with me, which will be lovely as always. But I have a very precarious feeling even about that, not because we are unhappy or less necessary to each other, but because he is showing his age; inevitably he must, even he must and will, but it is terrible to see signs of it all the same. He gets uncontrollably depressed, and since he's a strong and resolute – and very honest – person it is not just a matter of being comforting to him; the things he finds impossible you know are impossible, and so does he.

And it's partly Bill [Oliver]; I've found at last that I can't maintain my great pitch of excitement with his slow-moving responses (and distance) without using up something in myself that I can't do without. So in secret but important ways I've switched off. It may in the end be good for the relationship, but that's not why it's happened ... A letter from Bill says he's sort of disappeared, which happens to him quite often – perhaps I am experiencing something of what he feels. Perhaps this racing ahead in middle age is not after all as simple as it had begun to seem. Perhaps it's nothing much to do with age, but that one can never afford to misjudge one's own rhythm and speed, the shape of one's own cycles of development.

Later (handwritten):

A beautiful day, good intelligent talking (with Beeb), much affection; I feel restored – though nothing actually is changed, I still have work to do to get my equilibrium back.

A few months later, shortly after Trevor had moved into the downstairs flat, she wrote to me warmly of Beeb and their relationship:

> *How lovely that conversation was with you this morning – I told you it would make me want to write to you straight away – and it has … Indeed I feel there is 'a good time coming' sort of mood upon me at the moment. It won't last and the reasons for it are probably largely irrelevant – like that it's been a beautiful week of fine still weather, I've worked 'at home' a lot, liked to feel that I am in 'my house' (that sense of relief persists – and small nice things have happened like conversations between Trevor and me) that Beeb has been without Beatrice and rung me every day for long free talks, all building up to last night when I went to dinner with him and we spent at least half the night together. No, all those things are not irrelevant, are they? They are in a way deserved rewards for remembering to take note of other people's difficult claims, but remembering ourselves as well, and each other. How childishly pleased we were to be able to do this small thing – only it's not a small thing if you live – and love – in this way; dinner alone in a house (and his is incredibly beautiful) with all night and nobody to ring up or knock on the door, and not even any guilt because we have both put a terrible (I mean it) amount of ourselves into looking after our collapsed partners, was a very great thing. Yevtushenko says love is not bought but stolen apples and I know, I think, what he means (not anything to do with it being legitimate in the conventional sense) – but love is also earned, and I think what you earn by fully understanding the balance of claims the outside world makes on you, you make on yourself, you mutually make with a person you love – that, that is truly yours.*

Despite Beeb 'growing old', they maintained an affectionate friendship for the rest of his life. He died at the age of 96, a couple of years before she did.

Lauris met Bill Oliver (W.H.) in 1976, a few months before she left
on her first journey overseas. It was a relationship of great intensity
and, from its beginnings, troublesome – at least for her. Unlike
Arthur, Beeb and indeed Denis Glover, he was more her age – an
academic, a scholar, an historian and a poet. In her diary on 17 July
1977, she wrote:

> *Bill, dear Bill, I met you at the wrong time (I have always said
> that time and timing controls everything – only the people and
> events that come on the crest of their time can swing upwards
> and have body and power – the others dissipate at once). I
> thought you would ease my great pain, cure it even, make life
> whole for me again – and of course you could not. The very
> prospect frightened you, and indeed should it not?*
>
> *This diary writing has saved my life – it's early morning
> again, and again I am enabled by this to get up with some
> resolution and face the day. Rachel said just before her death
> that there had been two totally absorbing things – Gerard and
> her religion; both had passed and she waited for the next thing
> that would carry her completely with it. Terrible words, in
> retrospect. In a milder way, I think something rather similar –
> when I look back over these years since I made the first great
> discovery of myself in loving Arthur I think what has not
> happened? Is anything left to happen since so much already has?
> What does one do at such perils?*

In letters to me she described her endless agonies over him.
At the time he was also having an affair with my partner's older
sister, which no one – me included – seemed to find surprising or
unsuitable. Lauris managed to become reconciled to the idea, and
the fact that I was living in the older sister's house at the time gave
them opportunities to meet.

LE to FE, 8 April 1978:

> *When I come to Auckland, I hope to meet _____; I'd really
> like to, having no hang-ups about her now. It is truly amazing to
> me that intelligent men can be so ignorant about their own and*

everybody else's emotions, that the worlds of feeling occupied by others, often women, are totally strange ... Yet in a funny way he does love me I think, and feels me to be necessary; it's just that he has no idea about many emotional experiences because for so long he has sealed himself off from them. As you my dear funny Frances have often said, Jokers? Ah jokers!

And I? I offered endless advice, some of which she took. The usual pattern in their relationship was that the time spent together was intense and fascinating, the sex ecstatic, then Bill became preoccupied, seemingly indifferent, ignored her or fell in love with someone else, so she was by turns disappointed, indignant, bereft, betrayed, broken-hearted and, very occasionally, resolute.

At frequent intervals she reached a limit, wrote him a furious letter, or with considerable effort found some detachment and believed she has found equilibrium without him. It never lasted. He came back into her life, bringing chaos in his wake. At the end of a letter to me about him she wrote, 'How can you bear all this maternal (no, just other person) egotism?'

FE to LE, 28 May 1978:

You say at the end of your letter ... how can you bear all this egotism. It is not that and really you also know it is not egotism. It is the other half of the dialogue.

About Bill, I am tempted to say give it away, but I know I mustn't and anyway it is arrogant of me to say so ... but relationships where the balance is out are not really healthy. If one person gives more than the other because they can, or are better at it for whatever reason, then somehow I suspect they are not worth it (unless of course you want it that way – and I know you don't). I am taking a hard line but I don't mean to be callous or not understanding. After all we both believe that work comes first (or first equal) and if it suffers then the balance has to be put right somehow.

At that time, I too was a woman with multiple relationships – another mother/daughter parallel. Lauris took on all my men 'friends' without question, sent them postcards when she travelled, bought them little gifts as if they were part of the family, enquired after their well-being, while between us we drew parallels in our behaviour and theirs and offered each other advice.

Over Bill, equilibrium she did not find. A couple of weeks later, on 16 June 1978, she wrote:

> I am as usual struggling to be free of my difficult entanglements, which unlike yours … can have no good outcome … Bill I think is fairly neurotic. I am going to see him in Palmerston North next week, and that will be nice I suppose, but there seems to be a ban on his coming here, at least to see me, and it is something to do with his wife, or his own guilt, I don't know what – he is very strange and secretive about it, and when I rang him recently he was like a dying man, could hardly speak, just kept saying 'it's good to hear your voice' as though I was going to save him. I think in the end I will have to abandon the whole situation and leave him to his problems. I will hate that but I hate this too. Sometimes I feel like his psychiatrist – though we don't talk like that, but all his letters are about his great tumult and how he wants me to help with it but can't allow me to. It's very tormenting indeed. Does awful things to my concentration.

However, in early 1980 she told her diary:

> Everything has happened; I can say as though there had ever been any doubt! – that there is no way I can squeeze the breath out of my love for WH, no matter how hard I try. It's there, it's there for ever and ever, whoever else wants (and has) him.

And in December that year:

> A cool still afternoon, late in the year yet neither spring nor summer – a time that seems to belong to no season. I have been organising papers, letters, old poems, diary entries – reading them with the amazement I always feel at the extraordinary creature I once was. All that fuss about WH …

On New Year's Day 1981:

Glancing back over the hysterical tirades of the first part of this journal I am disgusted at my performance there – I would burn the lot if it were not that I am about to try writing fiction and my own psychological acrobatics could be useful to me. I'm to start today – I'm putting it off.

Throughout the 1980s, her struggle to achieve equilibrium over Bill was a constant and wistful refrain in her letters to Fleur Adcock, coupled with an admiration of Fleur's independence. In between, bemoaning her inability to make it 'stand up' all on her own, she complained about Bill:

Men are feeble creatures indeed ... full of man hatred at the moment (Bill of course being infuriating). Anger I've been thinking is a rather refreshing emotion – I've had it roaming though me for a week; it's like a hot spin in a washing machine, cleans it all out ... I don't think he's much use to me, he just joins the masses of old but ungrown-up men that one can bother about a lot (for rather illusory rewards) or not ... ravings about useless men ...

She also described herself – quite perceptively I think – as 'unreliable and foolish on the subject of men'.

She and Bill wrote poems for each other; 'After Chagall', 'Going to Moscow', 'Those Roses', 'Demande de Midi' and 'Driving from the Airport' are some of hers, reflecting on the desires, longings, fears and possible humiliations of love in middle age.

'After Chagall' is a more considered response to their relationship, written well after the early tumultuous months – the 'second tortured adolescence' riddled with agony and possessiveness. He had observed to her that the two elements necessary for love to survive are intensity and detachment. She wrote in *The Quick World*, '[This] poem took up this idea quite lightly – something I could not possibly have managed in those first months of lunatic enthusiasm.'

I remember Lauris having a print of Chagall's *I and the Village*, though the images in the poem, while evocative of Chagall's style, don't exactly match those in the painting. Intensity came eagerly and easily to Lauris; detachment was much more elusive. The images in the second stanza of choking, of stuffiness, of loss reflect her struggle to accept the strictures of the ordinary day to day – in love and in life:

> … There is no sound
> but the hum of our hearts. The painter
> is right, the real world could never
> contain us. This is intensity.
>
> Now the air thickens, the radiant company
> darkens – bodies, birds, cows, violins and
> harvest moons come drifting down, they
> coalesce …
>
> … I struggle, choking
> on the denseness of the air, look everywhere
> but cannot find you. When it no longer hurts
> to stand still and fit into the strict shape
> of my skin – that will be detachment.

Of 'Going to Moscow' she wrote:

As I sat eating raspberries and thinking about saying goodbye to my friend, it struck me very powerfully that we were behaving just like characters in a Chekhov play. They always seem to live in the country, their lives are full of farewells and futility, but sooner or later someone says, 'Ah if only we could go to Moscow, all would be well.' Well, I was leaving, I was in this sense going to Moscow: my friend sadly was staying in the country:

> At the last my frozen lips would not
> kiss you, I could do nothing but talk
> to the terrible little dog: but you
> stood still, your polished shoes swelling up

> like farm boots. There are always some
> who must stay in the country when others
> are going to Moscow. Your eyes were
> a dark lake bruised by the winter trees.

Lauris was not actually going to Moscow; she was going to
Menton and there was an element of relief in getting away. Her
agonies over Bill certainly have a Chekhovian quality of despair and
futility and give a particular potency to conjuring Chekhov's *The
Three Sisters*, with its characters' lives full of unfulfilled loves and
farewells.[3] The poem was published a couple of years before Lauris
actually did visit Moscow – if the visit did not inspire the poem, did
the poem inspire the visit? Perhaps she hoped that metaphorically
visiting Moscow might alleviate some of her distress over Bill.

'Those Roses', with its lustfully bursting, creamy, burrowing
images is, Lauris said quite explicitly, about sex, and is redolent of
intimate encounters.

> – and I
> notice a certain vegetable poise,
> not striated like the fibrous
> deposits of a more strenuous growing
> but smooth, opaque; placid testimony
> to the sufficiency of flesh.

She described it as a poem that 'put itself together as a complete
whole', as if she watched it happen. The obliqueness of the
metaphors is part of the joke about the privacy and intimacy of the
sexual act, she said. At a guess, it was inspired by the times she spent
with Bill in her Menton year, when he was travelling too; time when
their respective marriage partners (and other lovers) were well and
truly out of the frame and the difficulty of making arrangements
relied only on their own willingness and desire.

'Driving from the Airport' appears in her *Selected Poems*
(1984), the book that won her the Commonwealth Poetry Prize
the following year. The reference to poetry as a pale imitation of

life, a mask of smoke compared with being with a lover, was a
perennial issue for Lauris, and though she claimed to believe that
when the chips were down life trumped art, it's through her art
that she expresses the dichotomy. Her complicated and unresolved
relationship with Bill is implicit:

> oh tell him
> tell all those whose plane has gone
> over the cold horizon
> it is never a poem we want
> never this plausible mask of smoke
>
> it is the burning substance
> the shiver
> the sprawl
> the full spectrum of light
> on the poor bodily creatures
> that are for ever misunderstanding the way
> to be royally, ripely together.

Despite the fact that they fell in and out of love with other people
over the years, their relationship endured, though towards the end of
her life Lauris told me rather wistfully that it was 'a small thing, very
small'.

At her death, Bill told me (rather unsuitably, I thought) that they
had made love in her bed just a few days previously. In those last
weeks of her life, in January 2000, Lauris came down with a terrible
flu, one of the consequences of which was that she lost her voice
entirely. She could barely manage a wheezy croak on the phone,
so faxes – and sometimes letters – were the necessary means of
communication.

She also suffered an attack of grief when Bill went on holiday
with her friend and publisher Bridget Williams. She reasoned
with herself and I offered what support and advice I could about
detachment and letting others live their lives on their own terms.
Lauris was deeply affected though, and worried at the matter, but

she died before she had worked out what, if anything, she wanted to
do about it.

Out of a desire to 'do the right thing' towards those whom Lauris
had loved and, I suppose, a way of keeping her present, if not alive, I
visited Bill a few times after her death. They were pleasant occasions
when we talked of her and the world over a glass or two of red wine
in his rather spartan flat in Upper Lewisville Terrace, Thorndon, in
Wellington. But, as time went on, and his relationship with Bridget
Williams deepened, my contact with Bill dwindled. I had only
known Bill through Lauris and eventually it seemed better to leave it
that way.

Hubert Witheford was Lauris's grand folly. Here is her introduction
to me of her next love affair:

> *… You won't know who Hubert is, and this is a large part*
> *of what I want to tell you; it seems important to me to do so*
> *because what has been happening to me in recent weeks is by*
> *far the most central experience of my own life (as distinct from*
> *the one I share with dear persons like yourselves – if there can*
> *be such a distinction; there can't but at this stage it is something*
> *that is happening to me separately), for many years, perhaps*
> *ever. Hubert is a NZer I knew very slightly when I was first a*
> *student at Victoria and then didn't see for something like 40*
> *years, though I read his poetry, which is both beautiful and*
> *profound – his name is Hubert Witheford – you may know some*
> *of his work yourselves.*

She described meeting him again in London and his decision to
visit New Zealand and come and see her:

> *Well, that happened with astonishing consequences; we have*
> *been more or less living together ever since, though there isn't*
> *much time left for that since he goes back to London next week.*
> *However he has decided that he will come here to live, starting*

next year, and we expect from then on to spend most of our time together in some way, though much of the detail is of course unknown at present.

She went on to relate their parallel marital circumstances – partners they don't live with but maintain a relationship with – though Hubert had an added complication in that he lived with another woman as well:

However, it is for us both a profoundly shaking and widely reverberating experience, this late coming together, and arranging to make it continue to seem vital, even if difficult.

I haven't told you anything about Hubert himself, and there is perhaps no need since eventually you will get to know him, but nothing will happen for about a year. He is a person of tremendous wisdom and insight, not at all dramatic in personality but forceful in a gentle way; very emotional, full of a kind of inner adventurousness which is perhaps the thing I particularly respond to, though it is only one of many. And he takes my own work seriously and likes it which is rather a relief in a way, since he's so much more established than I am, and it would be embarrassing if he didn't! So there it is.

She wrote to Fleur Adcock of having 'fallen quite devastatingly in love … Bill (Oliver) has moved to some place on the horizon.' Hone Tuwhare wrote to her that he and Bill Oliver had commiserated over missing out on sex.

In her diary she recorded her feelings: 'One thing is for certain I truly love him, without the absurd fuss I made about WH, or the docility Beeb induced – he's simply the most towering person I've ever known.'

It didn't take a year. In the intervening months, Hubert wrote fulsome letters to her almost daily. Here are some of the phrases he used:

shrewd little sheila
crazy in love

the presumptuous feeling of being actually married to you has
   moved to the foreground
my adored, my totally adored one
My yet increasingly beloved
My once and now and future love
I have never properly loved anyone except you and will be with
   you and stay – if you want it – before long. H
There is nothing about you I don't love

Lauris would have found such adoration irresistible; he was everything she could have wished for in a man – a passionate adoring poet.

Hubert arrived in late August 1982. As he had in London, he divided his time between Lauris and his wife, who had accompanied him to New Zealand. It did not go smoothly. To Lauris's surprise and chagrin she encountered significant opposition from some family members. She wrote to me in elaborate detail; partly, I think, as a means of working out what she thought, but there was also an element of consciously or unconsciously gauging and/or attempting to influence my reaction. I have quoted from this letter extensively because it's also a fascinating portrayal of Edmond family dynamics. That I was unfazed by such a letter is an indication of how normal such confessions and family evaluations were:

> *… there is something I have to make clear to you before Hubert and I come to Auckland – though it is not as soon as I said; it's a fortnight later … does this suit you just as well for us to stay a few days?*
>
> *But anyway before you think about that, I want to tell you about the events of the weekend in Greytown. To begin with Stephanie (who may have told you something of this), I saw her last week and we talked, bitterly on her part, with much weeping on mine, about the difficulties we have at present in our communication. She told me among other things that she and Trevor and Virginia had all decided that in spending the main part of my time (that is the part that is not given to visits to Greytown or in other places with Trevor) with Hubert, I have*

*'made a choice' between this relationship and my family. This is
so far from what I think about it myself, that I was very upset
indeed, and being convinced that Trevor saw it much more as I
do, I rang him. He then spoke long and even more bitterly than
she had about the same thing – that I had made this choice and
now had to live with the consequences. I declared, as I have
all the time, that our separate living had been set up before
Hubert appeared, and that my condition for agreeing to the new
arrangement was that my Greytown commitment was not to be
disturbed. My feeling about it is unchanged, and in fact Trevor
and I have appeared to get on so well that I was convinced that
my different situation in my 'separated' life was having good
effects all round.*

    *Then I went to Greytown, earlier than I intended, so I could
talk to them all – because it has been obvious ever since she
arrived that Virginia is even more implacably opposed to me
than she used to be. Anyway, it seemed everyone's business, since
the 'making a choice' idea seemed to have been formed among
them as a group. I actually wrote down what I thought before
I went, as I do sometimes when I want something to be very
clear – mainly saying that I would never 'reject' any member of
my family, and that I had felt very strongly all the time that this
relationship must not get in the way of family loyalties, and for
me it had not. Virginia read it, gave a contemptuous snort and
that was all, Trevor said it made no difference to him, he still
thought the same, and Victor [Virginia's husband] said he knew
that was what I thought, and he didn't have a problem with
it – it was theirs, not his. The next morning Trevor and I talked
for ages – a most desperate conversation with him saying really
savage things and me weeping uncontrollably. I won't tell you
all the details – they don't matter anyway – but the main items
were that he felt as though our shared life which I regarded as
just the same was for him entirely changed, and in fact destroyed.
The main practical consequence was that he was going to change
his will to exclude me, should he die first, and leave everything
directly to the family, not, as at present, to the surviving spouse
first, and then to the children.*

*Then I talked to Victor – I went to get some coffee or
something and he was alone in the kitchen – and I said that
since everything was being said, and it was proving so terrible, I
had better say that I didn't know how I could go on relating to
him in a civilised and affectionate way, and to the children with
great warmth (which there is on both sides), and have Virginia
treat me like a blank space in the room – it was too artificial. He
agreed, and then said I should try to talk to Virginia. I observed
that I didn't think I could because she won't talk to me at all,
and I didn't see how there could be any future except for me not
to see any of them any more. He agreed with this too. As you
can imagine I was by now in a state of such grief it felt as though
I would never recover. I went back to Trevor's room and told
him this, and even he was appalled – he said he was aware of
Virginia's support for him but he had never intended it to go that
far. In the end we arranged that she would come and talk to me
with him there, which she did.*

*What followed was a long bitter tirade against me – not just
for the present situation, and in fact not really that at all. She
said that what I did with my private life was my own business,
and my only crime in that respect was to appear to demand
some sort of attitude to Hubert and she very much resented that.
She said she might well like him and get to know him well, but
wanted to do it in her own way and not to be set up for it by
me. I replied that I thought I had indeed done that when he first
came, and it was quite wrong and I regretted it, and there was
not the slightest chance that I would ever expect anything of her
again in that way. I meant it too. Then she said that as far as
Trevor was concerned the terrible thing I was doing was to live
at Grass St, and I should sell the house and give him his half of
the money from the sale and go and live somewhere else. Then
she said it hadn't been said or thought that I should never meet
them, but that on the contrary she thought we'd never get on
very well but it was better to find some way of having a sort of
communication. Victor later came and explained that he had not
meant to suggest this ultimate rift either – so that was settled,*

though by this time I was in such a state that I could not speak or eat or do anything for ages afterwards.

But it wasn't over yet. After she'd gone I told Trevor that I actually agreed with her, that the shared enterprise that created Grass St had always been thought 'fair' because he'd put more money into it but I'd done the bulk of the work. Now that was not so, and some of his resentment probably came from feeling that his claim on that old sharing was somehow violated by Hubert's arrival. He more or less agreed with this, so I asked him to say what were some sore places in his mind about that. I said I didn't want to sell the house and move unless I had to, and he that he didn't actually want me to, that had been Virginia's idea ... There were two – one that he'd paid for the most recent alterations (I was just back and had no money – but had thought it wasn't quite fair too) the other was that he'd had an overdraft for a long time when the earlier building downstairs was being done, and I had not contributed, at a time when he was worried about money. So, I asked him if I were to give him both those amounts – it's a bit over $3000 – those two old pains would be laid to rest. He said yes and that's what I'm going to do. I suggested paying some more, but he didn't think more was necessary.

Then we had a fairly good sort of day, on Sunday. I worked hard, as I always do there, in the garden first and then painting his room and some of the hall. I was to come home Sunday night but I felt so much that the idea, which I have never relinquished, that our shared life does continue to be good in just the same way as before, was in both our minds and I wanted to stay till Monday. This I did, though my departure was very miserable, after all. I told him in the morning that of course I would mind terribly, if it should happen, that all his affairs should be dealt with by Virginia as his executor and I was made a sort of non-person. I also said if the situations were reversed I would never dream of taking any of these actions, but would co-operate with him in any way I could – if he were ever to meet a companionable person, a woman, I would regard his house as hers, and would think myself lucky to be able to come there as a visitor – that in fact what I have been saying for years about our troubled ex-marriage I do most passionately believe, that all that is still good in it must not be denied, but that it leaves a large part of both our lives to be pursued independently. I added too that I was horrified at the Calvinistic quality in Virginia's obvious desire to 'punish' me. (I thought afterwards of all the things an affectionate and protective daughter might have said about support for him without it involving destroying me – widening his view in various ways ...) He said he didn't know what he'd do about the will – probably nothing in the end, but that if he did he would never make it so that I had to leave Grass St, which he didn't want me to have to do. He also said I could continue to come to Greytown for visits.

So, feeling that I had to leave since I'd cried so much in those days and was crying again, I went out to start the car and found it waterlogged! However, that was fairly easily fixed, and in a state of semi-collapse I came home.

I'm telling you in such detail because you have said that Hubert and I could stay with you, and thinking it over if you feel you don't want us, this gives you the chance to say so. It makes me start to cry again to say this (will there ever be an end to this misery?), and yet it does seem I have to – and indeed if you do feel that it divides your loyalties in a way you don't want, then we won't come, and I will understand. I just don't feel now that I can easily assume – as I have been doing – that anyone else in the family sees the situation as I do.

I was sympathetic; it wouldn't have occurred to me to question her motives or intentions – she was my mother. We spoke on the phone and I reassured her that I did not share the views expressed by my sisters, that I believed it was her right to live her life on the terms she wished and that I would neither threaten nor ostracise her. She and Hubert were welcome to come and stay. I also suggested that if she was finding the relationship with Virginia so toxic and distressing, perhaps she could give it a rest and see what – if anything – might evolve of its own accord. This was a piece of advice I regularly gave and it was one she was never really able to take. Leaving well alone did not come easily to Lauris.

Rereading these letters now, I am struck by another mother/daughter parallel, bringing to mind her description of me at 20: 'emotional floods and storms, her violence under the stress of drink and disappointment, the futility of her days, sodden with great wet waves of feeling and lacking the shape and firmness of any systematic work'.

A few days later she wrote again, 'I'm sending you a poem – I seem to be writing a lot and nearly all about Trevor!' It was 'Camping'.

> *It was good to talk to you the other night – even good to be lectured by you! I have thought a great deal about what you said, and have come to see it as not only sensible but the only possible way for me to behave … How primitive it all is. People keep telling me at present that I don't understand what the 'ordinary' world (whatever that is) is like. At least some people do – most of my friends are calm and sensible.*
>
> *But it is true that doing something out of place and out of time disturbs the whole universe, or the bit of it around you – I have a sense of things which were securely lodged in their place having come adrift so that they roll about like big rocks in an earthquake and keep hitting me. Each time it hurts like hell – and I suppose that will go on happening till they have all settled into some other, slightly different, new place and stay there. I have certainly underestimated the effect of making this sort of change – I thought that, since my life was organised the way it was, what I did with the bit of it (the largest bit) that I spent alone was of no great interest to anyone else – but I suppose if you want people to be part of your life then you have to let them be part of its upheavals. As far as the family is concerned, I suppose all of the upheavals have been other people's, and nobody is geared to them being mine. Or am I only talking about Virginia – perhaps …*

Lauris was indeed being reprimanded by her family for unsuitable behaviour, required 'to get back into line' because she inconvenienced them, made them uncomfortable. I have never agreed with the family attack on Lauris. It was her right – any woman's actually – to pursue personal and sexual satisfaction on her own terms, to take a live-in lover if she so desired. I suspect Lauris's fierce moralism as a younger woman seeped into her family and later, she had to bear the consequences.

She did of course 'get back into line'. Her next letter has a much more sober tone:

> I have just this minute put down the phone and come to write
> down in a letter all the things I couldn't, for various reasons,
> say. The main one is that the 'solution' to the family upheavals
> has coincided with a very severe reaction of mine against the
> durability (can one say that?) of this new situation anyway. The
> process, in brief, was that I decided to find out why I was so
> extraordinarily upset all the time about family alienation, when
> nobody else ever burst into tears at all, and in fact once the
> scenes had ended didn't do anything much. What I discovered
> was that I couldn't defend my altered circumstances because
> I didn't really believe in them myself. I have in any case been
> having a time of great withdrawal from my friend Hubert, and
> though this is no doubt partly one of the phases that occurs in
> any new relationship, it is also far more, I'm sure, and has to do
> with the realisation that he is, after all, a good deal of a stranger
> and it is far too soon for me to be sure I want to live with him
> all, or even part of the time – of course you may ask, why the hell
> didn't I find this out before it all began? Well, I couldn't because
> it hadn't happened, and it's no good anyone saying that I plunge
> into things in a crazy way because I KNOW that. What I don't
> know is how it will all turn out … For the present I am going to
> do nothing for several months, and give up crying, which I was
> doing every time anyone spoke to me … one of the problems for
> me (perhaps the problem) is that he gives such fixed attention to
> this thing called the relationship that I feel tied hand and foot
> by it – perhaps that can change; if it doesn't, I am sure I can't

last long. I thought being adored with total concentration was every woman's dream, but in fact it's quite unbearable – for me anyway.

So. We'll bring sheets and blankets and let you know exactly when we're arriving – probably some time latish on Monday November 22.

In a piece of magnificent irony, within a week the Hubert affair was over. On 14 November Lauris wrote to Fleur Adcock, her tone remarkably light in contrast to the tortured one that filled the pages she wrote to me:

My family simmered. Suddenly there was a colossal confrontation with them – Trevor and Virginia and Stephanie, the two daughters who are here; it was all about my having made a choice and how I must not expect that they would think of this as home, and though they spoke politely of Hubert (well, Trevor didn't) they didn't want to come and see him here, though they would meet in town, that sort of thing. I was frightfully distressed but in the end glad because it made me appraise this relationship very critically and in fact H is so devouring a lover that I was becoming emotionally and sexually paralysed from lack of air. This is how I've remained until he agreed to get another place ...

They didn't come to stay. I didn't ever meet Hubert. I have no sense of who he was and how they were together. Hubert was a preposterous folly on Lauris's part. Nevertheless, even endings one wishes for harbour regrets, disappointments, especially when an adventure embarked on with such passionate optimism, such ardent and impulsive recklessness so quickly crumbles into a dusty heap. In another letter to Fleur, she wrote:

Woe, woe, predictable, warned-against, known-to-everyone-except-me-as-inevitable disillusionment! Did you warn me? Of course you did, tactfully, courteously, uselessly. So did other people. And did I listen? A tolerant smile, meaning that these things are different for me ... Well, they're not.

Anyway – I'm ashamed of this, but I know it's true – I think I was in love with the idea of someone being so mad about me, more than with the person, whom I didn't really know. How many times, I've thought writers were dreadfully susceptible to flattery, but that I was not – well I am truly brought down over that. Indeed, I've learnt several salutary lessons, as I suppose one always does. Another of them is that I simply can't handle that sort of total togetherness, and I don't want it. I much prefer people who are interested in their own affairs and have some of their time – but not all of it – for me.

And in another letter to Fleur, she concluded that a good part of the attraction was

permanent security – I say I don't want it, but underneath I think I have a much more powerful craving for some lasting, reliable companionship than I have ever admitted. There are advantages of having tried it and failed though, because at least I now know that if I am lonely (and I am at times) I can remind myself that I've chosen it, the solitary life.

A year later, in January 1984, after reading over her diary entries describing the early passionate days with Hubert, she wrote in the typically extravagant fashion she reserves for addressing herself:

In fact all these recent pages are wrong wrong wrong! Whoever in … the world was wronger than I? I am the queen of wrongness, wrongness is my specialty, my flair, my power, my capacity. In wrongness I find myself most totally. Hubert was a flop. He was childish, arrogant, passive, opinionated, cold, insensitive – all at once! WH is my love, my love my love for all my life, whatever he does, however the world changes, declines, blows up; the sun can rise in the west and fall in the east and I will still love him. A thousand other women will be captivated by his gentle inquiring stance, his concealed certainty, his bodily impetuosity – it will make no difference. Did I need Hubert to make me understand this? To make me learn generosity at last, or that I love him (WH, that is) without wanting to possess him.

For Lauris it always came back to Bill, and the other unresolved question of her struggle to be reconciled to a solitary life. By 1987 she would conclude, in another letter to Fleur, that 'nobody in their right mind would find me marriageable':

It is certainly true, I get more interested in what I am doing myself and I don't care too much if the nearest thing I've got to 'a man in my life' is fairly marginal (in several senses).

That she was emerging from a second riotous adolescence and moving into more productive and settled years is an irresistible construction. Also, that she had provisionally recognised the inevitability of a solitary life even though acceptance of it was still some distance in the future. There's also the implication that she had been looking for another marriage, which she now concluded was unlikely. Even so, the dream of a coupled union never quite left her. It's not easy to maintain equilibrium while living outside the prevailing value systems of the society one has grown up in.

There were other relationships, and sex remained a driving force for Lauris, personally and creatively. Towards the end of her life, when an unwelcome awareness of 'waning powers' was beginning to surface, her wistful words were, 'I don't want to lose my beloved sexuality.'

After the Hubert debacle, her letters to me were much less about 'man trouble', though she continued to write to Fleur in this vein. I myself had abandoned having multiple relationships at once and moved into a more settled coupledom; this and her increasing interest in her work were both topics in our evolving communication.

Thinking about Lauris and love, I went in search of Drusilla Modjeska's coherent analysis of how a woman must negotiate her place from being the object in our Western patriarchal society to its subject. Modjeska's work has been influential to my thinking – perhaps to Lauris's too – but I couldn't remember where I'd read it. First I tried *Poppy*, her exploration of her mother's life. The copy

I found in my bookshelf had Lauris's name in it – perhaps she had bought it when she was writing her own life story.

Eventually I realised the book I wanted was *The Orchard*. Modjeska writes that 'a lover validates a woman', where 'being a woman alone invalidates her'. Lauris grew up with these ideas – love as the gift of happiness and fulfilment. Like thousands of other young women, she left home with copies of *Pride and Prejudice* and *Jane Eyre*, having learned that she wanted to be admired, pursued, loved, to find her Mr Darcy or Mr Rochester, romantically and economically. And yet to be neither wife nor mistress but woman on her own terms – this was Lauris's journey. And working in the arts without another job is risky and, except in a few cases, financially unrewarding. Lauris supplemented her earnings with teaching, editing and literary grants.

In her work life, Lauris faced the ongoing problem of established male hierarchies not really taking women seriously. Poet and printer Denis Glover was guilty of this. Despite 'taking her up' – it was he who invited her to edit the letters of his friend and fellow poet A.R.D. (Rex) Fairburn; assisted her with the publication of her first collection, *In Middle Air*; and subsequently persuaded her into editing his own work – and despite admiring her and finding her useful, Glover treated her with condescension – a woman writer! When he launched *In Middle Air* he was unable to resist 'asserting that all poetesses would be better to stay at home and concentrate on mending their husband's socks'.

In terms of her day-to-day living, Lauris resolved these questions – she earned her own income, constructed a working and a social life that sustained her. She also provided me and many other women with an essential and admirable role model, even though the dilemmas, the conflicts between life and art, love and independence, together or solo, never entirely left her.

8. Laughter and love at the centre

Friends describe Lauris as having a gift for creating intimacy; as compelling, charming and extravagant, with a great enthusiastic curiosity. She made people feel as though they were exactly the person she most wanted to talk to right then. No conversation was censored – you could ask her anything, talk about anything. She had a particular skill at being intimate in a collective context too, expanding the one into the many so that each felt special, as if she were addressing them individually.

A number of her poems are addressed directly to friends and lovers, Hone Tuwhare among them. Was he friend or lover? He was both, though his lack of commitment to any notion of fidelity elevated friendship as the more enduring. A line from one of his poems, 'Lament' is on the headstone of Rachel's grave. It's the second line of the final stanza, omitting the first word:

> I bear no malice, let none stain my valedictions
> For I am at one with the wind
> the clouds' heave and the slapping rain
> the tattered sky and the wild solitude
> of the sea and the streaming earth
> which I kneel to kiss …

Lauris and Hone met in 1975 while both anxiously tending to their psychically wounded children in Auckland Hospital's Ward

10: for Lauris it was Rachel, and Hone was visiting two of his sons. The choice of the line for Rachel's grave was Lauris's tribute to Hone and the warmth and support he offered her over the tragedy of Rachel, and indeed continued to offer her. They loved each other so they went to bed together when the opportunity presented itself, though it was opportunistic rather than a sustained affair. (One of my sisters was mortified to walk in on them making love in a motel in Dunedin).

When Hone was in Wellington researching in the Turnbull Library, he would stay in a motel nearby. Of a morning, Lauris would pop in for a quick visit on her way to the *Journal* office. One memorable occasion when she entered, Hone leapt out of bed, hitting the floor, the reverberation running up the walls and into the ceiling where the grand chandelier detached itself, and, with impeccable timing, landed directly on Lauris, who had to be rushed off to hospital! Fortunately, the damage was rather more to her vanity than her person.

In her diary, Lauris described their relationship thus:

> *Hone too was what was called chauvinistic, he didn't want me to challenge his authority in any way, his literary and personal superiority. At the same time he had a marvellously unpossessive attitude to sex, and I in turn never did, or could, claim his special loyalty. He saw sex, and used it as a natural expression of desire, refreshingly unconnected with jealous demands. There were actually skirmishes on the edges of this battleground (he had other relationships to attend to, and preserve), but they were a source of fun, kids' games which we played together. Hone's Polynesian quality – or what I thought of as that – was part of the new knowledge I found with him. He lived in his body, right down to the fingertips, in a way that no Anglo-Saxon (and therefore, as I saw it, inhibited) man could do. His physical, intellectual, emotional selves were one, or at least securely intertwined; when he sang in what I called his bumblebee voice, a musical purring, it happened everywhere – his fingers and toes sang as much as his vocal cords. I'd never known such a being at*

home in the body and it delighted me. Yet again it was a major new discovery.

'Sober Truth' was written for Hone:

> Yes, you're yourself all the way through,
> the breathing radiator I've often stood near
> in a spell of hard weather of the heart,
> warmed by some great buzz
> of laughter and love at the centre.
> This, old friend, is to tell you
> I got home safely last night
> after the party.

I met Hone with Lauris in Café Brava in Courtenay Place underneath Downstage Theatre in November 1997. The impetus was a trip to Rachel's grave in the Akatārawa Cemetery. Hone had written a poem for Lauris, published in his 1993 collection, *Deep River Talk*, and mistakenly titled it 'Frances, Baby' instead of 'Rachel, Baby'. It was corrected for his 1997 collection, *Shape Shifter*, and our visit to Akatārawa on Sunday 16 November was to lay the error to rest in the presence of all four of us.

Hone stood as we entered the bar, greeted me by putting his hands to my hips and ever so delicately aligning me so I was directly facing him. He eased us together, his genitals pressed against my pubic bone, and he kissed me on the cheek. It was matter of fact, intimate and affectionate – his manhood greeting my womanhood – but despite that, not overtly sexual. Over a couple of drinks, we arranged to collect Hone the next day somewhere up in Melrose or Mornington. Once in the car, he asked Lauris to drive slowly as he scanned the trees on the street verge. 'Here,' he suddenly said. Lauris stopped and he got out, picked a few leaves from a pūriri tree. This was my introduction to the significance of pūriri leaves for honouring the dead.

At Rachel's grave, Hone asked me to read from Eccles. 3: 1–8: 'To everything there is a season'. Then he read his poem.[1] He laid the

pūriri leaves, we cried, hugged each other, talked and remembered
her. As we walked away, he turned back, sang for her in Māori, his
great rich voice echoing across the hillside. We drove back to town,
to Café Brava for a celebratory drink. 'Afternoon at Akatarawa' is
Lauris's poem for that day:

> (for Frances and Hone)
>
> It was there, a silence within the wind, brushing
> lightly across that dedicated hillside
> holding its dead in its arms, each one's
> eternity contained in the long sleep of the earth.
>
> It was a colour – or no colour – in the quiet sky
> as we three knelt or sat on the grass looking down,
> my hand on the carved stone of her name,
> her years written there in brief relentless strokes;
>
> it was our tears, our shared remembering,
> our close-leaning bodies; it touched our skin
> with the wind, held us close in our stillness.
> It was – a mysterious knowing beyond knowledge;
>
> or perhaps the earth itself, where we will all
> one day lie with her, the voice of its silence.
> Then we stood up, heads bent, and meandered
> over the grass. But – there was one thing more –
>
> he broke, turned, breathed hard, his great voice
> suddenly filling that cathedral of hills with
> a muscular shouting, strange harsh music as though
> coming from some deep place beyond even himself.
>
> He ended. We walked to the car. Miles down the road
> in the silence we drew around us, each peering
> inwards to see what we could of her long-ago face,
> he told us: 'A salute. For a chief only. For her.'

I met Hone at a time when my life was in great disarray; it was, in Lauris's words in 'Sober Truth', 'a spell of hard weather of the heart'. He was gentle and kind; no doubt the details of what was happening in my impossibly difficult domestic circumstances told him by Lauris. He wrote to me in his rather spidery hand, bits of the letter spread over the page in an eccentric arrangement and eccentrically addressed:

Frances Edmond – with Holy Whanau
Tuesday April 28 1998
To Frances Edmond – from Hone
Dear Frances,
I've just arrived last evening after about a fortnight in the Wellsford area with an old friend.
  I'm on my way south on the night train to Wgtn. Where I'll be met by my publisher Roger Steele and with whom I'll be staying for one night before flying back to Dunedin for some kind of 'thingy' at Otago University. They're making me a Doctor! Shit!
  I'm pleased everything has finally been resolved for you domestically, and that the children are fine, Frances. I wish it sincerely for you. I'm coming back in July for the Montana Book Award. I think my recent book has been shortlisted. Write to me if you can get a babysitter – you've got a personal invite from me, okay?
  Arohanui my dear.
  Hone

PTO
My mail (heaps) was sent up to my Wellsford address (temporary) by the Postmaster/Shopkeeper at Kaka Point, South Otago. I'll try and ring your Mum to say hello too. I tried to ring you but you had no number under Edmond!
  Kia ora! H.

PS my blessing to your children too. I'm meeting a granddaughter, Moana, whose taking time out from Uni courses to pick up some Land Court papers off me!

PPS When you write, send me a photo, so as I will recognise you:
and with the children too.
    Hone

I sent him a photograph of me with my children but when the time came for the Montana Book Awards I couldn't go, it was simply too hard: my youngest child was sick, I hadn't found a babysitter, I hadn't written to Hone and he didn't ring. Ah well. Everything has its time and chance, whether we pick up the baton or leave it lying where we find it.

Hone died nearly 10 years later and Michele Leggott (at that time New Zealand's Poet Laureate) rang suggesting I join her, my cousin Murray Edmond and Russell Haley to go north for his tangi. In the car we discussed what waiata we might sing should the occasion require it. Murray and Russell came up with 'On Ilkla Moor Baht'at' as an offering on the life of a popular and much-loved poet. We spent the journey remembering the words and practising. In the event our efforts were in vain as there was no opportunity to sing.

We filed around his coffin, his body a crumpled relic of what he once gloriously was and I, uncertain of protocol, did not lay the pūriri leaves I had brought. I felt remote, detached, pleased in the abstract that I had gone north, both for Lauris's sake and for his, but we, or at least I, felt a stranger, an interloper from another world as he lay among his mourning whānau. We followed his body to the urupā and stood by as he was interred in the welcoming earth, then we left.

I have beside me as I write his collected works, *Small Holes in the Silence*, and a signed copy he gave me of *Shape-Shifter*. The inscription reads: 'To: Frances – with great thoughts and aroha to you always. Hone, 24 Nov 1997, Poneke.'

Same to you, Hone.

There are other poems for friends. 'Poem for a Marriage' was written for the wedding of her friends Lynne Dovey and Ben Gray. In the light of Lauris's many unresolved dilemmas, this is a poem that unequivocally takes the side of life, love and togetherness. It's a Lauris hymn to marriage itself, to steadfastness, to the recognition of its textures through the imagery of the natural world with its constant inconstancy – tides and seasons of weather as well as of the heart.

Lynne and Ben had asked her to read a poem for their wedding and, unable to find something she considered suitable, Lauris wrote this one. Specific in its genesis, nevertheless it has the Lauris touch: wisdom discovered in what we take for granted, the patterns and rhythms of mother nature, of the 'green world'. I read it recently at my stepdaughter's wedding, its timelessness and tenderness exquisitely fitting the occasion:

> Walk quietly here, observe how currents
> of wind and water have prepared you for a sign:
> the days, the years set out in a single
> composition, formed from the turn and wash
> of the tide, the spinning eddies of wind,
> the sun's repeated visitations.

Another take on the marriage question can be found in 'Sonnet for the Unsung' – the point of view of 'the other woman':

> she walked through crowds staring at where he'd slept
> into the garden his sons had helped him tend
> and sat alone and bowed her head and wept.

'Poem for a Mistress' it might have been titled, this forlornly perceptive description of the other woman, the outsider, the one with no claim, no right to grief or public consolation. The poem acknowledges her loneliness, the price she has always paid for the liaison. It reads as if it were written for a specific person and I have often wondered who. But it speaks to all women who have fallen in love with a powerful married man who promises more than he gives, who avoids the question of leaving his wife but who is nevertheless delighted by the attention of an intelligent and undemanding woman who is prepared to put up with the morsels available to a 'mistress'. I have considered the possibility that it might be about Lauris herself but it's uncommon for her to write about herself in the third person, and the wistful portrayal of an accepting woman does not have the ring of Lauris.

Bruce Mason was a friend from training college days. They were in plays together, belonged to the same circle – 'our cleverness / (the 'vicious little circle' marvelling at its / brilliance for a fragile, funny summer term' ('Round Oriental Bay').

After training college Bruce remained a supportive friend, particularly at times when Lauris was what she describes as 'adrift'.[2] In her diary of 1977 she wrote of him '[taking] me for a drink, seeing my distress … I was grateful for his enthusiastic offer of helpful conversation anytime I should need to ring him up and explain my need'. In a letter to me in 1978 she wrote:

> *Bruce has something that he calls Bell's palsy, but which looks like a stroke – all one side of his face has fallen. It's terrible; mortality making itself felt. He is, for what it's worth, (which is probably quite a lot) very courageous about it, makes jokes about being 'your friendly neighbourhood gargoyle' but you can see that to be grotesque is the last degradation for him.*

In the early days of Lauris's relationship with Hubert (April–May 1982), they spent time with Bruce: 'We went to Bruce and Diana's for lunch, an elegant affair, superior food, a slow pace playing some of Bruce's tapes of himself.'[3] By 1982 the diagnosis of Bell's palsy had been reviewed and he knew he had the cancer that was to kill him on the last day of that year.

Lauris relates a farcical tale of Bruce, Hubert and herself spending an hilarious day together:

We had Bruce to lunch – an amazing day, we drank a whole bottle of gin, got incredibly euphoric, kissed one another, rhapsodised about Hubert being back and us all being marvellously full of love for one another – then came out and my car was towed away and Bruce was picked up by the police [for drunk driving] … It was frightfully funny especially since he later became a little pompous about his 'eminence'. But during the night I was appallingly ill …

'Epiphany (for Bruce Mason)' was written towards the end of the year. He was only 61 and he was dying. Lauris took the newly completed poem to him at home – a last gesture in recognition of their long friendship and connection:

> I saw a woman singing in a car
> opening her mouth as wide as the sky,
> cigarette burning down in her hand
> – even the lights didn't interrupt her
> though that's how I know the car
> was high-toned cream, and sleek:
> *it is harder for a rich woman …*
>
> Of course the world went on
> fucking itself up just the same –
> and I hate the idea of stabbing at
> poems as though they are flatfish,
> but how can you ignore a perfect lyric
> in a navy blue blouse, carolling away
> as though it's got two minutes
> out of the whole of eternity, just
> to the corner of Wakefield Street –
>
> which after all is a very long life
> for pure ecstasy to be given.

'At the Exhibition: Gun Club, Eion Stephens' is based on a painting of Eion's:

> 'Yes I am having
> a good time. Interesting …',
> (the targets, the trophies) and stares
> at his square fingers holding the glass
> tight, like a toy; like a trigger.

Eion was delighted with this poem and remained in intermittent contact with me after Lauris's death. In June 2015 he sent me an anecdote recalling his first meeting with Lauris. Handwritten, it was slipped inside a card with a small painting of his on the front: a heart, a ladder painted in black over blocks of colour – orange, green, red, pink – and the words 'a ladder to heart':

> *I first met Lauris in 1984, at Wellington airport, while travelling with Hone Tuwhare, and as was the way in those circles, invited to stay at Grass St.*
>
> *Before turning in for the night, I was aware of a white cat called Brian, who tested my automatic affection for the species. He was not an attractive animal in any way, but assumed his position in the household with some kind of enigmatic exchange with Lauris.*
>
> *The next morning, Brian was nowhere to be seen, his breakfast untouched. Lauris always had a mock dramatic side to her. She stood in the middle of the kitchen and pronounced that, 'He's finally run away from home.'*

Brian – full name Brian McWhinnis – had been my cat until I abandoned him to Lauris after she returned from overseas in 1977. In fact, the abandonment was more his; I went to live further around the hillside in Grafton Road and Brian, an un-neutered tomcat, refused to accompany me. He and his sister, Valencia Whirl, had been classic white kittens, the kind that decorate many a chocolate box, hence her name.

Valencia accompanied me on my travels while Brian lived out his life with Lauris, lording it around her hillside, fornicating when he could and endlessly fighting other manky toms for territory and sexual superiority. I tried to persuade her to get him neutered, to turn him into a lazy, docile, gelded slob, but she would have none of it. Perhaps she thought he was better off in his natural state, preserving his adventurous feline spirit. Perhaps she liked the idea that he was getting plenty of sex. Perhaps she couldn't be bothered with the effort of getting him into a cat box and then up or down the hill into the car and off to the vet.

Once, when I was visiting, I made the mistake of picking him up and he sprayed the front of my clothes with revolting tomcat urine. He sprayed the pillows in the downstairs flat as well – when he found a way in. I wholeheartedly agree with Eion: Brian became a disgusting, bedraggled, unkempt, example of felinity, tufts of hair missing, ears torn, lanky, mangy body and haunted face. It would have been a kindness to neuter him, especially after he could no longer maintain his status as 'top cat' of the neighbourhood. Lauris recorded his demise:

> ... Where do
> they go, cats? – discreet as spies, no farewells,
> no unclean decomposition; just the silence,
>
> sharp, as this one is, with a thousand
> conversations, the taste and smell of little pieces
> of our lives: they stuck to him, I think,
> he carried them about, sweetened them perhaps ...

Fiona Kidman and I have spent many hours remembering and discussing our beloved Lauris, but one afternoon we sat down to attend to some specifics: I was curious about the journey of their long friendship. When Lauris was editor of the *PPTA Journal*, author and editor Ian Cross, looking for some new blood, invited her to join the committee of PEN (the writers' society). PEN held some riotous parties, according to Fiona, and this is how she got to know Lauris:

We took to each other, an enchantment; at the Western Park we would talk on and on and on about everything over G and T (me) and brandy and ginger ale (Lauris). We were both women moving out of the domestic into being writers, being 'in the world'. I had had no special friend since school so Lauris was very important to me. There were great gushes of emotional outpourings. Lauris had no filters, would talk about everything … it was a great gift but also could be a curse. She was charming and extravagant and I was charmed and happy to be with her. She was constantly engaged in developing her own intellectual prowess. She encouraged me to think in new ways, and into reading new things.

Then, in 1975, we both had our first books published by Albion Wright at Pegasus Press. Albion liked my book but not hers. He accepted mine overnight but Denis [Glover] had to go to Christchurch to see Albion and put Lauris's case (she may have paid for him to go.) It was some years later she told me this. Yet it was her book that won the Jessie McKay Best First Book Award (John Thompson was the judge and he was good). I realised that the 'exciting world of Wellington poets' was not really for me. I had to rescue myself … and write a novel.

We did have a major falling out that lasted a number of years. I don't really know what started it. Lauris made a strange attack on me about friends of mine she didn't like. I walked home after an hour in floods of tears. Lauris was 'with' Beeb at the time and he worked at NZCER. Alistair [Campbell] was there too and Leigh [Minnit] as well – she could be sharp. Part of it was Lauris making another life for herself. But, was she telling me not to be friends with Leigh? Possibly. It seemed there were irreconcilable differences. I was grief-stricken at the break, then angry. I summoned her to the Settlement and told her I didn't care if we weren't friends any more.

It took some years for the rift to heal. We had started out as equals beginning our writing lives together, discovering each other, but that had changed. It is also true that at the time of the break I was probably projecting my own difficulties onto the relationship. I knew five daughters who had died, of which

Rachel was one. And it was at a time when Lauris needed to be centrally focused on Rachel. She wrote to me from Menton; [that was] the beginnings of healing and after that we had a much better friendship that lasted the distance. We were close friends for all the rest of her life. And by the time we were friends there was also Vincent [O'Sullivan], Alistair and Meg [Campbell], John Thompson (JT). They were important for Lauris because she was recognised as their intellectual equal. Status and credibility mattered to her.

She discovered the sexual revolution in her fifties – later than many – in breaking through intellectually there was the sex too and it was 'okay'; it was the zeitgeist, it was 'of the times'. There was something quite splendid about her, her wildness, her breaking of the rules. She had intense intimacies, and there was a ruthlessness too. She saw her sexuality as an essential part of her being, once she had discovered it. It was as though she could do everything and have everything and Trevor as well. His candle for Lauris never went out.

Fiona and I discussed the idea that Lauris drove Trevor to drink.[5] We also talked about family attitudes to Lauris and her endless letters:

Her letters? They were reprimanding, overreacting, querying. She would fax them to me. I was drawn into grappling with her relationships with her family. She was an education for me, the mistakes she made in telling family stories made me very careful about what I said about my family.

In her last period she was no longer lonely and unhappy, she had grown up, matured, arrived at equilibrium. She got up early, worked in the mornings and had a real certainty about the quality of her work, a self-belief – she 'lived her poetry'. She was a great teacher, brought out the best in people, nurtured them, was helpful to so many who were trying to 'make it'. She was a flawed human being, as we all are, but she gave people of herself in her words and in her teaching. She articulated what they felt in her poetry. Grass Street was a 'salon'; people ate out of her hand, became radiant in her presence.

The two friends regularly exchanged birthday cards, Lauris writing to Fiona:

> *This card doesn't look as though it's set itself up as a birthday card but it seems to fit all the same my birthday message to you – my unchanging love for you (unless it grows, if this is possible), my constant pleasure in our shared understandings, our always illuminating conversations on all the subjects that matter. I simply cannot imagine life without you to sort out its complexities and idiocies with me. Have a really nice birthday my dear friend.*

In April 1999 Fiona sent a note to her old friend for her 75th birthday:

> *… But none of this is saying my dear and so loved friend, happy happy TRUE birthday. Every year I've known you has been a celebration and while counting years is not the done thing in one sense, all the same, as they are being acknowledged this year, I thought our friendship is about 27 years old … which makes us both youthful and old friends all at once.*
>
> *Anyway, have a lovely day, give love to Frances, and a card I've just sent will meander through the Easter mail, eventually.*

A month later she followed up:

> *I was going to say, and then I sidetracked myself – no you didn't do it yourself – the public part of being 75 – you had a party, like lots of people do for all sorts of reasons – yours was being 75 – and suddenly a great many people were moved to stand up and declare just how important you are in a literary as well as a personal sense.*
>
> *That's quite different from doing it yourself, and in a way, it's a more definitive statement than awards.*

After Lauris's death, in January 2000, Fiona and I, both bereft, reached across the empty space she left behind and found each other. In the beginning Lauris was the conduit, but as the years have gone by we have found our own close friendship. My life would be much poorer without Fiona's patient, thoughtful wisdom and steady affection as well as her sense of fun and her marvellous books.

I visited Fleur Adcock at her home in East Finchley, London, in August 2017. Fleur told me her favourite Wellington moment was arriving at Grass Street; she loved Lauris, missed her still, was shocked at her dying so young:

> *I am older now than she was when she died – 83, Lauris was 75 – and I regret that I didn't see as much of her as I would have liked. It was that 'bloody hill' that killed her … all that upping and downing being hard on an ageing body. But at least she was in the midst of her life, had all her faculties, a good way to go, though we all agree she died too soon.*
>
> *I met her in late 1975. Alistair and Meg Campbell introduced us at the Abel Tasman pub. We clicked; like so many people, I took to Lauris at once and we became friends across the globe. We had great conversations, talked about everything. Writers seldom talk about their actual writing – they talk of money, publishers, scandal, sex. You know she was always falling in love – with unsuitable men: Hone, Denis Glover, Hubert and who was that old man?*[6]

I asked Fleur if she thought Lauris was a poor judge of men. She replied:

> *Yes, of character in general. Hubert – he couldn't keep his hands off women … one had to put furniture between you and him! Do you know the story of the $10 bill? Lauris, Hubert, Louis Johnson and I went to dinner in a Chinese restaurant in Courtenay Place after a book launch of Alistair's … and when it was time to pay the two men got into a contest of masculinity, each of them insisting it was his treat. They passed a $10 dollar note to and fro across the table, arguing, until Lauris snatched it out of their hands and said, 'If you don't want it, we'll have it!'*

*Whereupon she tore it in two, giving me one half to keep until
we next met. Three years later I turned up at our rendezvous in
a Wellington bar with a roll of Sellotape; we reunited the two
halves and bought a bottle of chardonnay and two packets of
nuts.*

Fleur wrote in a review of *Night Burns with a White Fire*:

*One of her essential qualities was her open-hearted delight in the
world of nature, people, events – she was so often filled with joy
about something. This wonderment could occasionally verge on
the naïve, but that's an innocent fault, if a fault at all.*[7]

At the time I visited Fleur, I was beginning to think about the
memorial plaque now installed at 22 Grass Street. Fleur, knowing
that most of the immediate family would not put any money
towards it, offered a contribution and gave me the idea of asking
Lauris's friends and colleagues. When Fleur was last in Wellington,
she made the pilgrimage to Grass Street. She wrote to me afterwards:

*I thought you might like to know that although I wasn't able
to be in Wellington for the launch ceremony I did trudge up
Grass St with my niece Mia and her partner Kristen to inspect
and photograph the plaque before I had to leave for Auckland.
The sun was shining when we were there, but I'd have enjoyed
an excuse to go inside Lauris's old sitting-room, although I too
might have felt a bit tearful.*

In 1985 Lauris visited Fleur in London, recording in her diary:

*My last day evening in London. I keep saying I'm not ready to
leave and in a way I'm not – on the other hand if I were to stay
for longer I would have to start on a different programme, find
a place to live, think of it all in longer terms. As it is, it's been
a beautiful time, especially moving closer to Fleur, that delicate
fastidious yet adamantine creature; I have come to feel a great
fondness for her – I think it can be called love. She's more
vulnerable than you expect; she is also careful of herself … till*

you realise that she will always give away her rest-and-seclusion insistence if she warms to you – and she is very warm with a kind of discriminating appreciation that I for one value very highly indeed. The last thing that I did was go for a walk with her in the Highgate Wood this afternoon; then we had some tea at a little kiosk and she took me up to the station. 'It was lovely,' she said, meaning everything; and I: 'It was the best thing' – and of the personal ones it was.

PART III
Realisation

9. Wellington!

In my childhood there were names that exuded the exotic, the marvellous; places of which I had no conception, let alone any physical sense, but whose magical quality was projected through the tone of my mother's voice. Places from that other life she had lived, the life before Ohakune and us: Kelburn, The Terrace, Bowen Street, Plimmer Steps, Tinakori Road, the Cable Car – names that now seem so ordinary, so plebeian, it's hard to locate them in such an emotionally charged frame.

In my childish mind they bore the weight of myth and adventure, though goodness knows what I thought my mother got up to. 'Varsity' was another word redolent of mystery and excitement. Willingly, I received into my psyche Lauris's sense of Wellington's richness, ambivalence, glamour.

As an adult I lived in Wellington for only a few years and although its quotidian reality never held the fascination for me that it had for her, the aura of the exotic failed to be eradicated from those names. Once encountered, traversed, climbed, the absolute ordinariness of these places could not, did not, destroy the sense of wonder with which they had been imbued in my childhood.

In her letters, diaries and reminiscences, Lauris described her life as a young single woman in Wellington with a vivid and unselfconscious passion, giving affectionate reign to youthful affectations and pretensions. In a letter to Fleur Adcock in 1987, when she was Writer in Residence at Victoria University, she describes the beginning of this marathon of autobiographical writing:

> ... *I am getting some of the autobiographical stories I planned done – in the queerest way though; my mother kept every single letter I ever wrote to her, and when I was first away from home at 17 they were incredibly copious, detailed, star-struck, the country girl come to town and dazzled by everything. It's embarrassing but funny at times too, and I'm transcribing and editing them – a weird activity, and you might think suspect (for instance I leave lots of bits out, occasionally add a word or two, tone down a little of the gush about how much I love my mother and so on) ...*

When she left home at 17, she was shy, 'socially inept' (her words) and the age her grandmother, Clara, was when she married. Following in Fanny's footsteps, and those of her older brother Clive, Lauris arrived in Wellington to attend Wellington Teachers' Training College at the beginning of 1942. Like Fanny before her, she lodged in Victoria House (Vic House), 'gushing' over Wellington with innocent delight:

> *Wellington is a lovely place ... twice we've been to the dear railway station to have a cup of coffee and a ham sandwich. Then we went and browsed round in Modern Books, where all the enlightened Left Club Books etc are to be found, and a very interesting place too, I often go there.*

There's something unique, something incomparable, about the first place one lives after leaving the parental home, discarding childhood and dependence and stepping out into the wide world. To the young and unformed, eager to discover the world and one's place in it, the particular town or city where one first settles, however briefly, buries itself in the psyche through a kind of osmosis and remains there. Its odours and physicality hold memories of first loves, first angers and humiliations, first hurts and joys, first knowledge of all kinds of new and immediate ideas and experiences.

It's a first love affair. Lauris's was with Wellington; mine was with Auckland. And although I still (technically) live in Auckland (Waiheke Island), I long ago fell out of love with the city itself, though specific locations can evoke ecstatic recollections. For Lauris, however, the love affair lasted a lifetime, as recorded in these prophetic words:

> *In all my life, no matter where I live, I'll never forget this old path through the gorse, and the leaning stones of the cemetery, and the dirty green wall of the gym as you go on to the steps and up into varsity itself.*

In her poem 'Round Oriental Bay' she revisited other early Wellington experiences:

> This is my city, the hills and harbour water
> I call home, the grey sky racing over headlands,
> awkward narrow streets that stirred me long ago
> – it's half a lifetime since I first came in
> wonderment …

Lauris's upbringing was implicitly political, as was mine. In her case, her parents were committed social creditors; in their time it was not so outlandish or unusual. On first coming to Wellington, Lauris stayed true to her parents' beliefs, attending social credit gatherings and meeting 'important' people. Over time, in the face of scepticism among her peers and exposure to a whole range of new and exciting political ideas, her commitment to social credit waned. Her connections with the socially progressive Modern Books and encounters with the Left Book Club undoubtedly contributed to a broadening of her political horizons, including a flirtation with the Communist Party, though she didn't ever join.[1]

Lauris's strand of political activism is present in her Wellington poem 'Counterpoint: after Chernobyl', along with a critique of humanity as 'a careless species' implicitly referencing a failure on the part of those in power (men) to care for the vulnerable earth and the vulnerable creatures who inhabit it. It ends with a 'grand flourish':

> it's our place, our piece of the poor earth,
> loved and illusory possession,
> brief habitation
> in the violent nomadic passage
> a careless species takes
> across its given ground.
> This is its song.

One of Lauris's feminist motivations was to give voice to the voiceless, to what is not seen, lifting it out of silence, dragging it into public view, honouring the invisibility of 'mother earth', turning it from a 'possession' of mankind into a thinking feeling entity, deserving of respect and nurture.

'Scar Tissue' similarly recalls Lauris's past in her present, the passions of her youth dulled in the way a city heedlessly demolishes its past. She was with Denis Glover at the time:

> Wellington is an old crone
> all gaps, teeth knocked out;
> daily, watchers stare
> at waving arms that claw
> walls into rubble.
> A case of indecent exposure
> occurred last week:
> bed, wardrobe, blue wallpaper
> swinging high – drunken, ridiculous,
> skin peeled off and bricks falling
> into the crawling pit where puddles show
> the sea still seeps under the Quay.

In her autobiography, Lauris wrote about Glover:

*He was an old man when I met him, but still very good company.
We were walking along Willis Street, Wellington one day and
bemoaning the fact that fine buildings were always being
knocked down. I looked up and saw the exposed bedroom,
its wallpaper and wardrobe and was struck by their dreadful
nakedness.*

Hot October detailed the privations at Vic House, including cold
showers, though the habit had been established at home, such
rigours presumably by Fanny in the interests of robust moral and
physical health. Lauris also wrote of miserable Wellington weather
and of sneezing putting you in greater danger of your life than at
any other time. This is an odd assertion – an old wives' tale? No, she
was correct. A sneeze can have catastrophic consequences and Lauris
was not one to shy away from extravagant pronouncements.

Interestingly, she made only passing reference to that major event
of the mid-twentieth century, World War II, mentioning half-drunk
soldiers assisting her collect the contents of her case after it 'flew
open and everything fell into the gutter'. She wrote of the 'rotten old
war' taking second-year students off to camp, but otherwise the war
does not appear to have greatly affected her young Wellington life.

Her days were structured around the formality and routines of
the training college timetable and a tidy programme of hostel life
– no drinking or drug taking. She threw herself into student life,
joining drama and tramping clubs, writing for student magazines,
taking piano lessons.

After training college and her marriage to Trevor, it was 30 years
before Lauris returned to 'the place I call home'. I moved to
Wellington at the beginning of 1974, to attend Toi Whakaari (New
Zealand Drama School), and it was during my second year there
that Lauris and Trevor moved to Grass Street, leaving behind the

miserable years in Heretaunga. I remember the day of the shift; in true pioneering fashion we did it ourselves. It seems crazy now but I remember guiding that infernal Challen piano down the Grass Street zigzag walkway to the new house. The details of how we got it down the series of steps or indeed up the long front staircase and into the house I seem to have erased from memory.

Lauris wrote about the move in her diary:

> *February [1976]. A new house, something of a new life, a summer so full of living that I can be sure that moving here has already given us the 'sense of the future' we so much needed. And we have the hills, the trees, the sea often rough and grey, and the high winds of Wellington – in fact there is so much weather here that it is part of our lives as it never was at Heretaunga – that lovely graceful house is lived in now by people we know nothing of; and I care curiously little. It has been a great upheaval, but I am glad of it all now …*
>
> *November. A year almost later. A year of slow reconciliation and surprisingly vivid happiness.*

The Grass Street house was both lovely and impossible. The street itself is a hillside walkway, with number 22 perched dramatically in the middle, clinging to the side of a hill. To get to it one had to choose either 'up' or 'down', though it wasn't a real choice because you had to do the opposite when you left. For a young mother visiting from out of town it was a logistical nightmare. Lauris did not possess much in the way of baby hardware so one was obliged to transport it – carrying a highchair and cot down (and up) the zigzag pathway is not one of my favourite memories.

Once you got there, however, the house was light, airy, welcoming and comfortable, with a glorious wall of window in the sitting room overlooking Oriental Bay, the shifting waters of the harbour in the daytime and the sparkling lights of Wellington city at night. Lauris would regularly walk the short distance into Courtenay Place, the post office being a significant destination. There was also the matter of replenishing supplies of wine and food, all of which had to be transported by hand down the path – a regular, if not daily expedition. On principle she never complained about the path, though Trevor, when he was in residence, regularly did. He would walk 'down' on his way to work and 'down' at the end of the day by taking the bus to The Crescent at the top.

Friends were known to comment on the inconvenience of where she lived but her love of the location, the house itself, outweighed any inconvenience and she absolutely refused to listen to querulous suggestions that she might move somewhere more convenient. From 'All Possession is Theft':

> – the agent, natural for a moment, pressed on
> 'The elevation here …' I turned aside
> breathless, feeling faintly lecherous, closed
> my hand about that small old bag of gold
> and, with a quick tug, took it. I live here now.

'The Active Voice', 'Wellington Letter I' and 'Summer Oriental Bay' are three of Lauris's vibrant Wellington weather poems. She wrote, 'Most of my writing life has been spent in Wellington, in the presence of its geographical suddenness, the brilliance of its light, the ambiguities – and sometimes the trials – of its weather':

> It's true you can't live here by chance,
> you have to do and be, not simply watch
> or even describe. This is the city of action,
> the world headquarters of the verb –

This vigorous opening stanza of 'The Active Voice' is one of her best known and most often quoted, the last sentence one of her marvellous, poetically grandiose overstatements. It's set in concrete along the Wellington Writers' Walk that meanders around the waterfront – plaques with inlaid metal text, subject to 'the constant beating of the weather'.

'Wellington Letter I', the opening poem of the sequence dedicated to Rachel, is a poignant description of weather, the physical profiling the emotional and setting the tone for the whole piece, while 'Summer Oriental Bay' also uses the metaphor of the weather to reflect an emotional state of being – 'our brief encapsulated happiness'.

After drama school I stayed on in Wellington working at Downstage and then Circa theatres. While Lauris was away and I was looking after my father, I was in a production of Somerset Maugham's *The Constant Wife* at Circa, a play ironically (or perhaps not, considering Lauris's turbulent private life) about infidelity. I played Constance, whose husband is having an affair with her best friend. It was great fun and it was during this production that Lauris and I collaborated for the first time.

Circa Theatre was not yet a year old and full of youthful vigour, energy enough to branch out into lunchtime theatre shows, songs, poetry and prose readings. The cast of *The Constant Wife* performed three of these, one of which was readings of Lauris's poetry, performed by Prue Langbein, Anne Flannery and myself.[2]

Reading poetry aloud was a skill I learned from my speech and drama teachers.[3] Encouraged by Lauris, I developed a love of the romantic poets – especially Keats. Her influence also led me to other favourites of her own and Trevor's – Auden, Eliot – while at drama school the subtle delivery required for Shakespeare's sonnets was rigorously studied and executed.

In our collaborations it seemed as though Lauris and I had been made for each other: a lucky writer with an acting daughter and an equally lucky acting daughter with a mother who wrote marvellous, evocative and very performable poems. I wrote to her while she was in Africa in 1977 to ask whether she would mind if, as well as poems from *In Middle Air*, I used some from her new, as yet unpublished book, *The Pear Tree*.[4] She wrote back:

*Yes, of course, do use any of the poems out of the second
collection; it's often more interesting to read unpublished things,
and I am very happy to think of you doing it, and doing it with
grace and feeling, as I know you will.*

And:

*I am full of strange feelings about your programme of my poems
– I am perhaps not sorry not to be there for that, it is probably
more possible to do it without me, but I am full of curiosity
about it – what you've chosen, who goes to hear it (tell Dr Beeby
– he'd like to know, and the other PEN people), what it's like.*

The selection was not difficult, some poems simply leaping off
the page, language and rhythms fitting easily into the framework
required for a public reading. I felt connected to her writing,
understood it; in an essential way I knew what her poems were
about. In search of an audience, I sent out notices to all her friends,
including those at PEN. Beeb, dapper and full of wit, sporting a hat
and cane, did come to the show and lavished flattery on me. I wrote
to Lauris:

*It was lovely seeing Beeb. I did feel that he missed you a lot. He
said wistfully to me that he didn't have a drinking companion
and I felt strongly that his life was confined and he wanted you
back. I did so like him. If time permits, I'll take him to lunch.*

Time did not permit, but subsequently I had lunch with both of
them, an occasion where Beeb conducted Lauris and me in a mutual
admiring dance of delight, we turning, turning, turning, gracefully
extending our arms, pointing our toes, finishing our moves with
flourish while he waved his conductor's baton benignly over us.
There's also a note I have from him:

Frances,
Please excuse Lauris for being late for school. It was my fault.
Beeb

This arose after I had made vociferous complaint about being left standing for a good half hour in freezing weather on the corner of Taranaki Street and Courtenay Place waiting for her to collect me. What were they up to?

I also wrote that we had loved reading her poetry and everyone who came loved it too. Regrettably, audiences were small, I explained, but that was our own fault because 'publicity was bad and it was the week after Easter, not a good time, but audiences did build'. This was the beginning of a life-long collaboration, rewarding to us both, remarkably free of conflict when other aspects and interactions in our relationship were not always so.

As well as paying particular attention to some of her friends – like Beeb – at her request, I also acted as her 'literary secretary' while she was away. On 23 March 1977 she wrote to me from London:

I have changed my policy about letters and started to write them to those who write to me, which means I owe Trevor a letter but not you. (Give him my love and tell him it will come soon.) However there are things I must say to you; here they are: 1. Everyone says you are being me marvellously and I congratulate you on achieving such a high standard so quickly (you don't need to be better than me, it would be difficult in the first days of my return when like all travellers I will be obnoxious). 2. Have you heard from Albion [Wright at Pegasus Press] and/or the Lit Fund about the book? If the answer to both is no, would you ring Alistair [Campbell] and ask his advice about writing to Albion – it will mean, you see, that he did not get the MS to them in time for the Feb meeting and will have to be pushed, probably, into getting it in in time for the next meeting which will be May. If it is any later than that it will be too late for this year which probably means waiting another whole year. 3. When I was in Nairobi I met an African novelist called Ngugi and we (shyly) exchanged books. His was a play about the Mau Mau revolutionaries and I want to ask you or anyone else you say, if you might do it – perhaps Circa would? If I can afford the airmail postage I'll send it to you for your consideration; I think it would need a bit of cutting but would be tremendously strong and effective. 4. Love to your men. I mean to send them a message but have not found the right card yet. 5. Dearest girl, do write to me and tell me things you are doing – you can't imagine how much more neurotic than usual I am here about mail. Today I walked along Bond St – it's all exquisite jewellery shops, single diamond necklaces on dark blue velvet. I wouldn't even dare to enter one of the shops.

I replied:

I rang Maria today and she says to tell you that the March [PPTA] Journal is safely out … I will ring Alistair this week. Have so far heard nothing from Albion … or the Lit Fund and there is no absolutely crucial mail. A thing came from Dora Somerville about 2 Tui Books publications about 'NZ Games' and 'Homosexuality' which she wants you to contribute to.

The 'no absolutely crucial mail' was a reference to the fact that I knew she was hoping for communication from Bill Oliver. In a letter sent to me care of Ian McClymont she wrote:

Not more cries for help, nothing like that – just a short private letter to you. I suppose you realised from my last to you at Grass St that the 'lots of mail' meant that I had heard from Bill – and I did, and of course, I have recovered from all that panic and faint-heartedness. But it has made me think (I have been out walking in Deirdre's impeccable garden [in Geneva] with time to ruminate) that for a long time now you have had all the burdens of the 'home duty' you are doing and none at all of the support that I asked of you – by writing that letter.

We had been discussing men – Bill, for her part, and my complicated pairings with two men who were friends and colleagues. I wrote:

I have so much to say to you that I don't really know where to begin. Well here we go. Men are silly creatures. They seem to understand so much (ones like Bill, I gather) but are not so hot at putting it into practice. And withdrawal and neurosis about relationships seem to be the prerogative of men ... I suppose perhaps not knowing Bill (very well) you didn't really know what was happening. But you know, you can spend so much time and energy worrying about a relationship that your expectations of it become too great for the thing itself to bear – and it can't be sustained at that pitch and disappointment follows. Witness me over ____. Months of unnecessary heartache. Too much passion is destructive in the end. My words of wisdom for the day!!! So don't worry too much. I love you lots.

As Lauris was long gone from London when this letter arrived at New Zealand House in London, it was 'returned to sender'. Lauris arrived home in mid-May and her second collection, *The Pear Tree*, came out in September.

The following year, 1978, she first began to work on what was then titled her 'Ohakune Stories' which eventually evolved into her novel, *High Country Weather*, mostly written in Menton. She wrote to me in April 1978:

I have now started work again on my stories, and when you are here I would like to talk to you – or listen, rather, because the original idea was yours and I want to know some of the things that were in your mind that might be clear enough in mine to do – even if I remember them differently.

Wellington Letter is another of our writer/performer collaborations; I recorded it for radio in 1980, Fergus Dick producing. It was played on the Concert Programme of Radio New Zealand in September of that year. After Rachel's death in 1975, Lauris had wanted to write something for and about her. When she finally came to the writing of *Wellington Letter*, it came in a great rush and she worked feverishly over the January of 1980 to complete it:

It had been an extraordinary time; an upsurge, perhaps, of that old and primitive desire, in the face of a great loss, to create something new, as though this can assuage a small part of the world's hurt, and one's own.

Our next collaboration was *Between Night and Morning* (N and M as we called it), a play for solo voice (a one-woman show) that I asked her to write for me. At the time solo plays were popular, though many were based on the lives of famous people. Lauris's was not; indeed, the character had my middle name – Elizabeth or Lizzie – and some of the events were taken from my own life.

Around four o'clock one morning I had rung her in a distressed state because my partner had not come home. That he was with another woman was not in doubt; I had seen the signs and knew who she was, but it did not make it any easier to cope with. That I rang my mother was not surprising, given the intimacy that existed between us. Moreover, in such a state, who else would I turn to? The opening paragraph of *Between Night and Morning* read:

> *Four o'clock. You've been in bed for five or six hours, asleep for perhaps three. It's the far corner of the night where everyone's alone. The traffic's silent; even the tom cats have subsided. The very old die in their sleep. It's the time when your dreams are deepest and least recoverable, your hold on your daylight self so slight you've almost let it go. It's a ghost, a mirage, a spectre wandering over the white hills of your dream without face or voice.*

Such lovely writing. Did I feel violated by her use of a painful event from my life? Honestly, not at all. It wouldn't have occurred to me. At that time, I was still firmly inside my family's notion of boundaries, which meant that I had none. Indeed, the fact that I would ring my mother at 4am because my partner was off with another woman is a very good indication of their non-existence for us both. Lauris, reading over her tortured diary entries on Bill Oliver, wrote:

I'm surprised, and interested to see how much it contributed to the writing of the plays. I did not once think of it, but some of those terrible secret despairs and eventual discoveries did make me able to understand Jennifer in Deception and Elizabeth in Between Night and Morning.

She also wrote of N *and* M in her diary, in December 1980:

What a complete special life of its own that play has had! Let me go back to its birth and nurture (nothing of the kind will ever happen again I am certain) – Frances ringing up to say, 'I want you to write me a play'. L: 'Oh of course dear. How many people would you like in it? Her: One, Just me.' She had been trying to do it herself, knew it was to be about the emergence of a shy ignorant country girl into the fuller richer, but also more dangerous life of the town, and being an adult in it. Her own story, in a way, set in her own time; a story not really told, though surely a great part of the 'NZ experience'. I was touched – all the more since I sensed a rather painful kind of personal desire behind it; ambition I suppose. A kind I understand very well and have known in an acute form. Mine – the clearest example is Beverley Morris, educated, active, arrived, saying all those years ago to a meeting of women when she was 'appointing' me as a play-centre mothers' tutor (taking the course written by her) 'Here is ... and she has ... oh, you haven't a degree, have you? A few subjects, isn't that right?' I don't know why I should have felt so utterly mortified but I did – and began to think with some determination about improving myself, getting an education ... Frances, meanwhile, had had a series of parts in not particularly rewarding plays and continued to live with a person who has an attitude to success that is full of dark complications. As well, she is the one who has said before, that our Ohakune lives should be chronicled in some way – and of course she's right. The plays, the 4 radio ones and hers, do indeed make a start on that long and complex process.

Anyway she came to see me. We sat on my bed and she told me some of the events of her own life which could perhaps have a place in the play – losing her virginity, her early funny, touching boy and girl relationship with Ron. Her sense of inadequacy when she went to Auckland and University, to 'town'. There were many things I remembered that had had a different version for each one of the children – and indeed were paralleled in my own life. It did seem an important story to tell. But how was I to do it? I have never written a line for the stage, though of course I've acted on it; moreover if solo plays for radio had proved super-humanly difficult, how would I ever be able to make one dramatically 'authentic' in the theatre?

I didn't know, but I started anyway. When one draft was done Frances and _____ came round late one night and she read it to us, right through. She sat on the floor in the living room and that low beautiful voice mesmerised us with the story. Then there were re-writings, revisions – the only one I now remember was after a few weeks of not looking at it I re-read it and realised that there was a hole in it towards the end – a major event lacking, the motivation for Elizabeth's final action, her discovery of herself. What could it be? I worried endlessly, then devised the 'night voices' and her power to draw them with her assertion of her value, learned through caring for her father.
Then George [Webby] read the play, hated it – or thought it couldn't possibly work; wrote pages and pages of anxious criticism. Pause. Then Phil [Mann] – did he have time to read it? Would he be interested in it? Would such a distinguished producer even think of taking it on? Delays, delays; misery, disappointment. Then, suddenly, the news that he liked the play, would do it, rehearsals would begin the week after next. I couldn't believe it – kept fussing about, thinking that I should do something. Nonsense, said Frances, just wait. He means it, it'll happen. He's busy, but he doesn't say yes if he means no. And so it was – those long concentrated sessions in Drama House, with Phil saying 'Who is Harry? Who is Stanley? What does Terry look like? Is Mother educated? How and where? Is Father? What has Harry or Terry or Elizabeth or someone done since I last saw them? Where were they this afternoon?' And so on. A splendid earth-bound (but high-flying too) imagination; humanity,

wholesomeness, breadth, good fun. I so admired him – every day was like a huge lesson to me in how to construct a reality before people's eyes, on the stage.

Between Night and Morning had its opening season at Circa Theatre in January 1981 and was reviewed by Lauris's old friend Bruce Mason. His review was headed: 'Fine poet's work just not drama'. Bruce described both Lauris and me as gifted but the production as 'very busy', the lighting too complex and some conventions in the writing and production as 'muzzy', the implicit suggestion being that the play was overdressed, demonstrating a lack of trust in its ability to speak for itself. Certainly, Lauris and I had been swept up by Phil's enthusiasm and carried along by some of his complicated and occasionally inconsistent production ideas, though of course we all share responsibility for the play and the production.

Surprisingly, Bruce heard resonances of *South Pacific* in it: Mary Martin singing, 'I'm in Love with a Wonderful Guy', and 'I'm Just a Cockeyed Optimist'. A sentimental streak in Lauris finding its voice? Or perhaps the sentimental streak was in my performance. Or a combination of both? At the time, both Lauris and I were obscurely upset and defensive over Bruce's review and several others in similar vein, reassuring ourselves that there were plenty of people who didn't agree.

There were more positive reviews. Kim Hill, for example, described it as 'intensely moving, frequently harrowing and ultimately satisfying'. Bruce was right, though, about over-elaborate production. A solo play should be just that. We took his advice, stripped it back to essentials: largely abandoned the soundtrack; cut recordings of ringing telephones and voices of other characters addressing Lizzie from a cavernous darkness; stripped out atmospheric lighting and music too. For the *Gentle Annie Road Show* tour, and other later performances, the play relied on me, a chair and a few lighting cues.

Lauris and I continued to consider the play and what adjustments could or should be made. For the season at the Mercury Theatre in

June 1981, I worked with director Jonathan Hardy and assistant director Stephen Dee. I wrote to Lauris:

Stephen Dee who's working with Jonathan and me on the play most particularly wanted me to say this to you. That the play is superb and captures a kind of reality that few plays capture and it is consequently frustrating because Terry is the one weak link in it. He isn't real. I don't suppose even if you did agree with this you would feel like doing anything about it. I'm not trying to make you and I do understand. It's just that I have felt a whole new lease of life about it and it's gone so well that I still feel it can go further. In a nutshell, I think by paring down my performance, and the process of its maturing, the play stands firmer and much clearer than it did – there was too much of me in the way. People have talked much more about it and less about my way of doing it, which is how it should be. I am pleased and so should you be. Many people have said it's a marvellous piece of writing (except for Terry and he's not dreadful, he's just not as good as the rest).

Lauris replied from Menton:

Thank you so very much for your detailed letter about N and M – I so much wish I could see it now (but I will eventually) – and actually I do see the point about Terry. All the more since I have finished a draft of the Ohakune stories, High Country Weather, and I think the same thing has happened there. It's like Hardy (on a distinguished level) making Angel Clare feeble in Tess. I don't know what to do about it – I can't think here, away from you and without knowing the development there's been. All I can say is that I understand what you say about the thing emerging without the interference (although she does it) of the actress. It's very like what Katherine Mansfield says about her desire to show everything in perfection, yet not to be there herself, not a whiff – I know how right, how important, this is. Terry is a structural weakness, I can see that. Sometime I want to do something about it, but not here, not now.

Regrettably, the vital life of N *and* M came to a premature
end. The last performance I gave was at the Melbourne Theatre
Company on a Sunday afternoon in the early months of 1982.
Despite best intentions, Lauris and I both moved in other directions.

We continued to work together on other things. When she
recorded her three-volume autobiography for Radio New Zealand,
there were some pieces about Rachel that were too emotional for
her so I read in her stead. I also recorded the whole work for the
Blind Foundation.

The next significant project was initiated by me. I had taken time
out from performing to have three children but there came a time in
the early 1990s when I wanted to get back into some form of work
and I came up with the idea of recording a selection of her poems.
Schools, libraries and bookshops we thought would be a suitable
market for such a venture. It was a fun project and Lauris, in her
usual style, supported me absolutely and worked incredibly hard,
contacting schools and libraries, taking copies with her when she
went on promotional tours for other reasons. It sold reasonably well
but I still have a box of unsold cassettes in my garage.

In Position was another rewarding and satisfying collaboration.
Before it was even published Lauris sent the sequence to Fergus
Dick, drama producer at Radio New Zealand. Fergus discussed with
Elizabeth Alley, who was in charge of literary content, the possibility
of recording it; the upshot was that they commissioned the work
for broadcast on Concert FM, with original music by Dorothy
Buchanan and Lauris's and my voices. The recording took place in
October 1995.

In Position is the first section of *A Matter of Timing*, a poetry
collection published by Auckland University Press in March 1996.
Her first letter to me about the possibility of a recording is dated
Boxing Day 1994, when she sent a copy of the manuscript for my
consideration. She wanted to know if I were willing (of course I
was), and which poems I thought would sit easily in my younger
voice and which would not. She also consulted me over the order,

where I thought the music breaks should be and what kind of music would be appropriate. We shared a love of the process of investigating what happens to a poem when you read it aloud, how a little change of emphasis here, or a pause or a breath, can clarify or enhance meaning. In matters of performance and shaping she respected my acting experience. She was fun to work with: open to new ideas, new ways of doing things.

Lauris described *In Position* as 'twelve poems built around a common theme … and it being a new departure … it breaks some new ground for me'. In a letter she wrote:

> *It's been a long and in some ways gruelling process getting this together – it contains most of my current ruminations about ageing and dying. The last great preoccupation, I suppose … It's … another phase. I spent years thinking and in various ways writing about being alone – living alone – because I found it so alien, so difficult to do. In the end I came to terms with it, or as much as I ever will. This is rather the same – though I doubt anyone would ever claim they have found out how to grow old and die. I wouldn't. You just have to keep rehearsing.*

The last performance/recording project Lauris and I worked on together on was a CD: *The Poems of Lauris Edmond*, a whole new recording of the tape version I had made in 1991, *The Poetry of Lauris Edmond*. The CD project was Lauris's initiative, dear to her heart, and she put a lot of time, effort and money into it – though that could be said of everything she did.

The recorded sequence *In Position* was part of it, and the rest of the material – including a new version of *Wellington Letter* – was recorded at Radio New Zealand House in August 1999. Studio time, production facilities and technical personnel were provided free to Lauris and producer Fergus Dick, although Lauris paid almost $4000 in fees to those who worked on the project.

It was only six months before she died, though there was no hint of 'fading powers' except perhaps a suggestion of croakiness in her voice. I remember the two of us sitting in the front room at Grass

Street in the evening with our glasses of wine and a tape recorder, rehearsing for the studio the next day, making pencil marks in the margins to remind ourselves of emphasis, of where to breathe, laughing over our stumbles, consonants ever so slightly thickened by wine. Lauris died before the CD came out and one of my early duties as her literary executor was to launch it at Unity Books in Wellington in March 2000.

Later that year I performed *In Position* at the invitation of Coral Bognuda, who taught cello in the University of Auckland's School of Music. It was a memorable occasion in the Music Theatre, a venue with a wonderful live acoustic and generous resonance, with Coral playing Dorothy's music with a gorgeous warmth and flourish, while I performed seven out of the 12 poems.

The other significant collaboration, in the mid-1990s, was *Silent Tears*, the story of Pauline Brown, a woman Lauris met when she attended a prisoners' concert in Arohata Prison. Pauline was doing time for murdering her violent and abusive partner whom she believed had sexually molested one of her children. Lauris became interested in Pauline's story, in how she had come to commit this dreadful crime, and devoted an enormous amount of time and effort to find a workable form for the story. I restructured the text for her, helping define a narrative arc, and Lauris and I were both pleased with the results. However, the manuscript remained unpublished in her lifetime, turned down by several publishers on the grounds that the purpose of the story as unclear. It was also problematic because Pauline had committed murder:

> *Pauline's own words are not good evidence for the 'damage done to her by the system' – she is so clearly a 'victim', and so clearly blames everyone else for what happens to her, that her own telling of this story blurs any case that might be made for her being treated unjustly.*[5]

In September 1996, at the beginning of the project, Lauris wrote to Fleur Adcock:

… certainly there are issues that should be talked about – like that this sort of crime is never forgiven in a woman, no matter what the provocation, but in men is treated with great sympathy – by the Police and the Justice system, not to mention the general public.

At that time there was far less understanding of domestic violence, its nature and extent, and negligible understanding or acceptance of the idea of 'battered woman's syndrome'.[6]

In a note to me, Lauris wrote that the publisher's response showed 'a failure to even begin to comprehend the "extreme passivity underneath a fairly aggressive surface [that is] a known effect of long abuse".' At the time Lauris wrote *Silent Tears* this was neither known nor would it have been an acceptable idea. The story would get a more sympathetic hearing today.

Poems for Miss Black (i.e. Pauline Brown) was the title Lauris chose for her final collection, the middle section of which is a series of poems addressed to the incarcerated woman. Lauris sent the manuscript in July 1999 to me and other family members and friends, asking for feedback. Her accompanying letter to me read:

I think I want your opinion because you are the person who most reliably and astutely listens to what a poem is saying, and how it's doing it. I'm basing this on those interesting conversations we had when we were working on that In Position tape – do you remember?

My feedback was positive, with the proviso that I felt one of the Miss Black poems didn't work. I was not the only reader who thought so and she took it out. However, the manuscript had not been finalised when she died and it fell to me to put the final text together, write the introduction and oversee the design and production. I had no experience of this process and certainly had not expected to take it on. Lauris had recently said she thought she had a good 10 years left and I believed her, though with hindsight, I'm not so certain of the confidence with which she made the claim.

After her death, the title she had chosen felt too particular, too confined a reference, the more so as only one part of the collection was addressed to Pauline. The poem 'Late Song' had been written as a gift to her family on the occasion of her 75th birthday in 1999, and it felt like a more evocative title for her final collection. Four poems I found on her computer after her death were added to the last section: 'I Saw This Pretty Dark Girl' 'Some Conversations Continue Life Long', 'The Captive' and 'Languages'. She had mentioned to publisher Elizabeth Caffin that she had some new poems to add but whether they were the ones eventually chosen, I do not know.

The last poem of the middle section (addressed to Pauline) is one of what Roger Robinson calls her 'epiphanic' poems, 'Being There'. This is a poem I find irresistible; it absolutely reveals and revels in an unequivocally Lauris instant – the immediacy of the moment is all we have and it possesses us rather than the other way around:

> There must be a moment when
> a flower opens
> a bud splits
> a leaf breaks and falls –
>
> you never see it, you wake up to find
> mushrooms in the autumn paddock,
> a fully expanded pink impatiens cluster
> where last night one flower
> bloomed in the dusk,
>
> the speckled scarlet day lily
> a dried husk which minute by
> midnight minute shed yesterday's
> necessary sun. Nobody's ever there.
>
> But I was. I am, indisputably, here:
> the jasmine tangle on my shed wall
> moved, it just did, and a geranium flower
> opened its last petal. It's out. Now.

For a day, for a week; an invisible step
in the dance of creation
pointed its toe, put it down
tap, tap, without sound
on the shimmering floor of the world.

Bars, locks, fists of blood, bombs falling
couldn't stop it happening.

A few years after she died, I put together a play from her body of
work and I used it as the title, though I adjusted it slightly, dropping
the 'T' off 'There' to make it *Being Here*. It was workshopped by the
Auckland Theatre Company's Literary Unit and subsequently had a
rehearsed reading at the Christchurch Writers' Festival in 2005.[7]

Although *Late Song* was her last formal collection, there was also
Carnival of New Zealand Creatures to come. *Carnival* began its life
as a commission from the Bay of Islands Arts Festival with funding
from the Millennium Trust – text by Lauris and music composed by
Dorothy Buchanan. It was scheduled as the third segment of a three-
part performance at the April 2000 festival called *Birthplace of the
Nation* and performed on the Treaty Grounds at Waitangi.

In December 2000, Chris Orsman sent me a proof copy of
Carnival of New Zealand Creatures asking for comments or
suggestions. It's a beautifully presented slim volume of poems
about New Zealand's natural world and I had only admiration for
its creamy linen cover over a red inner, exquisite stitching, elegant
layout and finely detailed illustrations.

Lauris was to have read her poems at the festival, accompanied
by an ensemble from the Auckland Chamber Orchestra, with Peter
Scholes conducting. It was another of her commitments that fell
to me to fulfil. I have always enjoyed reading Lauris's poetry but
in this instance it was a pleasure touched with poignancy that she
wasn't there to do it herself. On the night, it was as if the absence
of both writer and composer signalled another kind of absence, as
if the piece itself were not really present. There were technical and

programming failures and omissions and I felt it keenly. *Carnival* is a delicate piece, a chamber piece, and in the early evening on the grand stage on the Treaty Grounds it got lost, the intimacy of the piece dissipating into the ether, leaving the audience mystified. There was worse to come; at the reception there was no acknowledgment of Lauris or Dorothy Buchanan or even of the commissioned piece itself.

I was not alone in thinking the event a debacle. The following year, Larry Jenkins, who had been instrumental in setting up the festival and involving Lauris, organised a tribute to her – a warm, generous, occasion that dispelled some if not all of the hurt and anger I had felt the previous year.

Lauris wrote of the ancients: 'Tuatara', 'Katipo', 'Frogs' and 'Dinosaurs'; of 'Insects', 'Fish' 'Birds'; and of creatures such as the huia, which are no more, concluding with an exquisite coda:

> The air's a wide transparent tapestry
> stitched by singing
> layered in light
> for ever formed, dissolved
> remade, resolved,
>
> by the fantail's flicker-ticker
>
> the ardent swoop of finches' wings
>
> a starling's two-step minuet
>
> and after dark
> the hollow morepork's drop of sorrow
>
>   immemorially falling, falling.

10. Here and elsewhere

where is it, the sun-drumming
dazzle they're after? Who knows –
not us – it's anywhere but here.

'Sunday Morning' is an early poem, from *In Middle Air*, the setting Upper Hutt. Lauris describes driving down to the corner dairy, sitting in her car, watching the morning's activity with a kind of secret glee, then writing the poem on the basis of her observations. There are, of course, many other perspectives on 'elsewhere' – and its antithesis 'here' – in her writing, in addition to the light-hearted irony she uses in this poem.

Lauris was a late traveller; she didn't leave New Zealand until she was 52, in the early years of 'life number two':

Everything about a first journey is miraculous. Planes on the tarmac were the biggest in the world; they towered over me like dinosaurial monsters, glittering in the February heat against the milky haze of the Sydney skyline. In my lifetime, I thought, dazed, Kingsford-Smith had flown the Tasman in a single-engine Tiger Moth with room for one in the cockpit.

At the airport she clung tearfully to us, worried about abandoning her dear ones, anxious about the adventure ahead, the mysteries of travel adding a frisson. Her first trip overseas was also, in a sense, a first for me – I had not done 'The Great OE' as many of my contemporaries had. I was fascinated, vicariously enjoying her adventures, her descriptions of the places she visited: Africa first –

Mombasa, where my older sister Virginia was living – then Florence, England, Paris, Geneva, Czechoslovakia. She wrote of arriving in London and Paris as kind of cultural homecomings, all the books and pictures she encountered as a child, as a young woman – all the places, names and landscapes – becoming fabulously real.

This first journey heralded many years of travel, intellectually and geographically; the early to mid-1980s were vital, exciting, turbulent years for Lauris. She visited Australia, England, Germany, France, the US and Canada, the Soviet Union ... her year in Menton she described as an *annus mirabilis*. Not only was it an honour in itself to have been awarded the Katherine Mansfield fellowship, but it provided new perspectives, contributing to a developing sense of who she was and where she belonged. She told Elizabeth Alley in an interview for her radio series, *Place*:

> *I was a New Zealander, and knew it with a sharp new consciousness. Simply by the act of separation, I had made my own country a single whole, round and complete and graspable at the end of a long corridor of distance.*

And:

> *I knew that all one most fundamentally learns – the treasures of wisdom – are not to be found in far off places, however dazzling, but right at home, whether home is Timbuctoo [sic] or Auckland, or Wellington, or Waipukurau.*

1985 was another *annus mirabilis*. While she was writer in residence at Deakin University in Australia, Lauris learned that she had won the Asia–Pacific section of the Commonwealth Poetry Prize. The winner was to be announced in London in November. She wrote to Fleur Adcock:

> *The world – or anyway the Commonwealth – is divided into five parts, it seems, and the five winners are to be flown to*

London to give a poetry reading on November 28 and stay there till December 8, give other readings (goodness knows what the details are, or who's organising it). Meanwhile the Chairmen of the five panels (they seem hung up on the number five) will also be flown to London and there they will decide which of us is really Miss (or Mr) Universe; having given us £1000 each, they will then give that Top of the Pops person another £5000. It is somehow rather hard to take this commercial extravaganza very seriously, but of course I have no intention of saying no to any of it.

Despite her deprecating remarks, she won; it was a significant honour, affirming her status not only in New Zealand but in the wider literary world. English publisher Bloodaxe Books published *New & Selected Poems* in 1992 – the beginning of a lasting relationship. As recently as 2020 one of her poems, 'Late Song', was anthologised in Bloodaxe's *Staying Human: New poems for staying alive*.

The constant travel exacted a toll. After the Commonwealth Poetry Prize adventure she wrote to Fleur, 'Next year [1986] I hope to stay home all the time.' And mostly she did. Later in the year she wrote again to her friend:

And I, like you, am enormously enjoying just being here, home that is. It's the first time in about 18 months that I've felt I had a future that I've got at least marginal control over – one day follows the next, and I can plan to do things and there they still are to be done the next morning. That seems to have been so rare a condition of my life that I've been telling myself I'm in love with ordinariness. But of course it's partly that Grass St isn't ordinary, and in fact Wellington altogether looks so spectacularly beautiful to me that I am constantly amazed by it; it's the light – every white wall lit up by the sun, even the trees on my hillside or the beach as I walk to town on grey days (and it's been a fiendishly cold winter) look clearer in outline than anything I've seen before. I suppose it's a bonus, to be able to rediscover your familiar places like this.

However, her avowed love of home and 'ordinariness' did not sustain her – 'I'm homesick for England when I think of my friends there, but I can't see myself moving out of the Southern Hemisphere for a year.' By April 1987 she was possessed by discontent and restlessness, complaining to Fleur, 'I'm beginning to feel that readers and editors and critics and commentators generally that I feel at home with elsewhere are not here.' And in January 1990:

> *Television standards in the deregulated market are simply dire and … without BBC World News on the Concert Programme and even more importantly the Guardian Weekly I would feel as insular as they [broadcasters] want us all to be.*

On December 6 of the same year:

> *I am so conscious of getting my world events from scrappy American-sourced television news, and comments on radio (much better informed) … Heavens, there's so much to talk about, and letters are so inadequate. I really believe I'll come to England next year …*

Lauris had apparently been considering the possibility of going to live in England, although I had no inkling of this at the time. Perhaps it arose from winning the Commonwealth Poetry Prize and becoming an international figure – the world was at her feet; her choices infinite. It would have been difficult for Lauris and her family and there are ordinary questions like where is one to live, how is one to earn a living? By 1989 she had 11 grandchildren, which was likely a contributing factor to her recognising that leaving New Zealand for any length of time was unrealistic. In her essence she was a New Zealander and belonged here, but for the rest of her life she was a regular visitor to England; indeed, she had a trip planned the year she died.

Intellectual status and credibility mattered to Lauris, though the intellectual snobbery that sometimes accompanied it was one of her less endearing qualities. 'From the South' (*Seasons and Creatures*) and 'Wellington Letter XVI' are both poems which have at heart this attitude, a commentary on living in New Zealand. The first has a sanguine, reasonably optimistic view:

> glimpse of some passionate uncertainty
> which is what we call daily living in these
> nervous, unfinished, beautiful islands.

The second is a harsher critique of the contrast between a beautiful landscape and its small-minded inhabitants:

> In this land of giant angularities
> how we cultivate mind's middle distances
> tame and self-forgiving, how easily
> we turn on one another, cold or brutish
> towards the weak, the too superior ...

Given her upbringing and New Zealand's cultural preoccupations during her formative years, her Anglophilia was, I suppose, not particularly remarkable. However, the idea that the English were more sophisticated, more cultivated than us rough and rude colonials was under remorseless and necessary interrogation, while her liberation into her own life also occurred within the context of a flowering of New Zealand's cultural nationalism, including a Māori renaissance, the powerful drive of second wave feminism, and a breaking down of traditional codes of acceptable public and private behaviour.

These changes aroused her curiosity and even, in principle, her approval, though her acceptance of some of its manifestations was slower. She surprised me by sharing in an old-fashioned moral panic, not just about my choice of career but its substance as well.

In 1980 my partner and I, along with Richard Adams (Nairobi Trio) and singer Stephanie Arlidge, put together *The Gentle Annie Roadshow*, which included a mildly risqué cabaret, some Brecht Songs and *Between Night and Morning*. As a kind of dress rehearsal, we performed it for our parents before we set off touring. They were disturbed, anxious at the risks we were supposedly taking, perceiving us as having stepped so far outside what they understood as cultural norms that we would be isolated, vilified, accused of – and possibly even charged with – indecency.

Compared with such acts as *Blerta*[1] and *Red Mole*[2], *The Gentle Annie Road Show* was relatively tame and well received by audiences. And Lauris's view of my chosen career broadened, recognition of the mutual advantages a useful impetus.

Lauris's journeys are reflected in many of her poems: 'Summer Near the Arctic Circle', 'Rhineland', 'In the Chemin Fleuri', 'Going to the Grampians', 'At Delphi', 'Going to Nepal' to mention a few. She wrote that there are some places that 'enter the memory and stay there, solid and secure, ready to be conjured, the raw material of the active imagination'.

'Summer Near the Arctic Circle' records her experience of a 'white night' in Leningrad (as it was then), as she lingered in a small park at midnight while waiting to catch a late train back to Moscow. It was early 1985, and Lauris was en route to read at a festival in Cambridge, the loosening of restrictions under Gorbachev facilitating the opportunity. She spent a busy few days in Moscow and Leningrad:

> Midnight and light still, Leningrad and I
> awake to another white night, that spare
> other world where each leaf and stone
> is not to be approached, scarcely named,
> so rare, so unearthly has it become.

She described it as one of the poems that

> *need a long slow, drawing-out, but do in the end declare*
> *themselves ready to face the world … It was almost as though*
> *the physical impact of that extraordinary reversal of the known*
> *order – midnight, and still light – was so great that for a long*
> *time I didn't know how to contain it in words. In the end, I*
> *seemed to come closest to the heart of the poem by following my*
> *own footsteps in a very simple way. I was in a small park, two*
> *lovers meandering ahead of me.*

Vincent O'Sullivan told me that while she was in Moscow, Lauris visited Lenin's tomb. Since his death in 1924, Lenin has lain in state in Red Square. I too have paid my respects to the father of the Russian revolution, queuing for hours outside Red Square as the line inched forward. Entering a darkened room, one walks down a ramp and into the space where Lenin lies, a pale, almost white corpse dressed in a dark suit, his face so well preserved it seems made of fibreglass. He looks just like the Lenin one sees in pictures.

According to Vincent, on the day Lauris visited, one of Lenin's ears fell off. I like to imagine the force of her presence finally severing what must have been a tenuous connection. She certainly had a seemingly infinite capacity for conversation, although one was required to remain respectfully silent in the presence of the great man, so it must have been the wild verbal gymnastics inside her mind that did the trick.[3]

This particular journey took place just after the birth of my first child, in March 1985. On her return, Lauris was due to leave again after a few weeks to take up her residency at Deakin University, so her house was tenanted. She spent the intervening period staying with various of her children.

While she was with me there was a rather unfortunate accident. It's a typically Lauris story. I see Lauris and me struggling to manoeuvre a large and rather unwieldy pram containing my baby daughter up the steps and onto the terrace of the house where I lived. I, with a firm grip on the pram handle, step backwards and pull, while Lauris at the other end – the hood end, her face and body obscured behind brown fabric over the high-standing frame, pushes. I feel a sudden lurch and hear a grunt as I take the full weight. I haul the pram up onto the terrace and turn to see my mother sprawled in an undignified heap in a lavender bush at the bottom of the steps. She is struggling to get up and making little coughing exclamations of pain. I run down to her. 'I'm all right,' she insists, refusing any assistance, displaying the usual family denial of illness or disability.

It was her leg. Unaware that the steps shortened as the path ascended, she had missed her footing, stepped into thin air and landed hard, her shin scraping along the lip of the concrete. It looked nasty. I attempted to persuade her to go to the doctor but she refused. 'I'll keep it covered. It'll get better.'

It didn't. It festered and became infected, and on her return to Wellington she had to go to hospital for a skin graft. It took weeks to heal and delayed her departure to Deakin. I felt a mild guilt at my failure to insist on medical attention, though I did extract a promise that she would be more responsible in future.

At the other end of Europe from the Soviet Union was Greece: hot, convivial and a mythological and political cradle for western civilisation. During Lauris's Menton year, she and Margaret Scott visited Greece. A trip there is not complete without visiting Delphi:

> Climbing slowly in the heat to the shade
> of a cypress, I have entered three thousand
> years' silence; but the sacred Kastalian
> spring is still the sound of a woman weeping.

'At Delphi' is a personal favourite. The mythical city radiates a psychic power that reverberates in my conscious and unconscious mind. I have visited twice and would return again and again if time and chance permitted. Lauris felt its power as I did. Lying on the southwestern slopes of Mt Parnassus, its location is startlingly grand, precipitous, overwhelming. The town hangs high on the side of a deep rift valley that runs down to the Gulf of Corinth.

On my second visit I stayed in a hotel whose rooms looked out over the valley; leaning out the window into the soaring silence of the late afternoon – the giddying drop into the valley below, the enfolding hills and sky – I heard the faint melodious chime of a goat bell drifting up from the scrub and cypress trees, timelessness embracing me and the landscape. The sanctuary, which folds and

climbs up the steep side of Mt Parnassus, is a short walk from the
village and is, as Lauris described,

> *a miraculous place, the one that, of all others on earth, the gods*
> *would choose if they were going to speak to mortals. The great*
> *echoing hills standing around the temple ruins, the high, sweet*
> *hush of the air when I climbed up to sit under the cypresses – it*
> *was as though it entered my very soul, and stayed there. And I*
> *learned that the Oracle was always a woman, always past her*
> *middle years, experienced at living; how could I not hear her*
> *speaking to me on that wide bare hillside?*

In Lauris's poem the priestess – the pythoness – is an older
woman, a crone, past her childbearing years. Of blameless character,
she was chosen from the local peasantry, though who was charged
with choosing her is not easily discoverable.

Lauris visited alone, her solitude no doubt magnifying and
intensifying the experience. For her, as for many women (including
me), visiting Delphi had a refreshing potency. War, heroism,
the power and sacrifice of men, are the usual stuff of ritual and
celebration, whereas here it's the psychic wisdom of women being
honoured, revered. You can – I can – hear the voice of the oracle
calling, and, yes, it is 'the sound of a woman weeping'.

Lauris had a long and productive relationship with Australia.
Her first visit was to a PEN conference in Sydney in 1977, in the
company of her old friend, playwright Bruce Mason. They read
to relaxed, responsive, outgoing Australian audiences where she
overcame an initial reluctance and found the beginnings of a 'public-
reading' confidence. The following year she asked my advice about
going on a poetry reading tour. My reply was direct, unequivocal:

> *I think the main reason for your not doing it is that it is a waste*
> *of time. You want to be a writer not a performer, don't you? Is*
> *five weeks with people you only sort of like and who are much*

younger than you worth it, for the few members of the silly old general public hearing you read your poems, and a bit of money in the pocket? I doubt if you will be able to get much work done during that time. It's got nothing to do with being a 'stuffy old conservative' and a very different thing from spending a week at the PEN conference in Sydney. I feel quite strongly you should say no.

She did. With hindsight, I think my advice misguided and, as an actor, my dismissal of the 'silly old general public' rather short-sighted, shooting myself in the foot. Later that year she wrote to me again:

Poetry readings are in the air. Sam [Hunt] and Alistair Paterson and I are arranging a major one for charity (writers in prison) and you Auckland people are to have one for some good cause in October. I am fast getting over my prejudices and practising my patter. It is, after all, an alternative to publishing.

Over the years she developed considerable performance ease, travelling widely, reading to the many who gathered to hear her and to buy her books – and not only in New Zealand and Australia but further afield.

'Going to the Grampians' is a poem she often read aloud; it has the anecdotal quality that she was so skilled at, inviting you into the immediacy of the story she is sharing, its humour, its pathos, its anthropomorphism:

the animal in you is quiet too
before creatures you thought ridiculous,
acknowledging a kind of grace
in an alien desire that uses
our most intimate gestures, brutes blessed
by the bodies they know as
love's most true, most wholesome domain.

She wrote:

The Grampians are mountains in Victoria, a few hours' drive
west of Melbourne. I have to admit that the kangaroos I saw
there were half tame; they lived in that bit of Australian bush,
were often visited by tourists and to some extent cared for by
park rangers. I suppose if this had not been so I would never
have seen those extraordinarily touching scenes of intimacy,
nor known how suddenly and improbably human these odd
creatures could be, or appear to be. Human love has infinite
refinements, but its physical manifestation is still fundamental, or
so it seems to me.

Fruitful, life-long friendships came out of her 1985 residency at
Deakin, one being with Judith Rodriguez, who had a quirky story to
tell. In November 2003 Judith wrote to me:

… I re-met Fiona Kidman at the Brisbane Writers' Festival, and
she has kindly sent me your email address. I would like you to
have the attached poem, 'The Year', which I wrote during the
months after receiving the one-year-late news of [your mother's]
death.

As the poem explains, I had the feeling of her being THERE – as I
knew by the jolt. I am clearly not one of those who receives secret
signals before the news confirms the event! But as I have also tried
to explain to your sister Katherine, I prefer the other certainty –
that having known Lauris, I go on with her as part of my life.

I replied, saying I thought Lauris would have very much enjoyed
the idea that she had lived on for another whole year in the mind of
her friend.

Lauris's first visit to Germany was in 1986, when she attended the
Association for the Study of the New Literatures in English (ASNEL/
GNEL) conference in Laufen. There were a number of subsequent
visits – to Wuppertal several times, to Kiel, to Trier – and she forged
some enduring friendships.

I had not visited Germany at that stage, and Lauris did not talk to me in much detail of her visits, though I do remember her saying she was shocked by the lowly and docile status of the women she encountered – the academic wives. I know more of her German experiences from others – Lynne Dovey in particular. Lynne worked for the Ministry of Foreign Affairs and Trade based in Bonn, and organised Lauris's German itineraries, including her first trip to the conference in Laufen. Lynne, thinking quite rightly that writers didn't (don't) earn a great deal of money, invited Lauris to stay with her. 'Rhineland' was written at this time; it shows Lauris's recognition of the environmental abuse rivers such as the Rhine have been subjected to, tempered by her faith in the regenerative powers of nature, never forgetting that death is an intrinsic – nay, essential – part of that process:

> and it was as though it turned and looked up
> from its liquid trudging, to remind me
> that a continent's dying still richly harbours
> the knowledge of ancient endurance …

After Lauris died, a memorial meeting was held in Aachen as part of a subsequent ASNEL/GNEL conference. Norbert Platz said it was

> *an essential part of the original plan that we should open this*
> *memorial session to Lauris's European and New Zealand*
> *friends as well, so that we could all share our recollection of this*
> *outstanding poet across physical and cultural distances.*

What struck me forcefully while reading the transcript of this 'In Memoriam' session was the consistency of response from those who met and engaged with Lauris, irrespective of country or community. Lauris was 'strong', 'wise', 'she touched the heart of things in her poetry', she was 'not interested in talking about herself, she would glean information from others'. Ken Arvidson, a New Zealander who attended the session, said of her:

I always remember the very strong impression that her personality made on me then, and on everyone, I think, that she met. The personality which was partly formed by her appearance and her voice, which has been remarked on, and a particular quality of vivaciousness and a wide-ranging interest in everything that was going on.

Gordon Collier wrote of Lauris reading her work to his students:[4]

… they never seemed to have to ask what it was about when Lauris read something. It was always a total experience, and then there was always the segue over to Lauris's enfolding the class and maybe getting them to extend themselves. The boundary between art and life kept getting dissolved.

Norbert Platz spoke in conclusion:

… all of us who have assembled here have generously provided plenty of 'allowable (imaginative) space' for remembering and honouring a superb poet and a human being with whom we were privileged to have happy encounters when she was alive.

Joseph Swann's final words are a moving summation: 'We rejoice that she has lived and that we have known her.'[5]

11. Willows and catkins

Willows and catkins are two common images in Lauris's poetry. In the poem I asked her to write for me, 'Learning to Ride', she has me 'tumbling / among willows' and 'catkins fall on [my] hair'. They are Hawke's Bay images from her childhood; the Tutaekuri (dog shit) River runs along the southern edge of Taradale and sections of the river are lined with willows. I imagine Lauris, her siblings, perhaps a friend or two, on scorching Hawke's Bay summer afternoons, biking down to the river, swimming togs rolled up in a towel and hooked under the bike carrier, or in a basket hanging off the front handlebars. At the river, bikes lean against willow trunks, boisterous boys swing out on the rope hanging from the willow branch, water pluming as they let go and the rope swings shoreward, while sedate girls ease themselves into the cooling stream. Idyllic childhood images unsullied by adult woes or anxious prescience.

Many of Lauris's poems take as their source the natural world – earth, air, fire and water; the plants and creatures that inhabit it; the life force of the planet itself as it suffers from desecration by a 'careless species'. The rhythm of weather and seasons, their physical and psychic messages, and parallels with the human condition, the passing of time and its inevitable depredations, weave through her writing: birth, growth, flowering, seeding, death, dormancy (the winter of the soul) and inevitable rebirth. She wrote, 'I am permanently in love with the New Zealand countryside, but the only bits of it that get themselves into what I write are those I have somehow populated.'

There's a quaint story Fleur told me about Lauris coming to visit her in winter and being rather mystified as to why Fleur's garden was so barren. 'Where is the garden?' she asked. Returning in the springtime, Lauris said, 'Ah, now I see!' A studied ingenuousness at work, since her rural childhood in Greenmeadows, and mine in Ohakune, ensured the fluctuating immediacy of the natural world was always present, impinging on daily life in ways that city living can protect you from if you wish to be oblivious.

One of the ways the family experienced Lauris's love of the natural world was in the annual camping excursion, a tradition inherited from Fanny and Lewis. In our family it meant parents and six children piling into the stationwagon, which smelled of the dust of the road, of carsickness. The Dramamine pills – passed out before setting off in an effort to keep carsickness at bay (they didn't) – tasted of nausea; in fact, the taste of vomit was in my throat before we had left, before the car doors were even closed.

The big green canvas tent loaded into the trailer, we headed to the beach or lake for days of sun, swimming, playing. It never rained. I remember a summer when it was so hot the sand on the Taupo lakeshore burned my feet. I regularly got badly sunburnt, once so badly that my pyjama top stuck to the seared flesh on my back and had to be painfully prised off.

Lauris's poem 'Camping' – addressed to my father – captures the intimacy with the earth that is the camping experience, as well as connecting it to her sense of loss. She wrote it during the tragic months of the Hubert affair when she was wrestling with grief over the loss of family cohesion:

Do you remember how we woke
to the first bird in that awkward pine
behind the ablution block, and leaned
across the knotted ground to lift
the canvas as though it was
the wall of the world
and ourselves at the heart of it
lying together
with the fresh grass against our faces
and the early air sweet beyond all telling –

As we grew older, when there wasn't enough room for the ever-expanding Edmond family at Christmas or other festive gatherings, I sometimes took my tent as extra accommodation. It was reasonably common for Lauris and I to share the space – we were regarded as an 'unproblematic fit'; we would cope with, even enjoy, each other.

The sun shines, it's summer, we're at Katherine and Bruno's farm in Hawke's Bay. It's a beautiful place where for many years the family gathered, swam in the Tukituki River, played 'go home stay home' in the redwoods. At night the kids would spend hours playing 'spotlight' while we, the parents and grandparents, drank wine and shared the delights and sorrows of our daily lives. 'The Outside Room' is a poem from this time – a Hawke's Bay poem, a family poem and an environmental one:

It was the moon poised with a bright patience
low over the paddocks, the silence standing
about in surprise as though newly arrived,
the constant soft bleat of the sheep
and the earth, most of all the earth itself

sending up its unaccountably tender emanations
and winey smell, telling me what dew can do
to sap-heavy grass and sheep shit, and
to the sheep too, obscurely coiled
in the oily emollients of their wool –

all this, as I crept out in the no-time
after midnight, going to pee by the fence
squatting in the cool heady freshness, night's
elbow flung over the hill and the strange
spare light of the stars beyond –

At the time this poem was written, my sister and her husband
hadn't built their house; they lived above the barn and the toilet
was a long-drop some distance from the house. At night, when
one needed a pee, it was out on the stony driveway or over by the
paddock fence, Te Mata peak casting an ethereal shadow over the
silent landscape. Lauris wrote about the poem:

> *I suppose you could hear this as a political poem: it speaks of*
> *the beleaguered planet, it celebrates an unspoiled natural scene.*
> *It's true that my mind was full of suspicion and alarm about the*
> *danger of chemical poisoning, but in the end the sweet freshness*
> *of that country place made this a very personal, almost a love*
> *poem. I loved the words too, 'oily emollient' – delicious. Whether*
> *the hope expressed in the poem – that the earth has not 'given*
> *up' – is justified, I don't know.*

I too have always loved that couplet – all the 'o's and 'l's that roll
around the mouth: 'obscurely coiled / in the oily emollients of their
wool'. Whenever it has fallen to me to make a selection of Lauris's
poems, this is one I include, if at all possible, because it evokes those
years and an implicit, unquestioned acceptance of dependable and
loving family relationships.

In Lauris's young life it was the seductive attraction of the family
farmlet at Pyes Pa, while for us, her children and their families, it
was gathering at the 'farm' in the Tukituki valley. Both locations
have memorable potency. But nothing lasts. By the time of Lauris's
death, only one of her children's marriages was intact. This wasn't
something that happened only in our family, of course. Attitudes
and expectations towards marriage were changing all over the
Western world: women no longer had to make do, stay in unhappy

relationships. Lauris had been a trailblazer for her generation, but I don't think that prepared her for the chaos that ensued when her daughters followed suit. The last lines of this poem contain her hope not just for the planet, but for her family: 'holding once again safe until morning / their dream of a lifetime to come'.

The natural world also evokes the lives of rural women whose days are ruled by the seasons. I interviewed Anne French, who said that Lauris's writing validated rural women and their lifestyle; that by writing about ordinary things, she brought their experience out of the realms of silence, out of the unseen and irrelevant, honoured it, gave it meaning and dignity. Hence her popularity. Anne also told me that when she was Lauris's publisher at Oxford University Press they would print 5000 or 10,000 copies and be prepared for a reprint. These are extraordinary numbers for poetry. Lauris herself sold more of her books than any bookshop did. She was just as successful at this 'cottage industry' as she had been as a mother and housekeeper.

'Threads' and 'A Desirable Property on an Elevated Section' are two poems that bring women's work out of the shadows, the former employing it as a metaphor for writing itself, for the precision that words demand, while the latter uses detailed attention to gardening to gently push towards the idea that if men learned the lessons of nature it might make them more peaceful, less likely to exercise 'power and control and all that male shit' (as a friend once described it to me).

Lauris's concern for the injustices perpetrated on mother earth is implicit. The 'obedience' of the earth to conquering, colonising man is an imposed one, but to 'hear' the resistance one must be willing and know what to listen for. If you decide not to, or refuse to, the 'price of all possessiveness' will be exacted: 'the hard / and unpersuaded clay, clod by clod, / will turn its back on you and slip down hill'. The clay hillside on which Grass Street stood delivered this piece of wisdom.

In her lifetime, climate change was not yet a major issue, but nuclear pollution and the poisoning of the planet by the prodigious use of pesticides and chemicals to manage every environmental inconvenience, to 'tame nature', was already problematic. Her disquiet about nuclear pollution is expressed in a number of poems, including 'Nuclear Bomb Test Mururoa Atoll' and 'Latter Day Lysistrata'. The 'latter' poem took her in a new direction about which she felt uncertain. In early 1978 she sent me a copy, asking for my opinion:

> It is late in the day of the world
> and the evening paper tells of developed
> ways of dying; five years ago we would not
> have believed it. Now I sit on the grass
> in fading afternoon light crumpling pages
> and guessing at limits of shock, the point
> of repudiation; my woman's mind, taught
> to sustain, to support, staggers at this
> vast reversal. I can think only of
> the little plump finches that come
> trustingly into the garden, moving
> to mysterious rhythms of seeds and
> seasons; I have no way to conceive
> the dark maelstrom where men may spin
> in savage currents of power – is it
> power? – and turn to stone, to steel,
> no longer able to hear such small throats'
> hopeful chirping nor see these tiny
> domestic posturings, the pert shivering
> of feathers. They know only the fire
> in the mind that carries them down
> and down in a wild and wrathful wind.
>
> I do not know how else
> the dream of any man on earth can be
> 'destroy all life, leaving
> buildings whole ...'

Let us weep for these men, for
ourselves, let us cry out as they bend
over their illustrious equations; let us
tell them the cruel truth of bodies,
skin's velvet bloom, the scarlet of
bleeding. Let us show them the vulnerable
earth, the transparent light that slips
through slender birches falling over
small birds that sense in the minuscule
threads of their veins the pulses of
every creature – let these men breathe
the green fragrance of the leaves, here
in this gentle darkness let them convince me,
here explain their preposterous imaginings.

I replied:

*Your poem I really like and I don't see why you are embarrassed.
I think you are right – it is a new direction and it seems to me
it's the kind of direction you've talked about moving in. It is less
'personal' (in the sense of being less specifically about you) –
more general or universal or whatever the word is ... a women's
poem with a sense of it being an age-old women's cry but of
course in a present context. If you can follow my meanderings,
good on you. You should ring me up and I'd talk about it.*

Lauris responded:

*I am so glad you like the poem, your helpful remarks brought me
to a sudden decision; I sorted out about 45 poems that seemed
finished and good (I hope) and sent them to Vincent for an
opinion about whether I could possibly have another collection
published so soon – though of course it wouldn't be soon, it
would be next year.[1] Bridget [Williams] has made hopeful sounds
about being willing to publish them, though since she hasn't read
them that isn't much to go on. I am pretty crazy about the game
at the moment, but no doubt someone will pour cold water on
me soon and cure all that.*

Another poem that uses the natural world as a parallel to human experience is 'The Beech Tree' about which the ever practical, communicative writer said:

> *Here is another image doing its useful work, bringing together very different activities that yet have a common characteristic. In this case, it's the growing of a tree, layer by layer, likened to human growth. I have always liked the idea that our feelings and behaviour live on in us, physically as well as psychologically, and the chopping down of the tree brought this powerfully to the surface:*

> I tell you, friend or lover, all
> who touch my life, I cannot lose you
> even by forgetting until death destroys
> the ordered secret kingdom of my body.

Her creature poems occupy similar territory to her nature poems, paralleling and contrasting human and animal behaviour. 'Mister Dog', 'Cows', 'The Condition', 'Mynas' and 'Going to the Grampians (Kangaroos)' are examples. 'Mister Dog' is a 'half nonsensical address' to the family dog from her first book, *In Middle Air*.

> Thank God he'll never speak.
> We love him for his inability:
> our antics he approves, apparently.
> But if he said with sudden honesty
> our snarls and whines are all futility –
> he'd have to go. We require servility.
> Thank God he'll never speak.

When she was editing the Fairburn Letters, she and Denis Glover spent a great deal of time together, he sometimes visiting her at home. Denis proclaimed love for all of Lauris's family, but his favourite, the one who aroused his greatest affection, was Mungo, the dog, named by Martin after the Scottish explorer of West Africa, Mungo Park. It was perhaps Denis's somewhat sardonic canine preference that prompted Lauris to show him this poem. To her surprise, Denis's response was that if she had others like it, he would help her to get a volume published. This proved to be the genesis of her first collection, though ironically there are no other poems like 'Mister Dog' in it, and very few in her entire canon.

'Cows', from *Seasons and Creatures*, is probably the closest. This poem had its origins in the time Lauris was a Wellington-based tutor for Massey University, involving many car trips to Palmerston North, often necessitating a very early start. Lauris said the writing of 'Cows'

> *happened on the spot … I can vividly remember stopping the car on a country road (it's the by-pass road behind Masterton, not Woodville, but the real name mucked up the rhythm) in that wonderful early morning freshness and sitting there looking out at the steaming black and white cows. And I remember laughing secretly as I began my dialogue with myself which is what the first part of the poem really is. Then I got involved in my own argument and began to refute it – look here, don't act the poet!*

'Cows' is much loved by the public and I have often been asked to read it at public occasions. It has an easy flowing rhythm, trips off the tongue. I take issue with Lauris's assumption that cows 'cannot quarrel / or kill, have never fallen in love'. My experience contradicts the idea that emotions are exclusive to human beings. Was it a case of an irresistible idea and to hell with accuracy?

I am reminded of her poem about trout fishing, 'The Condition'. Lauris spent a weekend with Beeb in Taupo; his mission was to teach her how to fish. It did not go well – each time he passed her the rod he would grab it back almost at once, telling her she was holding it wrongly. A childish quarrel ensued, she packed her bags and set off walking down the road, he followed in the car. Peace was eventually restored though only after, in Lauris's words, a bout of 'huffing and puffing'. In her poem there's no quarrel or humiliating running away; she keeps fishing. He tells her, 'If they go with the current they suffocate … a quick dash is sometimes possible, but only / by holding their breath, so to speak …'

It's a nonsense – it has to be. If trout can only swim upstream, there they would all be gathered at the end of the road (so to speak), with no possible way out or back. Anne French told me she had pointed this out to Lauris, suggested she change it. Lauris refused: it would wreck the poem. Undoubtedly, she has a point, but it raises the issue of art versus authenticity: if you ignore one do you invalidate the other? As with 'Cows', I confess to being bothered by the inauthenticity. However, I am also aware that ideas of 'immanence' in creatures and the natural world are much more part of current environmental awareness than they would have been in her day.

'Mynas' is another popular poem: the risks, follies and delights of late love affairs (probably Bill Oliver). There are a couple of other follies connected with this poem – one is spelling. Lauris incorrectly spelled it Minas; in preparing the text of *Night Burns with a White Fire* we took the liberty of correcting her. The other is the story she often told of reading the poem to a particularly attentive audience in Masterton. The other two readers were Alistair Campbell and Rachel McAlpine, with whom Lauris was staying:

> *We glowed, each of us, standing about afterwards while individual enthusiasts came to talk to us. One who approached me was a man with an eager face, rather broken speech and a strong foreign accent. He had particularly liked my 'Minas' [sic] poem, he said.*
>
> *It was 'Good,' said my new friend I like – 'I used to be a miner myself, once.' And he grinned broadly.*

It was the morning after this poetry reading that Lauris, admiring a beautiful oak tree in the garden, close enough to touch she imagined, walked straight through Rachel McAlpine's very clean plate-glass window. Blood poured out of cuts on her hands and legs so fast that by the time they got her to hospital, there wasn't time for an anaesthetic; they stitched her up and filled her emptying veins with other people's blood.

'The Heat of Summer' and 'Enter a Messenger' are poems of exquisite immediacy arising out of a compelling moment. Lauris cultivated this attitude – a 'poet's training' she might have called it: if you gave up being surprised, you would give up writing. Of 'Enter a Messenger' she wrote:

> *I am not the first person to see fire as a rampaging animal; when it is leaping towards you as this one was, it does have a savage predatory quality. It was summer and a nor'wester was blowing – Wellington's prevailing wind – so everything seemed to conspire to give all power to the fire, none to me. It wasn't hard to see it as a messenger from that ultimate and invincible predator, death:*

> They caught and drowned the thing
> you know, within the hour; but this morning
> regarding the dead trees
> three or four yards from the house
> I know it is only a matter of time
> till it comes all the way …

Messages from other worlds – the natural one, the dream one, including warnings about death – Lauris took seriously. Well, her rational, twentieth-century post-enlightenment mind might have resisted but I think her poetic, intuitive mind received them, partly because her inner life was so readily and vitally accessible – it was finding its expression, its manifestation her challenge.

As an aside, Lauris always eschewed counselling, on the grounds that her 'chaos' was her creative source and imposing order would destroy it. Perhaps she was right. There's something in permitting oneself to become a force of nature.

Michael Harlow told me of a disturbing dream Lauris had not long before she died. She came to see him – 'agitated' was the word he used to describe her state of being – and told of her dream of waves rolling into the shore, over and over her, overwhelming her, submerging her, an exceptionally vivid and compelling experience. According to Michael it was a death dream – a premonition? – about 'the shadow' and having to come terms with it; about the need for reconciliation with her shadow self, with death, with Michael too (they had had a falling out).

As a young person I was unaware of the range and extent of my mother's emotional life – its turmoil at one extreme and its ecstasy at the other – but from her writing and from my later knowledge and experience of her I am able to recognise the patterns and their force, as well as their distinctness from the quotidian. My father was wont to describe my behaviour as 'histrionics'; I can see now that Lauris inhabited the same realm. I think it plausible that her attempts to wind back my emotional excesses were driven by her recognition of how difficult they were to live with.

Yet it's the vigour of her inner life that gives her poetry its potency, its truth and wisdom – the 'grand last line' syndrome. It's what caused her blind and irrational panics around the safety and well-being of her children – not just in relation to physical injuries but around the risks they took in relationships. It gave her that maddening capacity to go on and on and on about something that bothered her, that she could not get out of her head, that seemed insoluble.

It's summer here in Berlin where I am currently writing about my mother. Today is hot, oppressively so – 32 degrees according to the small weather station on my windowsill; the air is heavy. Even the fan blowing across the room merely stirs rather than mitigates the heat. It's too hot to think, too hot to work. A flash of lightning, a great crash of thunder just outside my window and rain, blessed cooling rain, falls from the grey skies over Berlin. Another flash and crash have me jumping out of my skin they're so close, so fierce.

The temperature drops 10 degrees in half an hour. The next thunder crack is a little further away, the storm passing on to threaten someone else. You can see why the gods wield thunderbolts – something so wildly unpredictable, so immediate and possibly lethal in its majesty cannot help but inspire awe in mere mortals. It's the very force of that natural chaos that Lauris found in herself and would not tamper with, nor allow anyone else to do so.

12. Becoming a writer

At the end of her year in Menton (1981), Lauris wrote:

> My 'life as a writer' is so short – I wonder if it has a future,
> if I have the power to take hold of my experience, and give
> it one? A woman of fifty-seven is beset by vanities, pretences,
> fears, protections – well, I am. The thing that concerns me most
> constantly and painfully is growing old. And being alone of
> course. But I don't write about that yet – there, I think, is where
> my next conflict lies. At the moment, whenever I try, I skulk
> around the question, eye it balefully, too frightened to close with
> it. I believe I have to move outside myself, yet hold to myself –
> it's always the same thing, always. Not just the excitement, or the
> pain, but finding the objective evidence, the detail.

Her writing life, her 'brief incandescence', was 25 years. At the end of 1981, when she wrote the paragraph above, there were still 19 years of writing ahead of her, a proliferation of work including a dozen more collections, her autobiography, essays, criticism, anthologies, the joint founding of the literary quarterly *New Zealand Books* … But thoughts around being older and female, being alone, her sense of time running out were powerful forces.

The photo on the front cover of this book was taken in summer in the garden of my home in Riversdale Road, Avondale, beyond what the kids called the great 'poisonous' pear tree. A delighted

Lauris, a glass of chardonnay in hand, and I are enjoying a moment of shared pleasure while my young children play. The photo captures her exquisitely in the moment – radiantly, gleefully alive, and it was not just the wine, though wine was a constant and a pleasure.

Moments of personal illumination, of epiphany, a 'being there', are common in her writing. Once considered dubious, lowbrow and female, writing in the first person, or 'confessional' writing, has achieved literary respectability, though in some circles it still carries those overtones. Poets whom Lauris greatly admired are in this tradition (Sylvia Plath and Robert Lowell, for example), but how did she negotiate this tricky territory? One advantage was that she learned to believe in her own writing, convinced that what she had to say mattered (though that is not to say she didn't have doubts; at times serious ones).

Some of her early writing has an unquestionable confidence, a certainty of perception. It's here in this brief excerpt from *Hot October*, taken from her diary of January 1943, when she was 18, after a week in the Marlborough Sounds with friends from training college, exploring, fishing, swimming: 'This you felt, was the heart, the centre of all seas and hills.' It was perhaps an early experiment with the grand evocation at the end of a poem. Such enviable certainty is a quality Lauris seemingly wore lightly. As Fiona Kidman remarked, 'She had a real certainty about the quality of her work, a self-belief. She "lived her poetry".'

Anne French concurs. And yet like any writer, Lauris had to grow into herself, discover how to say what was most crucial to her and then find the courage to say it. An encounter with Alistair Campbell offered her a significant step along this pathway. At the time she had only published one book, *In Middle Air*. They met for a drink and she gave him some poems to read. He told her she wasn't writing about what mattered most – the worst, the hardest things in her life were what she must write about. This, of course, included not only Rachel's suicide but her marriage to Trevor. It was 'too awful', she confessed tearfully; she couldn't possibly write about it. 'Real poetry is about the thing you can't say, can't bear,' Alistair told her sternly. It was a sustaining lesson she came back to again and again.

Travel also allowed her to grow as a writer. In July of her Menton year, after she had finished a draft of *High Country Weather* and returned home, she wrote in her diary:

> *There are new experiences, new habits, a new rhythm; I am more in my world, my children (and even my friends) are less to me – I have to know what this means. I perhaps have to be more unscrupulous about the 'using' of experience; I have to look to myself for more strength. But not too much – I must be weak – is it weakness? – as always to allow life to flow through me and come eventually to the page. The whole of the previous process was unconscious. I was not a writer till towards the end. Now I am one every moment, sleeping and waking; I have to live with this – it's a kind of torture, since it can so easily corrupt. It's the touch of Midas turning everything to gold; sometimes I want nothing but to escape from it, to go back to simply living – however hard that was, at least it had a kind of logic about it that this new life (what Denis called my 'new life of talking and writing' – ah how much I owe him) lacks. This is full of craft, of artifice, of deviousness – yet the ultimate goal is simplicity. I was simple before without trying; I shall never recover that artlessness, it's gone forever.*

And in December 1984, the year before she won the Commonwealth Poetry Prize, she was critical of her own poetry:

> *Poetry has ceased to be a discipline and become an indulgence. I must turn away from it, the hardest thing to do. No, it's not poetry I reject – it can never be that – but my own clumsy, self-encouraging ways of approaching it. I am a child, an ignoramus, a fool; none of my knowledge, the skill I thought I had, will do. It's all in the past; I must find new ways, a new language. I am hopelessly imprecise and confined in the language I have. I cannot write again until I have new materials, and have re-invested the old with value they have never had before.*

A few years later, at the age of 64 in 1988, after the publication of *Summer Near the Arctic Circle*, she was still given to bouts of soul-searching over her writing and its place in her life:

> *I have lost all my nerve over the writing of poetry. I am afraid of it. I have betrayed it and myself and it knows, as I do. Why such moralistic terms? – well, I forced the finishing of 'Summer', dragged some of those last poems (the last to be finished) out of a reluctant consciousness like heavy boots out of mud. I knew I should leave them, go away, wait for a change of weather, a change of season. It was all to do with a terrible habit, a practice anyway, of leakage in my mind so that over and over something happened and I'd think 'it's a poem, it could be, it nearly is …' as though I'd become a poem factory. So I thought I'd impose, and take, my proper punishment – to write nothing till I'd got rid of all this self-consciousness.*
>
> *And what have I found? Something almost worse – an easy pleased return to conversation and social fulfilment. Of course I never gave up conversation, but when I am writing I have a double life – the secret and secretly nourished one where poems discover their truths, and the other, the public courtesies, the serious play of friends and events. Is it partly age that allows one to leak into the other as they do at present? More, they merge, and the always seductive sociable one quickly gets the ascendant. I said to myself months ago that I had to go back to it – that ordinary outward life – because there ultimately is the source of every insight. But something is wrong; it's no longer the life of struggle (as it was in the first 'round' before I began to write properly at all – and I do see this as a reckoning at the end of a whole huge productive time, about 14–15 years of it). It's more superficial, more controlled.*

The first volume of her autobiography was published in 1989, so in a sense she did abandon poetry for a time. Her next collection came out in 1991 and it was a 'new and selected' (with the emphasis on the selected).

As a woman writer, Lauris understood that she had to compose the version of herself she wished to present to the world – a conscious construction – and while this is not unique, it is particular. As woman, as writer, she rehearsed a studied unselfconsciousness, a calm unflappable exterior and a marvellous delighted curiosity beneath which lay her tortured emotional excesses and agonies. These she channelled into her writing and recorded in her diaries, allowing her to face the world with equanimity.

It might be tempting to ascribe such self-conscious presentation of self to her maturity and her late arrival in the public world, but this is only partially true. Certainly, she always wore scarves or high-necked blouses to conceal wrinkles – her 'chooky' neck. She never wore rings, nor any other jewellery on her hands, and carried them palm upwards to conceal the veined, puckered, pigmented skin on the back. She wore longish skirts or trousers to conceal the disfigurement of varicose veins. Right up until her death she dyed and permed her hair, as well as having it washed and 'set' every week. I often wondered what she would have looked like if she had allowed her hair to be as it naturally was: straight like mine, and probably grey. Was this entrenched female vanity coupled with the classic cliché of wanting to look younger? I think, rather, she was determined not to draw attention to her age; as far as possible to make it irrelevant so it wasn't what defined her.

Lauris was fully aware that for the older woman, the recognised and countenanced role at the time was one of service – caregiver, grandmother. A motivating force in her self-construction was an absolute refusal to be so defined and restricted. If some of her techniques were transparent, her success in standing her ground, demanding visibility, that she be taken seriously, must be recognised, admired, even lauded. As a 60-year-old woman in 1984 she wrote:

> *It's a clear, still sun-filled afternoon in late autumn and the house is totally silent as so often, and I have just turned 60 (and behave as though I haven't – and by God will continue to do so), and I am not reconciled to my life.*

Her conversation was practised too; she often rehearsed important conversations. In the words of her friend, Lynne Dovey:

> *With Lauris conversation was an art form; she developed it, worked on it, with her beautiful voice, her way of talking which was like her poetry … poetic conversation.*

There were occasions when I had a different, less flattering view, when I found her a 'remorseless conversationalist' (and told her so – good humouredly). When my children were young and she came to stay, discussions were regularly interrupted by their demands; she would wait until I was available and carry on where she had left off as though possessed by an unflinching determination to reach the end of her thought process, 'Bars, locks, fists of blood, bombs falling / couldn't stop it happening' ('Being Here').

Lauris's much admired way of engaging in conversation, the 'tell me', rather than talking about herself that many of her friends describe, is, on one level, a classically female listening skill, part of the training that she and I, and generations of women before [us], received, if not directly, then at least implicitly. Lauris describes it as 'using to advantage, in the new life, habits I'd learned in the old'.

Imperatives for Lauris's self-construction included her origins in a rather odd family who had a layer of socialised skin missing, and a paralysing shyness she suffered as a young woman. Fanny suffered from it, and so did I. Such self-consciousness forces one into preparing oneself for social engagement. It is a gender affliction. In 'The Third Person' a woman tailors her self-image, attending to the façade in order to be acceptable. The powerful male is the axis; she is the acolyte.

The gendered nature of power and influence meant that Beeb and others of Lauris's 'grand old men' were undeniably useful to her, facilitating her entry into a world she wanted to belong in. But women writers could easily be dismissed for having the temerity to speak up in public.

The Bloomsbury flat saga is an example. In the late 1980s a substantial and beautiful architect-designed house on an island off

Ōhope beach in the Bay of Plenty was offered at a reasonable price to the government as a residence for artists. The Minister of Arts, Michael Bassett, expressed interest, and consulted with some writers, including Lauris. C.K. Stead was then asked to look at the property and report back to the minister.

After some months and no further consultation with the initial group of writers or the wider writing community, it was announced that a flat had instead been purchased as an artists' residence in Bloomsbury, London, on Stead's advice. When a group of 26 writers, including Lauris and Fiona Kidman, wrote a letter of protest over the lack of consultation and apparent secrecy around the decision, the media outcry and public abuse of Lauris and Fiona, who were vocal in their opposition to the purchase, was breathtaking. Both received hate mail.

In their defence, they composed a letter to the *New Zealand Herald*:

> *… we have both actively distanced ourselves from the affair, taking the view that those who wished to use the London flat should be allowed to do so without criticism by those who did not. We both declined the opportunity to sit on a committee to administer the flat, for the same reason. For the most part we have declined further public comment, although numerous newspapers have pursued the matter quite independently of us. At no point have we indulged in personal references of any kind.*
>
> *In return for this restraint we have been variously described through the media as 'garrulous', 'graceless', 'hysterical', 'divisive', 'envious', 'egotistical'.*

The subsequent sale of the Bloomsbury flat by the next National government was also laid at their feet. In Lauris's words:

> *Somebody must be to blame. It's not the other writers who protested, not the National Government, not Mr Stead who dreamed up the London location in the first place, certainly not the ex-Minister himself; no, the entire blame for the Government's action rests with those two amazingly powerful*

> *political schemers, Fiona Kidman and Lauris Edmond. They*
> *alone convinced the Government it could not afford to keep the*
> *flat. Who knows what these Machiavellian women will do next?*

The tone of the letter is ironic, but I know from talking to Lauris, and more recently to Fiona, that they were both shocked at being scapegoated and at the vitriol poured on them – by other writers, by women and men from the general public – for publicly questioning a process that many writers had felt was not open or constructive.

Irrespective of her personal vulnerabilities, including her family background, her age, her late arrival in the literary/public world and of course her gender, Lauris's detailed attention to her public persona – wanting to look nice, be nice, be seen as nice – was part of her magnetism, her charm. It also helps explain her public discretion, her circumspection over her personal life and lovers. She knew she must maintain her dignity.

Another quality that served her well but could also lead her into troubled territory was her impulsiveness. She possessed a fool's courage, accompanied by a determination to lead her life on her terms – to be the 'subject' of her life, including resisting public subjugation to 'woman as object'. In this she was blessed with considerable support from other women, writer colleagues, publishers and her extensive readership, many, though not all of whom were women.

Elizabeth Caffin told me that Lauris was a 'beacon': she took risks others were too timid to take. Of course, the corollary was taking the flak when she overstepped the line, or was perceived to have done so. What did she do? She suffered, she agonised, she talked and talked, over and around and through the issues, 'wrote it out' in her diary, until she found understanding and equilibrium. Then she carried on, stepped out again.

In an interview with Elizabeth Alley for *What Makes a Poem*, a radio series broadcast throughout the 1980s and 1990s, Lauris reflected on her writing process:

> *The American poet Marianne Moore says that a good poem – a real poem she calls it, has imaginary gardens, with real toads in them. It is in other words, a new world, come into existence for the first time, yet when you enter it, unaccountably familiar – strange, disturbing perhaps, but your world after all. This could be said of any kind of imaginative writing. For me, it's true of poetry, because of the sharpness, the quick take-your-breath-away of a good poem, its instant action. I'm talking about short poems, the kind I like to write best myself. I want a poem to change the world, to change forever my perception of it in however tiny a way, and I want it to happen now.*

In Ken Arvidson's introduction to *Selected Poems 1975–2000* he wrote:

> *Lauris Edmond's poems are usually written in the first person, sometimes as lyrics of celebration or lament, sometimes as meditations, but more often than not as autobiographical recollections, anecdotes or narrative vignettes …*

'Epiphany (for Bruce Mason)' is a good example, as is 'Composition with Window and Bulldozer', an anecdote of an unusual sight on the Grass Street hillside, observed by Lauris with her eldest grandchild. To quote Arvidson again:

> *The air of spontaneity which is such an attractive feature of her poetry makes it seem like a clear window on her world and her life. Her poetry is in fact a constant process of exploration and selection from experience, creating in language the 'substance' she seeks.*

Lauris told Elizabeth Alley:

> *The pleasure for me of writing a poem, comes to me as a*
> *springing to life of a little piece of my own experience, as though*
> *a bright light has switched on – something I know, yet don't*
> *know, am familiar with, yet have never seen before, leaps into*
> *dazzling outline.*

'Composition with Window and Bulldozer' contains the title of
her third volume of autobiography, *The Quick World*, while the
last lines bring the cold breath of mortality – or at least the risk, the
temptation of it – into the frame: grasp the glorious moment, it's
only a 'brief incandescence' and is all you have, 'Even you / do not
have very long in the sun'.

'Catching It', 'Biography', 'Trapeze', 'Crossing the Rimutakas' are
in this mould too. 'Catching It' is a Menton poem:

> I saw three men looking
> towards the sea:
> they were on a seat, laughing –
> three small brown foxy Frenchmen

She wrote of it:

> *… two moments in time are never exactly the same, each is*
> *unique, and I set about looking at the details that proved the*
> *uniqueness of this moment. I called it 'Catching It' because I*
> *think a poem is often there, just out of sight, and if you watch*
> *out of the corner of your eye, you 'catch it'.*

She used the title of this poem for the collection in which it
appeared, the phrase easily read as a kind of wilful ingenuousness
– catching what? Venereal disease, suggested Vincent O'Sullivan!
Lauris would have none of it. I thought the title of the first volume
of her autobiography, *Hot October*, sounded like the name of a porn
star. In her inimitable fashion she would have none of that either:
both titles stuck.

'Crossing the Rimutakas', another 'poem of the moment', has a
fragile immediacy:

> this happiness
> looking about
> and speaking with
> a soft breathlessness

The happiness is certainly not to do with my father; his was the house where she often cried. But when he left she was surprised to discover she missed him, missed the fact of his enduring presence downstairs. She wrote in her diary:

> *And I – do I miss him? Yes, I have spells of sudden sadness because even the frail tie we had is gone; but I've been practising separateness from him for so long now, some of it doesn't change.*

With Trevor gone, it was as if their shared past had departed with him and the only way she could hang on to it was by visiting him.

It's another manifestation I think, of ingenuousness. Her vigilant curiosity, which she revered and nurtured in herself, sometimes came across as wilful and determined naïvety, though she would argue it was a means of leaving herself open to whatever might occur: perception, event, encounter, love affair, thus making it possible for her to revel in the immediate present. She was endlessly engaged in the exploration of her own ideas and imagination and shared them generously, wanting others to be as fascinated, to see the world as forever dynamic, newly recreating itself moment by moment.

Janet Wilson conducted a delightful interview with Fleur Adcock about Lauris's writing soon after her death:

> FA: *... and this wonder she had about the world, everything. She was always ...*
> JW: *I know.*
> FA: *It was great – the first time she saw trees in the woods without any leaves.*
> JW: *I know. Remember when we went walking in the woods?*
> FA: *Yes!*
> JW: *Just down here?*

FA: *Yes, yes!*
JW: *And she saw a squirrel?*
FA: *Yes! And a robin.*
JW: *And I took a photo of her; it was obviously such a big thing for her. LAUGHTER.*
FA: *That's right – she'd just seen a robin and now a squirrel. PAUSE.*
JW: *I think she lost some of that in her last years.*
FA: *Yes, I suppose she got like the rest of us. She'd seen it all. She'd done all the things she needed to do.*

Lauris fiercely resisted any slide into a world-weary state of having seen it all, and yet the effort, the energy required to maintain such a high level of 'vigilant curiosity' I suspect became unsustainable even for someone as determinedly positive as she, and lurking despair overwhelmed her at times. In 1988 she wrote:

> *… we were wise, and where did it get us? We – I – became authoritative, and so what? The world moves on, is more awful than it was even, can be contemplated but hardly explained. To do that – explaining – you have to send up a great cry of mourning. Or blow your brains out.*

Perhaps the energy required simply wore her out. Which raises the question, if she couldn't have that anymore, did she, in fact, want her life to carry on? The 'fading powers' question is a hard one to answer, though, frankly, I cannot imagine Lauris as old, frail, querulous; in my mind she will always be energetic, dynamic and voluble.

The thought of living alone was a major hurdle for Lauris, but when the upstairs/downstairs arrangement with Trevor ended in 1981 she finally had to confront her anxiety at the absence of settled, familiar patterns and dependable relationships. She struggled with this during the year in Menton, and now 'aloneness' was a permanent condition: 'The giant fear that had waited outside the door for my whole life at last turned the handle and came in.'

The day itself could be filled with activities – work, people. The end of the day was the time of dread – 'That time when the solitary day has to look in the eye that silent beast that has sat out the action, the lassitude, the urgency, and now when it all ends is ready to spring.'

'The Susceptibility', from her 1984 *Selected Poems*, wrestles with this 'silent beast' in the lightest manner, capturing the agony and inconstancy of the solitary life. She was in her late fifties, struggling with purpose, entitlement: 'oh love oh danger / the world spins fully round / in half an hour'. 'The Henri Rousseau Style', from the same collection, grapples with the predatory grimness of silence and aloneness. From her bed she looked through a wall of glass over the Grass Street hillside with its 'massed Pohutukawa' toward Oriental Bay: a 'static pageantry'. The day as a Rousseau painting, with its lurking dangers.[1]

Until her time in Menton, Lauris had never lived alone. On leaving her close-knit family home she had lived in a hostel while attending training college, then married and had a large family. Is fear of loneliness something to do with one's identity being tied up with the external affirmation of being seen? If I see no one and no one sees me, do I exist? In Lauris's young life she had watched her mother's struggle to find a place for herself after Lewis died, and she did not want to repeat the pattern. And with such a rich and fertile inner life, she needed social discourse as a means to bring that life into focus and thus understanding.

An associated fear was penury. In her late fifties Lauris found herself a writer without a 'real' job, and thus without real means of support. Before her Menton year she'd had the PPTA job, and with Trevor living downstairs they shared the expenses. Now all she had was a small income from the downstairs tenants. This must have raised the spectre of dependence, possibly homelessness – of having to succumb to the indignity of a room in the house of one of her children in return for 'services' – a terrifying idea. She hurtled into and out of the affair with Hubert partly out of a need for security, both personal and financial – and it was that debacle that finally provided the necessary perspective: she realised that living alone was desirable and she had to make it work.

Despite learning to live alone, to make the necessary accommodations, occasional bouts of loneliness and a sense of loss never entirely left her. She wrote in *The Quick World*:

> ... *a sense of loss still underlays each step from the old secure predictions to the new and variable practices that I made up for myself. This had never left me; perhaps it never would. And of course I still felt lonely and dispirited, I still occasionally looked with pangs of envy at the placidly married ... And I had never quite cured myself of that sudden rush of sadness as I turned the key in the lock and came into my own house alone and silent, after being with friends.*

There are a good many poems that explore the potency, the inevitability, of other forms of aloneness: loss of sustaining love, for example, in poems such 'On the Te Awamutu Road', 'Spring Afternoon', 'Dunedin', 'One to One' – poems that take their inspiration from the end of her marriage.

'On the Te Awamutu Road' is particularly poignant, arising as it does from the drawn-out disintegration of the relationship – the mistakes and misunderstandings, the heartless cruelties, small or not, intended or otherwise, that are inescapable in the ending of any relationship: 'Some of my sorrow and complexity found its way into 'On the Te Awamutu Road', a poem which for a long time I could not read without coming close to tears':

> It was a dark bird, silvery
> in flight, coming quick
> and awkwardly – low too, as though
> already maimed; but that is useless
> now to think of since without
> apparent impact, no thud nor

syncopated interruption
of the wheels, I killed it.

I saw a turning tuft like black
and silver petals in the wind
and thought for something like a mile
that I should stop – and then
forgot. So it lies
without reproach, without defence
among the larger carelessnesses
left about my life.

One of the foundations of Lauris's solitary life was to ensure she maintained regular contact with friends and family – by phone particularly, letters and postcards, as well as outings and activities, along with regular Sunday night family dinners at Grass Street. All means of communication were significant bedrocks and she embraced new technologies as they arrived:

> *I've got a fax! I'm madly excited about it, and want to send messages to everyone – I've just done one to Kathy, but got it slightly wrong and picked up the receiver, whereupon she said 'You're not supposed to be there; press Start and hang up.' So I did and it went. Do you have one, and is it the same number as your phone? I hope so – I'd love to send you one. I know people who go on about their new technology can be very boring, but honestly I can't help it, for the moment anyway … It will be lovely to see you all again, not too long after Raetihi. Did I tell you that I came back from there with my head full of rocks and water and air – but of course you know that already. It's why you go yourselves. I'd forgotten how important holidays in the summer, in the country, really are – there were quite some years when I didn't have one, but these two this year brought it all back, the marvellous refreshment of the real country, the real away-ness.*

Other developments such as such as bankcards and ATM machines delighted her too. She wrestled with some aspects of the logic of modern technology – when your page disappears from your computer screen where has it gone? – and required regular assistance from grandchildren or, when that wasn't available, the hired skill of computer repair men. Nevertheless, she was amused and engaged by the multiple facilities technology offered her. In February 1999 she got email.

For many, the turn of the millennium and the anticipated disaster of Y2K was a non-event; not so for Lauris. She had very quickly become dependent on this new form of communication and her bereavement over the temporary loss of her email was no affectation – she felt cut off, alone:

> *This is just a note for you to find when you get back home, to tell you that if the whole of the rest of the country – and the world – got off lightly without trouble from Y2K I didn't! It's attacked my email, which will neither receive nor send anything – it stopped on 31.12.99, and I don't think I can get anyone to look at it till Wednesday.*
>
> *I posted you a letter today, and will fax this – there are still a few communication options open to me, but I do have a sense of loss and frustration.*

Friendships, literary occasions, lunches, dinners, parties, 'the public courtesies, the serious play of friends and events' all formed part of her well-managed life – she kept her appointment diary full. There were regular phone calls too – she and Fiona would talk often, sometimes every day. Lauris and I spoke on the phone at least once a week (unless we were in one of our 'fallen out' phases): long, satisfying conversations generally after 10pm when toll rates became cheaper. When she died we put a telephone in her coffin – it was inconceivable that Lauris could function in the afterlife without at least one means of communication.

Lauris may have wrestled with identity questions, agonised over the life of a woman writer and the acceptance of a solitary existence, suffered, and made mistakes, but she achieved, with style and aplomb, a literary identity and a richly satisfying and economically dependable life. She told her diary on 18 December 1988:

> *Grandmother in the family, figure among friends (I don't mean status, I mean assurance), good at coping in other people's dilemmas – vicariously of course – I have learnt more than survival. Comfort, means of composing contradictions, the long view.*

Not only sorrow and complexity but the predations of time become increasingly common themes in her writing; how time, as it shortens, both limits and expands perception. How does one live within and without its strictures? 'The rules change, a single hour can grow huge / and quiet, full of reflections like an old river' ('In Position').

'In Position' is from *A Matter of Timing*, her 14th collection, which appeared eight years after her previous one, *Summer Near the Arctic Circle*, though in the intervening years there had been two 'selecteds', her volume of Wellington poems, her *Five Villanelles* (a chapbook) and her three-volume autobiography. 'In Position', 'Take One', 'Going North', 'At Grass Street', 'This year 1000 Americans will live to be over 100' and 'Evening in April' are all poems that hint, suggest, or even explicitly reference, how she lives in the time she has, and the nearness of death. I'm fond of the first two, 'In Position' having a marvellous mix of humanity and humility, irony and wisdom, the last verse particularly:

> the queer outline of what's to come: the bend in
> the river beyond which, moving steadily, head up
> (you hope), you will simply vanish from sight.

In my mind the river is the Tukituki in Hawke's Bay because we spent so many summers there. I can see Mum, head tossed back, laughing deliciously at the images she has created, yet I also know that alone in the middle of the night she was beset by terrors. In her last few years, when she came to stay, I too worried about her, worried that I might go into the room where she slept and find she had died in her sleep. Like a mother anxiously checking her child I would peer discreetly around the door, looking for the gentle rise and fall of bedding, proof she was still with us.

'Take One' and 'Going North' take another perspective on time and opportunity. In the first, Lauris, on a summer evening at Grass Street, takes ownership of her unique and entirely individual experience, her physical occupying of her time and space. It's also an affirmation of what she believed was the profound and unbreakable relationship between 'life and art', that the experience of one's life was the stuff of which poetry was created. I have read this poem in public many times. Lauris believed as I do that a poem is not just on the page, it lives in the voice as well and this is a particularly potent one to read aloud, especially the final lines:

> … but whatever it does, while I'm here nobody else
> can have it. They wouldn't feel its kick,
> nor understand the gleam in its eyes – and I do.

The question of 'How do we live in the days that we have?' ('Going North') continued to engross her – what is a good life and how do you live it? Despite searching for the definitive, answers inevitably turned out to be provisional and had to be continually reassessed.

There are also poems about betrayals of perception, such as 'A Matter of Timing', and of ageing and the loss of beauty, as in 'Femme âgée'. The latter is a Menton poem, the grief and vanity French in character and evocation – young woman as object of desire, receiver of adoration, while the eventual weakness and infirmity of age not pitied or consoled but found disgusting.

'Evening in April' and 'At Grass Street' maintain her late preoccupation with mortality. The lines engraved on the Grass Street

Memorial Plaque located on the street frontage outside what was her house and unveiled during the Verb Festival in 2019 are from 'Evening in April':

> Sometimes on autumn evenings
> I walk around the house, outside,
> looking up at the trees ... and
> I feel the closeness of the green world
> with me in it

'At Grass Street' connects her physically and emotionally to the energy, the vitality, of the weather on the hillside where she lived, an energy that nurtured, sustained and delighted her for 25 years. It also delivers a kind of, if not exactly peace, then acceptance of herself and her mortality:

> ... my body, apparently still, follows
> each cell of earth, air, in a moving emulsion,
> ordered exhilaration so fierce
> it can only be quelled by this setting it down –
> for you who will later stand here, and of course
>
> not care at all, having your own weather
> and trees, hills falling and finding their
> eternally temporary poise ... all the same,
> we leave best what we have truly loved, and now
> I turn easily away, one second nearer my death.

Lauris and Rachel are both buried in the Akatārawa Cemetery north of Upper Hutt and the line we chose for Lauris's headstone comes from 'At Grass Street', 'we leave best what we have truly loved'.

13. Writing her life

In a letter to Riemke Ensing in December 1976, Lauris expressed gratitude for comments Riemke made on two poems published in *Landfall* that year: 'Directions' and 'The Pear Tree':

> *I was greatly touched by your comments on the two Rachel poems in Landfall; no need to say anything about the mixture of agony and relief there was – and is – in writing about her; you understand it. I have all sorts of problems, as you will know I'm sure, about publishing anything so personal, but have come to think that what happens to you has to be what you write about, and if it is as terrible as that well you have some sort of added desire to make something positive and perhaps alive out of the devastation.*

Here Lauris touches on a subject that not only she, but family members and some of her friends also wrestled with. With only one collection published, it's very early in her writing career and her thinking about boundaries is exploratory and experimental. Fifty years later, in the age of social media, life is lived and displayed online; personal outpourings are not just legitimate but gloried in, consumed and sometimes savaged.

In contrast, in Lauris's youth, as in mine, such displays were firmly linked to the 'low arts' (the social media of the day) – newspaper gossip columns and the 'Women's Page'. In a broader social context, New Zealand society approached the idea of writing or talking about oneself with a patronising snottiness – it wasn't the done thing.

A year later, in 1977, Lauris's thinking had evolved. Riemke had edited an anthology of New Zealand women poets, *Private Gardens*, whose purpose was 'to showcase unpublished and hard to find work'.[1] Lauris's work was included, and in a private communication with Riemke she said:

> *This is not to say that private experience is in any simple way the stuff of poetry (though women writers tend to use their own consciousness as a very positive reflector, I think; Sylvia Plath is an obvious example). I see in my own work a good deal of referring back, not exactly with nostalgia, rather with a sense of the limits life comes to impose, and an awareness of contrast.*

Lauris's ponderings here are ones she continued to refine and redefine all her writing life. She also saw the writing of poetry as a process of discovery, of finding the thing that is almost there, just at the edge of perception, and if you pause, stay still and breathe, it may come into focus – 'Catching It'.

There's also her sense that being a late starter meant she had to clear away the accumulated clutter to find the essence of what it was she wanted to write: 'There are obvious disadvantages about saving up something important and then starting to live it as a second life. One is very aware of age, of lost opportunities,' she told Riemke.

By 1988, when Massey University conferred on her an honorary doctorate for literary achievement, her thinking was much more clearly formed. In her address on being a 'working writer' she said:

> *Once I say to myself that art is one thing, life another, I believe I do irreparable damage to both. I have learnt not to try. The consequences are that my working life is cluttered, sometimes confused, marred by postponements and prevarications. I never think I have the life/art balance right, and I don't suppose I ever will. But this, I have come to think, is the only choice I have. It is within this muddled and amorphous framework – indeed at*

the heart of it – that I must look for the still centre from which writing comes. Katherine Mansfield, in a wonderful letter as yet unpublished, calls it drawing upon 'one's real familiar life' – to find the treasure in that.

Her way of blending life and art has left me with no strong impression that she had a defined working routine and/or workspace – an office. Of course, I lived in another city and, when I visited, her work was not centre stage. She had a desk in her bedroom – somewhat untidy, with piles and scraps of paper and folders – and sometimes she worked in other parts of the house, at the dining-room table for instance. There were often stacks of papers on her bed and in the spare room which, for many years before the arrival of computers and printers, was dominated by her beloved and alarming photocopier – a monstrous old baggage that regularly required maintenance and devoured ink cartridges. There were unlined writing pads and little square coloured paper notes disposed around the telephone and in the living areas and on her desk bearing scribbles, thoughts, messages and lists. I still have a few examples, taken from the house after she died.

It sounds chaotic but it wasn't. Lauris perfected the art of seeming casually unconcerned about anything except the immediate present. Beneath this careful artifice she was determined and driven, virtually impossible to deflect once she had decided upon a course of action. In her diary of 1996 she wrote, 'tenacity, that crucial – and often underestimated – virtue. I often say it's the one that's got my work where it is.'

Her vast archive at the Alexander Turnbull Library is testament to her belief in the importance of her work and the legacy she wished to leave. Seemingly, she kept every letter ever written to her, from writers, friends and lovers, all deposited in her archive – apart from the correspondence with her children, which was returned to each of us after her death. Her archive also contains a great many notes about whatever she was writing or thinking about, as well as numerous drafts of work in progress. It bespeaks a thoroughly impressive devotion to detail, to preserving the concrete evidence of a working creative life, as reflected in 'Greek Antiquities: First Floor':

> my fingers touch
> the tiny perforations that mark
> the spots upon your coats of clay
> and find them rough and hard. Will any
> dream of mine so run, wakeful
> through more than twenty centuries?

This poem has its genesis in her first overseas trip in 1977. She did not visit Greece on that journey but she did go to Paris, and on Level One of the Sully wing of the Louvre she found Greek Antiquities. She wrote in *The Quick World*: 'And in the Louvre, I felt again, as in Florence, the wonder of recognition of a tradition I could claim as mine simply by sharing of old knowledge.'[2]

Lauris understood implicitly how to fit her writing around engagements with her children and grandchildren especially, but also friends, lovers and colleagues. She worked whenever she could, whenever she felt like it, whenever the muse possessed her, whatever the hour of the day or night. When she came to visit, she would bring bits and pieces with her, though she never allowed it to dominate.

Did she have role models? I can't answer that. Nevertheless, I agree with the view she expressed in her graduation address at Massey:

> *... in honouring me, you honour all the other women – and some men – who, like me, have not tried to distinguish between the importance of their children, their households, their close relationships, the jumble of their lives, and the books, stories or poems that had to be written ...*

Only a woman could write that. Lauris, in writing her autobiography, bears witness to this – art and life wounding and bleeding into each other. The first volume, *Hot October*, aroused no adverse familial reactions because it was about Lauris's early life before she married. Over the second, *Bonfires in the Rain*, the temperature increased alarmingly, some family members furiously unforgiving. Lauris wrote to Fleur in May 1991:

> *I am so fed up with my three-volume self-searching, that as soon as I've got a draft finished of the third, I want to go right away for a while. There's been family unrest too – some of the kids are fine about it, others are very touchy and inclined to think I should have kept quiet. I can actually see their point of view, but even if I'd anticipated this (which I didn't) I would probably have gone ahead and done it anyway. That unpleasant ruthlessness at the heart of most writers and writing has to be acknowledged in this case. Mostly I look the other way if I suspect it of myself.*

Shameless, unapologetic, admirable. I recognise the truth of her words – within the seemingly adaptable and conciliatory woman there was an implacable will, a core of steel. I knew when I had run into it. It's not unique to writers of course, though it can certainly serve them well. More reasonable to suggest that ruthlessness is an attribute of successful people.

Later that year she wrote to Fleur again:

> *1 October 1991*
> *Stephanie and Virginia took a strange indignant line as though I'd stolen something from them by writing about them as babies; well, I thought it was strange. Kathy and Frances think more as I do, that it's my story and not theirs and anyway I say nice things about them; Martin prefers to stay in Australia and not know too much about it.*

Lauris had both an inner and an outer self and in many ways they were not and could not be integrated, though the distinction between them was sometimes blurred. The outer person was the woman born in the 1920s into a culture where the roles for women were strictly defined. The inner woman was a wild creature with a passion for a life on her terms without compromise or apology and an absolute determination to pursue it irrespective of the cost.

I would have loved her to honestly *be* that woman, the inner on the outer, or at the very least to be a working blend of the two, but I think it was not possible. For her to openly admit to her family – as she did to Fleur – the existence of the inner woman would have been to betray the mother in her. She wanted her children to love her, to maintain the kind of lasting intimacy she had shared with Fanny. The pathway to that love was motherly and grandmotherly concern, attention and advice – all of which she possessed and offered in greater quantities than were at times welcome.

In her diary, writing of *Bonfires in the Rain*, she described the reaction of one of her daughters:

> *It was like Trevor all over again – this terrible grievance against the world, nothing of the good part of it remembered or acknowledged. I was deeply shocked by it. 'You just got yourself stronger and better, having affairs with other people but going on living with Trevor, until you were ready to leave and then you did' she said. Is this how those years of torment are perceived? Because I wanted each of us to stand alone, shed these terrible dependencies, and I did and Trevor didn't, am I to blame for this? Yes, it seems. I had done a terrible thing to 'break out' as I did and then to write about it, and she would never feel any differently – she will never change in her anger and resentment about my writing my autobiography. Does she feel the same about Martin? No, because she agrees with his portrayal of Trevor and anyway he's just her brother – it's worst when it's your Mother doing these terrible things.*

> *I know now how the other two must feel, I know that everything I do – and most of all writing my life story, including miseries and tragedy that [were] their story too – is somehow capitalising on the family's pain. I know Trevor thought that, because of his outburst a few months ago in which he said he 'utterly despised' me for what I did and do. But I dismissed it as the mean-spiritedness he exhibits, I did not think of it being carried on in the next generation. But it is. I am full of disappointment and sorrow. I will learn to live with it and it is*

just as well I know, but I think it is terrible that they can't see the larger dimensions of the history of a life like mine, passing through the huge social changes it brought and suffering from them, and benefiting too. They just see that it's an ego-build-up for me. How paltry. Really. Useless to say that I and hundreds of readers, and some of the family, saw it as my version of events not hers or anyone else's – she sees no distinction: it's the family nothing more. But I know I must do what she said, accept, accept. There's nothing else.

If *Bonfires in the Rain* caused trouble, there was an even greater furore over the third volume, *The Quick World*. Not merely opposition from within the family, though there certainly was that, but resistance from some others who found themselves at odds with their role in Lauris's narrative. Her relief at finally having finished it rapidly turned to distress. I was not the only person in Lauris's immediate circle to be pursued by a journalist for 'inside information'. The one who contacted me asked for my comments on the letter Stephanie and Virginia had written to the *Evening Post* after *Bonfires*, in which they dissociated themselves from Lauris's version of family events. Were there family feuds over this book as well? he wanted to know. Could I confirm that Lauris had changed some names to protect identities? Would I like to comment? No I wouldn't! She had indeed changed names to protect sensitive egos but that was not information I was entitled to divulge, even had I been so inclined. To every reframing of the question he posed as he tried to find a way around my guard, I replied with a firm 'No comment'.

Lauris wrote again to Fleur in July 1992, not long after *The Quick World* came out:

… there was a nasty piece in the Sunday Sun, a dreadful raggy Auckland paper, the next week another; and now, I'm told, there's a furious review by [C.K.] Stead saying everything in the book is lies, and it's done just to revile my poor husband who can't answer back.

> *… Frances was very strong in her attempts to make me full of stuffing instead of the limp thing I often am in the face of all this.*
> *… you will dismiss it all as trifling which I try to do myself all the time – and intermittently can manage to do. But in between I really squirm, wish I could be on the other side of the world, doing and thinking about other things …*

My advice had been to remember that reviews are written by individuals with agendas; that it's not only unhelpful but folly to extrapolate one opinion into the view of many; that it's the people who buy and read your work who are the real judges, if judging is what you require. The same principle applied to the family:

> *You are allowed, nay entitled to tell your story as you know and understand it. You are not telling theirs; if they wish to write their version then they can do so. It is a mistake to regard 'truth' as absolute.*

An added layer of irony lay in the coincidence of *The Quick World* being published the same year (1992) as Martin's book about Trevor, *The Autobiography of my Father* (from different publishers) – a further reason for speculation about our family dynamics and allegiances and a veritable feast for gossipmongers. Learning that Martin's book was imminent, Lauris became acutely aware of possible complications:

> *… we are going to have to suffer being a much-talked-about family; my way of dealing with the gossiping of a small community is to ignore it, I know of no other way of surviving. However, in this case reviewers are not going to be able to resist the temptation to associate the two books, and the two authors, and ignore may not be enough.*

Her decision about Martin's book was to say (publicly):

> *I know of it, have read it, think well of it and beyond that have no connection with it. The obvious family connection does not imply a literary or professional one …*

As further explanation she wrote:

> *I don't want to sound pompous about it, but I know from*
> *experience that the only way not to be embarrassed by publicity*
> *– or caught on the hop by it – is to be well prepared in advance*
> *for what it may do.*

Savvy Lauris was covering her bases. The truth is there was a
communication breakdown between Lauris and Martin at that time.
I will not discuss it here but I was embroiled in it, if in a minor way.
In March 1992 I wrote to my brother:

> *I am enclosing a letter that Lauris asked me to post on to you.*
> *Lauris wanted your postal address which I didn't give her*
> *because you had asked me not to – so reluctantly I have agreed*
> *to send this on for her. But I am not happy about being 'caught*
> *in the middle'. I've said as much to her. However you and she*
> *sort out your means of communication or lack of it, I do not*
> *want to act as a go between. It's too easy to get involved in the,*
> *'Yes but he says …' or 'I thought you said that she said etc etc'*
> *and I prefer my relationships simpler than that.*

Martin's book won third place in the 1993 Wattie Book Awards
that year. The cover blurb describes it as 'a pioneering work of
creative non-fiction in which Edmond transforms his grief at the
death of his father, Trevor Edmond, into a fascinating memoir and
love letter'.

Lauris's diary records the lengths she went to in order to clear her
text before publication:

> *My book, Oh God my book – this third volume, with real people*
> *in it, coming close to the real present though all the 'exposures'*
> *that upset people happened about ten years ago; what turmoil*
> *it's causing. I sent pieces (with them in them) to: Vincent, who*
> *was sensible and professional, claimed to be surprised at my view*
> *of him, expostulated a little about his quarrel with Margaret, but*
> *otherwise said 'it's your book, go ahead'. Virginia, who ignored*
> *it till I asked for a reply, then stonewalled; just said 'I won't have*

my name in it' ... It's all civilised with Kathy and Frances – they just say (like Vincent, like all my extremely balanced women friends, Margaret, Fiona, Bridget) 'it's your book' ...

... there are other dramas. First there was Beeb, who flew into a rage and a panic, was horrified, shocked, appalled – couldn't sleep at night, couldn't bear to think that I would quote him saying (while betraying her) 'I have always loved my wife' and was in a paroxysm when I quoted 'I believe in telling the truth about everything except sex'. I went to visit him, I told him all about how people saw it as a loving respectful portrait, I agreed to take out those horrifying bits; then we were left with the bit about his main subject being himself – which I agreed to rewrite – and the quarrel at Taupo, which I offered to take the blame for, so it became 'I' not 'we' being childish and silly. There. I rewrote it, sent it to him and what do I get? Complete recapitulation, complete acceptance; he is moved by it, it is gracefully told. We have arrived at the other side of the negotiation that I knew it was.

Now there's Bill. Just as panic-stricken, though more sedate about it – a long pained letter, asking questions about whether 'it has to be like this' – and do I really mean to publish it? He can't believe it of me ... the implication is of course that there is something a bit weird about a person who wants to tell the world their private hidden inadmissible secrets. This is the point – I don't think it's inadmissible and he does ...

One part of me is hurt at all this – might not these wretched fellows feel quite proud to be thus associated with me? Did it not occur to them that they could say to their friends, and to the lousy journalists who are enjoying their gossipy speculations, 'yes the story is true – nice isn't it?' That would have shut everyone up. But that too would be to agree to being part of my story, rather than me and everyone else being characters in theirs. A transfer of power that is thoroughly terrifying to them. Hubert, at a distance, is just the same – he was frightfully angry when I talked to him in England. Oh well. Do I laugh or weep? Am I flying a flag for freedom, querying male hypocrisy or betraying a sacred trust? ...

In Waitara, staying with Lynne and Ben, neither of them liked my book, and it took some time to find out why – the result is illuminating and to my surprise makes me seriously consider a fourth volume. They thought it wasn't me – the me they know – but a shallower, more frivolous, less 'rich' personality. This is a new response, yet it echoes the various remarks about how I'm 'hard on myself', 'lay myself open' and so on. It does make me think that the story – the growing up one way, breaking out of it into a quite different, independent life, and the consequences of that – is not after all the whole of it. The second-time adult, the later maturity (the person Lynne and others know) should have a place. I don't know quite how I'll do it but I think now I probably shall. One thing I can see that it must contain is the process of joining together the lives that seemed so separate, and the periods of change between them – yes Lynne's right, there is something important missing …

She wrote further about Bill in December 1992:

He doesn't even speak to me now, feeling betrayed by The Quick World. I understand his rage and mortification now, as I didn't a few months ago – but too late. Not only that; I think now that there was a strenuous blindness held its hand over my eyes for months and months – as long as it was necessary to get the job done, the story told. The muse as giantess, as goblin, as traitor to me, its victim. I can't reject it, it served me with unerring judgement. It's just that it lost me my friends. Hubert too, though I care less about that, less about him.

Lauris and Bill reconciled a few months later when he sent her 'a funny self-deprecating poem about Edward Green'. It occurs to me she must have had fun thinking up pseudonyms for these silly paranoid men who would not allow their real names to appear: Edward Green is fairly tame, but Chester Wadsworth (Hubert) reeks of pretension. Beeb, at least, was prepared to be himself.

Lauris's autobiography brought her personal life directly into her art, and therein lay the source of the conflict. However, there are many poems where she takes the opposite path and brings art directly into her personal experience: 'After Chagall', 'Rodin Sculptures', 'Lake Tutira', 'The Kynges Englishe', 'Greek Antiquities: First Floor', 'The Henri Rousseau Style', 'Threads'.

While writing this, I was surprised to discover that 'Rodin Sculptures' is from her second book, *The Pear Tree*. I knew the poem was an early one – it has been included in every volume of selected poems – yet it's one I have passed over without it getting under my skin or into my psyche. Finding it in its original, I discovered that she rewrote the second verse and made a few line and word adjustments to the other two verses for later publications. The timing would suggest that the rewriting was for her prizewinning *Selected*, published in 1984. The original version of the second verse read:

> Yet to stand close was to feel in each
> an intensity so fierce it breathed from some
> centre stronger than fact or faith;
> to find in head and hand, puzzled
> or despairing face all poise and passion
> to hear cry the very voice of man.

All later versions read:

> Yet to stand close was to feel in each
> an intensity so fierce you had to step back
> pain struck so deep
> the abandonment dislodged each foothold
> the muscles of every back
> ached in its eloquence –

I did not see the Rodin exhibition in Wellington that inspired this poem, but in 2012, many years after Lauris died, I visited the Rodin Museum in Paris and finally this poem came to life for me; her words resonated: 'an intensity so fierce you had to step back / pain struck so deep'. Particularly the explicitly sexual *Iris*, a sculpture that continues to arouse controversy. Rodin's *Iris* is headless and her single (right) arm lies along her right leg, hand around the foot, pulling it up and away from the left, drawing focus to her genitals. The force of its intensity, its vitality, is palpable, yet there's something disturbing – not the explicit sexuality but woman dismembered and headless as if, to the artist, she *is* her genitals and her ecstasy, the rest irrelevant.

I speculate that Lauris changed 'to hear cry the very voice of man' because it was a troublesome line in relation to her evolving sense of the plight of women, and because by the late twentieth-century the idea of 'man' being an inclusive descriptor of humanity was coming under increasing critical fire.

In 'Lake Tutira', 'The Kynges Englishe' and 'The Lecture' Lauris reflects on how one negotiates one's personal identity, one's 'truth' in relation to art and language. Lake Tutira is in Hawke's Bay, on the road north to Wairoa, perhaps part of Lauris's childhood – Lewis and Fanny may have taken their children there on outings in the car, Sunday picnics. Certainly, her grandfather, William Price, at one stage of his varied and peripatetic farm-managing career, owned some land with one of his sons at Tongoio on the Lake Tutira road. It's a late poem from *A Matter of Timing*:

> Late afternoon. Two black swans
> glide to the edge on flawless glass.
> There they pause, erect, austere
> in their Modigliani slenderness …

Ken Arvidson says the poem encapsulates the idea that 'Life might well be provisional, but there's nothing provisional about the indisputable evidence of our senses': 'appearance / and reality harmonised at last.'

The language is quintessentially Lauris – don't play games with me, just tell me what you really mean! I can hear her saying this when there was disagreement or confusion or misunderstanding.

Her assertion that in the ordinary, the everyday, the truth can and must be spoken could be a mixed blessing – exhilarating when the aspired-for harmony flowered, but troublesome when the versions of reality were in conflict.

'The Lecture', which first appeared in *Seasons and Creatures*, is an ironic, self-deprecating take on the public/private dichotomy. On her way home from the Cambridge Poetry Festival, Lauris stopped off in America, spending a couple of days with friends in Kansas City:

> *I will never forget the evening on their terrace where our enormous mid-west steaks were barbequed, and where we sat in the dusk after eating them watching the fireflies darting – no floating – about in the warm air on that wide grassy hillside where their house stood … And then, as we talked, one flew right up close, under the sun umbrella which was still up above the outdoor table, a little whirring creature with a tiny body and short broad wings, flying silently and winking, winking. It came so close you could see it easily when its light was on and in between too. And then miraculously I caught it in my hand and held it inside my cupped palm while it flew round in there, lighting up, putting it out, lighting up again. Then I let it go …*

> > 'Up there in the quiet room
> > where the fireflies are to be seen
> > at work in their luminous trees
> >
> > there is my truth, my candour, my courage,
> > there I too can shine with the natural
> > intermittent light of myself,'

> – and then I shall go on holding forth.

In the poem Lauris references the confines, the expectations of what is required of her in the outer world, the codes of proper behaviour – 'lies' in the sense that formal behaviour is constructed, can never be a natural expression of the 'true' self. In the privacy of the upstairs room, however, she has the freedom of her inner world, the firefly world. She prods, rather gently, at the pomposity of the expectations of her and at her own ability to participate, to behave suitably, to deliver, to 'go on holding forth'.

It's a poem that has raised hackles. A couple of years after Lauris died, C.K. Stead published a collection of essays on New Zealand writers titled *Kin of Place*, in which he accused her of a 'false voice' in this poem. In his introduction to *99 Ways into New Zealand Poetry*, Harry Ricketts wrote:

> And one could certainly argue, as theorists and critics often
> have, that – in any kind of writing – honesty is as much a style
> as anything else and truth in any absolute sense a delusion. Yet,
> this does not quite get around the point that we do value poetry
> whose main object is to try and tell us a personal truth, and what
> persuades one reader may not persuade another.[3]

Lauris's appeal to her substantial audience was indeed her ability to write in a manner that conveyed a mutually shared and recognised 'truth'.

In the same essay on Lauris, Stead wrote:

> Lauris Edmond, for a number of reasons, including her own
> literary-political strategies which were complex and skilful,
> had a dream run as a poet. One often heard anxieties privately
> expressed in literary circles about her work but they were never
> given a public airing. The social politics of the time meant that
> anyone – and particularly any male – who dared to doubt at
> once put himself into the generalised camp of bomb-makers who
> believed that women belonged in the kitchen.

Of course, Lauris never read that essay, but in her Book Council lecture in 1999 it was clear she was familiar with the attitude:

> In the ten years after 1975, even more obviously if you make it
> 20, women's voices became in New Zealand, as they were doing
> in other older countries, the carriers of vital messages about our
> life and times. Where women's poetry had often been dismissed

as 'domestic', 'confessional', 'inward-looking', it increasingly became a true and valid reflection of real-life experience. It was also wonderfully recognisable to the reading public, though the prejudice of established male writers who felt they had territory to protect did not immediately die down. Indeed in the persons of some critics and academics it has not completely done so yet.

Elizabeth Alley believed Lauris's 'sense of authenticity and honesty' was a key to her popularity with readers:

Over some years, she transformed from being over-modest and self-deprecating, a little shy and tentative as an interviewee, to a position of certainty and clarity, and someone whose response to questions was always thoughtful and challenging. She was always able to go to the kernel of a question, frequently taking us – and her – into unexpected places, often finding that a certain line of questioning led her into paths she explored with an intensity and originality that surprised even her. Unlike some authors who sometimes felt that an interview for a new book was their right, her natural modesty, her sense of responsibility to her craft, her authentic voice and perhaps her genuine surprise at the extent of her success, made her a favourite writer for many.

14. The shadow world

In the photo on page XII a smiling Lauris, her blonde curls somewhat untidy, looks as though she's due a visit to the hairdresser. She looks tired, a little forlorn – old. She would hate me writing that word, yet, despite her efforts – indeed, despite anyone's – it's impossible to entirely conceal age. In Lauris's words, 'practising an expansive smile / at faces you've never seen that glow with recognition / and chatter about familiar occasions ('This year 1000 Americans will live to be over 100').

On 28 January 1999, a year to the day before she died, Lauris wrote to me about feeling exhausted and struggling with an excessive workload. In addition to her own writing, she was editing two anthologies: *New Zealand Love Poems* for Oxford University Press and *Essential New Zealand Poems* (with Bill Sewell) for Godwit:

> *I've actually had quite a collapse of my own over the last week or two; I've cried a lot, felt muddled and sad and exhausted, didn't want to see people … I think what has happened is that, in a quite different way from yours, last year has been catching up with me too. I had those two enormous jobs, the anthologies, never felt I got anywhere near being on top of them (and of course I'm still not), so seem to be always pushing a weight up hill.*

> *I think there's a kind of vanity in me that makes me reluctant to admit my age, or any weakness or incapacity, and when people asked me to do these big things I was so flattered I said yes to it all. I know nobody, of any age, who thinks you can reasonably do two such projects at the same time – but me? Oh yes, I could … and now I'm paying for it. At least it's a kind of relief to say to people 'I can't … leave me alone … I'm going to cry …', and they are, as everyone knows (I know you know all about this), nice about it when you do.*
>
> *Anyway, I'm trying to pace myself more realistically this year, as I know you are. A* Listener *investigation says the whole country is pushing itself too hard – are we just reflecting the times we live in?*

Lauris pacing herself more realistically did not come easily, especially as the road ahead shortened, while the amount she wanted to achieve expanded and unresolvable matters such as Rachel's death still demanded her attention. It remained an abiding focus in her writing, though it's often too simplistic to say a poem is 'about Rachel'. It's more that these poems explore the rising and falling tides that a devastating death creates in those left behind. 'Time of Silence', '3 a.m.', 'The Pear Tree', 'Wellington Letter', 'Another Christmas Morning', 'Rain in the Hills', 'Family Group' – all are poems that find their source in the death of Rachel. Lauris regarded it as essential – she required it of herself – that she write about death, about grief, with a straightforwardness – with the attitude of 'I am looking you in the eye and seeing who you are and what you intend', finding in her writing an approach, even an equanimity that she struggled to find in her day-to-day world.

'Time of Silence', '3 a.m.' and 'The Pear Tree' are geographically located in Fergusson Drive, the house from which Rachel died, the house so pervaded by her absence, her tragic death and a family's grief there was no option but to move. 'Rain in the Hills' is Lauris's testimony of how to survive without those you love, how they become part of you and how any denial or repudiation diminishes them and you. The poem captures a strange inclusiveness, an elemental connection between the living and the dead, how the one inhabits the other. Grief and loss flow through you as blood flows through your veins – without them you would yourself die. I remember those days of struggling to accept the simple reality that Rachel had died, that I would never see her again; the very air in the house, its walls, imbued with fragility and impermanence. To assume continuity, certainty, even familiarity was no longer possible; all that was gone.[1]

In the poems from *Wellington Letter*, Lauris reflects on life's transience, searches for some optimism and finds solace for her grief in Rilke:

> … in the morning mail a small
> orange-covered book, Rilke's
> requiem for his young poet – 'you
> gladly, you passionately dead' –

In her diary of 1975 Lauris wrote:

> *Rilke – I have been reading his poem about the suicide of a young poet. Alan [Roddick] wrote and said it would be good for my understanding of Rachel and indeed it does do something important – confirms my gentler feelings about her, enables me to face for the first time the harsher facts in its cataloguing of what the death has destroyed. A poem of great courage and compassion. Will I ever be able to address Rachel as honestly, with such control?*

And of Rilke, she wrote in *Wellington Letter*:

> He was my voice in the silent
> morning, he burnt my timid evasions
> as a fire in the slums destroys and
> cleanses; he took me outside
> to breathe the biting air.

In front of me as I write I have a slim, orange-covered volume of Rilke's poems, the front bearing a partial, shadowy picture of his intense eyes and moustached mouth. The requiem Lauris quotes is on page 55 and dedicated to Wolf Graf von Kalkreuth, a promising young poet and translator who shot himself at the beginning of his military service. Is it the copy that Alan Roddick sent to Lauris after Rachel died? I have many of her books but I don't know if this is one of them. It was usual for her to write her name on the inside cover of a book but the only identifying mark on this one is a faint blemish on the front cover, a ring perhaps left by a mug of hot tea. Nevertheless, I like to think the book was hers, a kind of comforting continuity as I write about her.

In the final poem in *Wellington Letter* she found an optimism, a way forward from terrible grief, by stepping back, seeing life and death, love and experience as eternally entwined, imagining herself and Rachel and indeed all of us as part of time, the earth itself, and the shifting tides of human experience and endeavour. It doesn't change anything but makes it bearable, which is all that can be hoped for out of such a tragedy.

'Family Group' is a Hawke's Bay poem, the family having gathered to celebrate Christmas on the farm in the Tukituki valley in 1985, 10 years after Rachel died, most likely the Christmas Lauris shared our family tent:

> The sun
> is hot on the hills: here by the walnut trees
> we will light a fire in the evening, eat out on the grass.
>
> Conversations bloom all about with instant colour
> like nasturtiums sown in the wind. We have all
> travelled a long way. The old jokes are heard
> in echoes and fragments, as we see forgotten summers
> in the crumpled rugs on the grass.
> And of course she is here too, the one who
> for ten years has set us the hardest lesson –
>
> to find what it is even death cannot take away ...

Despite shifting allegiances and undercurrents in family relationships, gatherings at the beautiful farm in Hawke's Bay continued to draw us together. Lauris gave a benign, maternal overview of family dynamics, hinting obliquely at conflict, making light of it, preserving in her 'art' an idea of a treasured collective family memory, a sense of unity, continuity and wisdom which, if we ever had it, we had long outgrown, individually and as a unit.

'Family Group' first appeared in *Summer Near the Arctic Circle* (1988), a couple of years before Dad died. At his death, in October 1990, she felt a kind of a shock of loss. They had come to an irreconcilable parting of the ways years before she found herself yet again searching for some kind of internal acceptance and reconciliation. 'One to One' is one of the poems she wrote:

> Love ends, as it began, in a flash.
> Lightning splits the heart, breaks root
> and trunk at a stroke and scatters
> debris everywhere. Driving across
>
> a bridge on a winter day, the water
> dark below, I came to this sheer end.
> No warning. Two unfleshed tendrils
> in the brain leapt their tragic gap …
>
>   … My loss I thought
> struck then, midway across the bridge,
> all later compromise the merest fiddle.
>
> Your death is my correction.
> It is as though you said why then
> hold on to anything – the loss
> of love is all, and lasts for ever.

Lauris wrote to Fleur a few weeks later:

> *… there was a cataclysmic event in October – Trevor died.*
> *Although he'd often been sick, and goodness knows his life*

*was a pattern of illness and alcoholism in the last few years,
his sudden death was a huge shock. Rather like the death of
my parents – and indeed I'd come to think of him in some
ways as an ailing and querulous elderly relative. But that was
before it happened. When it did I found myself really stricken;
and the turmoil of sorting out his life in relation to mine
keeps going on at high speed and temperature. There are some
good things – well, I suppose that's how one says it – for
instance that this releases me from the present and into the
enthusiasm and love and hopefulness of the earlier years ...
I have been thinking of him as a kind of tragic hero, like the
Mayor of Casterbridge or someone, a person with enormous
influence and fulfilment in his early life (I am deluged by
accolades from people who were taught, and they say,
changed by him), and a fatal flaw. As usual, ambition, and the
lack of self-knowledge that goes with it. Then the years of loss
and struggle, and, quite recently, a kind of recovery on a more
modest level of the best of himself, affectionate relationships
with his children and his community – he'd become a central
character in Greytown life; and then he died. It really fits, and
it helps me to be less tangled up with the 'could it have been
different if I ...' agonising, which I don't think is necessary
but I can't help doing.*

The Edmond family gathered in Greytown for his funeral:
daughters and son, their partners and children, Trevor's brothers
from Hamilton and friends from far away. The numerous
grandchildren found a collective and vital energy in enthusiastically
collecting flowers from all over the neighbourhood and piling them
into his open coffin till it was overflowing. I remember noticing his
ears were quite remarkably enormous, a thing I had not been aware
of when he was alive.

His death inspired many poems as Lauris worked to come to
terms with what it meant to her: the middle section of *A Matter of
Timing*, under the subtitle 'Subliminal', contains poems reflecting on
him, their relationship and his death. 'The Pace of Change' describes

the afternoon she and I visited him the day after his massive stroke, the day before he died. Lauris was staying with me in Auckland when we received news of his stroke, on the night of 19 October 1990. I had spoken to him earlier that evening, so it was unexpected. Lauris and I and my youngest child, who at 10 months old was still being breastfed, flew to Wellington the following morning. We collected her car and drove over the Remutaka Hill to Arbor House, Greytown, the retirement home where he lived. We found Dad lying on his side on the bed in his room on life support, an oxygen mask over his face as he gasped in great shuddering breaths, his body fighting for life.

Unselfconsciously, and I suppose out of curiosity, Lauris lifted the bedclothes, revealing the catheter attached to his penis, commenting that she was the only woman he had ever made love with. I was embarrassed; I did not want to see my father's genitals, and even more powerfully I did not want to be drawn into this act of intimacy between my parents.

We stayed with him a while; I held his hand, murmured words of love. The nurse explained that he was effectively brain dead and it was probably only a matter of hours before his heart and lungs gave up. My instinct was to stay. We had not stayed with Rachel as she died; here was an opportunity to atone, to be with Dad as he did. The nurse assured me sleeping arrangements could be made for us but Lauris did not want to stay. She would drive back to Wellington, return the next day. I asked her to reconsider but she was adamant. Overwhelmed by the circumstances, I gave in and left with her. The phone rang at Lauris's around 3am on Sunday morning. It was Katherine to say Dad had died.

In the poem, 'Subliminal', Dad lies in his coffin in his best suit and tie, at home in the house in Greytown he had bought but hardly lived in. He had sold his first house – 129 Main Street – because it was old and needed maintenance, and the large and lovely garden was too much for him to manage. Shortly afterwards, however, he had moved into the retirement home:

> So like him, and so cruelly unlike, this
> pale thing dressed up in the grey suit,
> white shirt, dark tie he always chose for
> funerals – presumptuous facsimile, no more ...

Having the body at home was a departure for our family –
Rachel's having lain at the funeral parlour – but times had changed.
Lauris wrote of it in a letter to Fleur:

> ... *the body [lay] in the house between its embalming and the
> funeral; none of us had any experience of this practice but of
> course agreed. And it was a revelation, I must say; some of the
> family stayed there the whole time, some, like Frances and me,
> with her baby, travelled backwards and forwards and spent the
> days there. It was very frightening at first, but by the end of
> the three days I found I'd moved through a cycle of emotional
> events that allowed me to realise the death as I never could have
> otherwise. It almost domesticated death; there he was in his
> room, and people visited him all the time, including outsiders
> and children – of whom there were a great many – and at the
> same time cups of tea and conversations and just living there
> went on all through the house. By the end, when we said
> goodbye – it was that, and very distressing in itself – we had
> all come to know, in a way I never have before, that this was
> a thing, not a person, and going into the ground was the best
> outcome for it.*

It was a strange difficult time, not just for the sadness of his
death at the relatively young age of 70, but because such events
expose complex family dynamics, reopen psychic wounds and impel
a family into an uncomfortable process of realignment. My response
was to beg my own family to stay at home where they were safe
and protected, an odd thing to have wanted. Perhaps there was an
element of wanting to do this difficult thing on my own. Facing my
father's dead body taught me, in a way that Rachel's hadn't, that it's
only death, and down that road we all must go at some time.

After Trevor's funeral we gathered at his house and his will

was read – he'd left his entire estate to Lauris, who observed with
undisguised glee, 'Now I have you all in my power!' We were all
in our various ways aghast at such a breathtakingly inappropriate
response. Some were genuinely outraged, expressing their fury in
a blunt judgement of her right to even be at Trevor's funeral, let
alone to claim a place in the life of a husband she had abandoned in
favour of a string of lovers and a life on her own terms. Obviously,
she did *not* know her place, and for that I did, and still do, admire
her. But what was she thinking? What did she expect? That we
might appreciate the irony, enjoy the witty joke – that she could still
invite us into a place of shared identity, this family she remained part
of, at the centre of even? She was profoundly mistaken, which she
understood in an instant.

There are poems about other deaths too, or impending ones: Arthur
Sewell's, Denis Glover's, one I believe is about Beeb. The number
of poems in this vein in her last two books persuade me that not
only was death a regular companion but she was increasingly aware
that her own was probably closer than was comfortable. In my
introduction to *Late Song* I wrote:

> … *I thought [the book] had a more reflective tone than some
> of her earlier work. Its contemplations of youth and age, its
> observations of the delights and painful ironies of intimate
> relationships, with their frustrations and forgivenesses, are all
> familiar subjects in Lauris's writing. However, there is a greater
> detachment here, a sense of being at one remove, as if she was
> already on the way toward that place which is 'too far for any
> remembering' ('Evening in April').*

Vincent O'Sullivan told me a story of Lauris attending Arthur's
funeral in April 1972. Apparently, she was known on the Waikato
campus as 'Arthur's girl', a curious epithet and a typically belittling
one for a woman in her middle-forties. Instead of behaving as

everyone thought she ought at his funeral – that is with the discretion of a 'mistress', with no rights, possibly not even the right to be there – Lauris brazenly sat near the front in the seating generally reserved for family. Did she know what she was doing? Vincent thought so but I'm not so sure. It has that fatally ingenuous quality she possessed of sweeping boldly into a situation without having any sense of possible opposition or opprobrium. Her view would have been that she was a 'good friend' of Arthur's, so she took her place among those close to him. Lauris often failed to anticipate the devastating consequences of her actions – another version of 'Now I have you all in my power!'.

She wrote to me:

> *It was a very good funeral (as I get older I acquire more precise standards in this matter!) – no service of any kind, just two papers read, and at the end of the second one a beautiful piece of one of Donne's sermons – about death, and a favourite of Arthur's. Then lots of people came to lunch, and after they all left Rosemary and I and a friend of hers who stayed too sat up most of the night and talked and got more or less drunk, which was a good idea.*

'Before a Funeral' is the poem she wrote about his death. She wrote in her diary:

> *Dear Arthur, how much I have to be grateful to him for – not least, the first successful published poem about the day of – or after – his death:*

> The great bright leaves have fallen
> outside your window
> they lie about
> torn by the season from
> the beggared cherry trees.
> In your room, alone,
> I fold and hide away
> absurd, unnecessary things ...

Apparently, while she was there for Arthur's funeral, Lauris slept in his bed, so 'I fold and hide away' is literally, poignantly true.

Arthur died today. As so often before, he rearranged the pattern of my life in a way that was always unexpected – even this very last time. Yesterday I got the most appealing letter from him; he had written me a long one – on bad paper and hard to decipher but as always full of challenging new directions in its thinking. I had not replied because I hadn't had time to think clearly enough about it and be ready to ask him some reasonably intelligent questions in reply – and yesterday his note in perturbation with much warmth a need for contact. How nearly I rang him yesterday – when I did try this morning (I stayed home for this) it seemed so strange that there was no reply that I kept on – and finally got Rosemary who had sent me a telegram telling me of his death earlier this morning.

I could write on and on about him – what else is there now but the residue in my mind and a hundred others? He has changed the world for me, for good – I would like to have told him but his (and even in a way my) insistence on style required that we said whatever deep and solemn things there were to say through light, or polite, or funny ones. Anyway, whether he ever knew it or not (and in fact that cannot now matter) he has given me a kind of freedom to live as myself which I will never give up, no matter what it leads me into. If love is entering into the life of another person then indeed I have loved him. What he felt for me I never tried to define and don't want to now – there were very sweet moments of happiness for us both in the meeting of deeply felt needs. I cannot imagine any experience at all like this entering my life again, but at least I now know something of the possibilities (which I would never have believed in) of the comfort of love for people who are old enough to be familiar with pain and frustration and bitterness. Being young and hopeful gives one the sparkle of love but age gives it – even if only briefly – its generosity.

Arthur died when Lauris's writing career was embryonic, while
Denis Glover, a significant contributor to its launching, died eight
years later, in 1980. I attended his funeral with her, a strange
occasion with scant reference to his life as poet and publisher, as if
those frivolities had nothing to do with true masculine pursuits. It
was a pompous, religious affair run by the navy, which lauded his
career as an officer – he received a Distinguished Service Cross for
bravery on D-Day, while in 1951, as a member of the Royal New
Zealand Naval Volunteer Reserve, he reached the rank of lieutenant
commander.

Lauris wrote of her friendship with Denis in *The Quick World*.
As the *Fairburn Letters* project was in its final stages of preparation,
she saw less of him:

> *I was too busy to go to the club. I'd heard all his stories, some
> many times; now there was nothing for it but to finish the
> wretched thing. Moreover, I had younger friends for whom I
> was not the pupil-nursemaid-admirer-secretary I sometimes felt
> I'd become in Denis' company. Yet he'd been a major liberating
> influence, and if our time for being valuable to each other was
> gone, I still felt a good deal of gratitude, and an exasperated
> tenderness for him, when we were together.*
>
> *I think I didn't realise how much he taught me of the craft of
> poetry, and the honesty and good sense one must bring to it, till
> after his death ...*

I cannot be absolutely certain but I believe her poem 'Finale'
is about him; it reads like Denis, the vital images and descriptions
evoke him and the timing would be right. It takes an altogether
different approach to the end of a life – a theatrical one with the
'character' still occupying centre stage as the lights go out one by
one.[2]

The story of Denis's death, as told me by Lauris, further
encourages me to think this poem is about him. He was infirm
from years of excessive drinking and one morning fell down some
steps at his house in Breaker Bay and broke his hip. He was taken

to hospital where he learned that recovery from such an accident could not be guaranteed and even were it possible it would be a struggle. Denis declined over the next couple of days and died of bronchopneumonia. In Lauris's version, he decided a disabled life was not for him, and 'he held his breath until he died'. It's generally considered impossible to hold one's breath and die, but Lauris assured me that's what Denis did – strength of purpose to the last ragged breath and suitably romantic enough to appeal to her.

The last of her 'grand old men' was Beeb. 'Late Dinner', first published in *Summer Near the Arctic Circle* when Beeb would have been well into his eighties, is a poem I have always found particularly evocative for the mythic scope of its landscape; the philosophical kindness set alongside vivid images reads to me as if it's about him:

> … dropped from the great beak of destiny,
> as it swooped low over the earth,
>
> oh my dear, how are we to speak of your thin
> covering, the everlasting expanse of the plain
> and the violent sky, the keening of the wind —
>
> Long as the journey was, and wonderful
> the mountains and seas, the ledges where you
> were almost devoured precarious and strange,
>
> and the silence that looms up beside you,
> look you now quietly, it is only death.

'Late Song', a passionate 'hymn' to her family, was written on the occasion of Lauris's 75th birthday. It's the last poem in the collection of that name, in the *Selected 1975–2000*, and in *Night Burns with a*

White Fire – her late song. It's also the poem I read at her funeral, just under a year later. I find it a marvellous poem, 'the tribal chorus that no one may sing alone'.

The celebration of Lauris's 75th birthday in 1999 was a family initiative and the planning quickly and predictably degenerated into tumultuous chaos, a perfect expression of typically fractured family dynamics. Lauris hadn't wanted to mark the milestone of 70, but at 75 she was willing. The idea came from my youngest sister, Katherine, in late 1998. A weekend date was suggested, to which everyone agreed except me – it was during the school term and I did not have the resources to fly. When I did the unforgiveable and asked for the date to be changed to sometime in the school holidays, I found myself in a familiar role – the difficult one, the selfish, unyielding one who tramples over everyone else's feelings due to her own over-weaning self-importance and need for attention. Faxes, letters, purple with moral judgements and insults, were hurled back and forth. Lauris shouted at me; I shouted back; my sisters remonstrated. They couldn't possibly change the date.

Lauris offered to pay our airfares, my anger and distress over the interminable infighting annulled by her generosity. She infuriated me but I loved her and it was her birthday; we flew to Wellington for her party, held at Wareham House on 2 May 1999. Despite everything, it was a great party. Family and friends came together and Lauris was generously, graciously celebrated and honoured. On the initiative of Fiona Kidman and Bridget Williams a hardback book of her poems titled *50 Poems: A Celebration* was produced for the occasion. Lauris read 'Late Song' to the assembled gathering, then one after another each family member went up to her as she stood on the stairs at Wareham House and she presented us with a signed copy of the book, a folded A4 page with 'Late Song' on it slipped inside the front cover. Later, Lauris described the occasion as like being at her own funeral and listening to all the eulogies.

On my return home I wrote to her:

I do not think as a family we know very much about simple human kindness or tolerance or forgiveness but an awful lot about judgement, about what people ought to do, not what they actually do.

She wrote back:

… about your saying that 'old stuff' between us had come up and clouded the issue. I half felt this too, and have gone on thinking about it, and believe I now see what part I probably played in that. I want to acknowledge it, in the interests of being more careful next time. When I was talking to you about that wretched date – and shouting at you – I didn't see, but I do now, that there will have been an undercurrent of my trying to pressure you to agree with me, and that's what I've done in the past, and it puts you at a disadvantage. I believed we were in the clear, that this was a disagreement between two 'free' people, but I think it wasn't; we were replaying bits of old scenes. I know how insidious old family patterns are, and I think now that this was a time when, though I hate to say it, I fell into one of them, and I'm sorry. Of course, we're both in it, I have to be watchful about not doing it, you to be independent of it.

In another letter on 26 June 1999 she wrote:

… of course, always central, is your relationship with your children, which changes, on the whole for the better because you have a fuller life, but none of it is simple. (This is the aspect of my middle-aged new growth where I performed worst, I think, I was so adolescent – as you are not – that I simply didn't see how I was for them).

I suppose I too feel this new open-ness in you, and a new maturing, as you develop and learn your own powers more and more. And, of course, as one of your friends who happens also to be your mother, I am endlessly interested in the parallels I see with my own middle years, the ones you're having now. The tribal song I talked about in that poem, I guess.

Rereading these letters brings back to me her thoughtfulness, her willingness to change and learn, alongside her unconditional support and the intimacy we shared. I would take issue with her claim about me being less adolescent than her – she's flattering me; I had plenty of growing up to do.

Drusilla Modjeska claims that we don't like our mothers because we don't want to end up like them. When her own mother died, Lauris wrote:

> *My life-long conversations with Fanny had been most fundamentally about the mysteries of people's lives, their motives, the cause and effect of every kind of behaviour ... I saw that there would never be a time when I would give up wanting to tell her whatever mattered, was funny or absurd, perplexing, frightening; she was the person in all the world it had always been best to tell.*

My thoughts exactly – a Price/Scott/Edmond legacy down through the generations. It is my mother I have always chosen as my role model, my mentor, my source.

Fleur Adcock on mothers: 'We don't appreciate them. I never valued mine, who was a fine piano player. A pinched nerve in the back ended her career and she became a piano teacher. I wish I had appreciated her more.' I have taken Fleur's words to heart.

15. 28 January 2000

Afternoon, around 4pm. I went outside, sat alone in the lovely expansive garden at Riversdale Road. That evening I was to go out to dinner with my new partner, Peter, to celebrate a year to the day since we had met. I thought of ringing Mum; I wanted to talk to her. In the morning I had been to a session with yet another counsellor, who was supposed to help me move on from the violent relationship I had escaped 18 months earlier, find some solutions to the seemingly insoluble difficulties that festered over the care of our children and the division of our shared property.

The counsellor was confrontational. 'Why don't you just buy a house of your own and get on with your own life? You have the resources.' Her frustrated impatience had the opposite effect. I didn't want to sell Riversdale Road – it was my children's home and I wanted to preserve some continuity for them out of the brutality and chaos into which the family had descended. I felt defeated, ineffective, burst into helpless tears that went on and on. I remember being aware through my distress that it was about 10.30, halfway through the session. I recall the counsellor waiting until I managed to get a grip on myself but I don't remember the rest of the session. I certainly didn't come out of it with any equanimity or sense that it had been of any benefit. I felt misunderstood, as if I were wasting her time.

These were my uncomforting thoughts that Friday afternoon as I sat in the sun. I needed my mother; it would have alleviated my distress to hear some wise and consoling words. Nevertheless, I stayed passively in the sunny garden because of the thought that followed: I had asked so much of her recently; she had given so generously of her time, her wisdom, her resources. Not only had she been a constant source of emotional support for me through the messy torment of separation, but she was even investigating finding a way to buy my ex-partner out of his share of the house, perhaps by raising a mortgage over her own. I decided I would leave her alone.

I drove to Peter's about 6.30. As we were dressing for dinner the phone rang and Peter answered. His tone immediately indicated something serious, though I had no inkling of what was to come. 'It's for you,' he said, handing me the phone. 'It's bad news – I'm sorry.' He put his arms around me as I put the receiver to my ear. It was my sister Katherine. 'I'll just tell you straight,' she said. 'Mum has died. She was found dead this evening, at home.'

My first thought was, 'Oh well, we can still go out to dinner,' some part of me believing that if one just carried on as if nothing had happened then of course it couldn't have happened.

I don't know whether I asked when or how, or if those questions came later. They came to be discussed in minute detail as we put together the fateful morning of her death. Lauris was standing at her dining-room table preparing to go out when it happened. It was instantaneous – she was dead by the time she hit the floor. Her aorta dissected, her heart broke, literally and I would say metaphorically, the accumulated grief in her life eventually taking its tragic toll. I found this in her diary: 'And sometimes I do feel the deep grief of too much disillusionment, too much lost hope.'

I knew about her heart – for some years she had had atrial fibrillation, subsequently an enlarged heart – I sometimes used to address her as 'my large-hearted mother'! That last summer she had confessed to shortness of breath and asked me for some breathing exercises. Naturally I agreed, but she died before I got around to giving her any. I hadn't realised that her shortness of breath was an indication of the seriousness of her heart condition.

We'll come tomorrow, I told my sister. Peter offered to drive. We collected my children from their father's. I remember waking about 4am and, in the dimness of an early Saturday morning, crawling out of bed, pacing the house in my dressing gown lost in grief, talking to her, begging her to come back. 'It's too soon, Mum, too soon,' I said over and over. 'How will we … how will I manage without you? Come back … please come back.'

But she was gone.

She died between one phone call and the next. Her friend Janet Wilson rang her at about 10.20am and was the last person to speak to her. The first message on her answerphone was at 10.40. Her time of death was calculated to have been around 10.30am when I was in the counsellor's room weeping copiously.[1]

It was Lynne Dovey who found her. Having dinner together was one of the things she and Lauris did regularly. Lynne left a message on Lauris's phone that morning to say she would bring dessert. The fact that Lauris hadn't replied didn't set off alarm bells; she didn't always. When Lynne arrived at Grass Street that hot summer's evening she thought it odd that all the windows were closed. Lauris had always said, 'Come in, the door's not locked', so Lynne went in and there was Lauris lying on the floor with a fallen chair beside her.

It took her a moment to realise something was terribly wrong, though she was not instantly certain Lauris was dead. She rang 111; they told her to give Lauris CPR but by then Lynne knew there was no point. She sat down beside her and, although Lauris was cold, Lynne felt she was still there so she talked to her, told her she would do what needed to be done. She rang my sister Stephanie, and though Lynne couldn't bring herself to say the words on the phone, Stephanie guessed or 'knew'. She came at once, police and ambulance arrived, and as the news spread, friends started to arrive. Lynne remembers being in shock, shaking so much she couldn't sign the forms. She needed a cup of tea to calm her down before she could.

Riemke Ensing wrote this poem about the night of her death:

A Change in the Weather

(for Lauris Edmond)

Last night the sky turned red. It seemed
to bleed. The wind got up and a storm blew
itself through the surf breaking on the beach.
Trees keened and clamoured in angst.
I thought of earthquakes, some terrible destruction,
a national calamity, and turned on the teletext.
It read you'd died just then. For a moment
everything seemed very still
then tempest raged again. All night
I worried on mortality, but drifted
off to wake to rain and clouds in mourning.
Further south, floods are closing roads.
A deepening depression is expected
across the country.

I keep her with me. I can still hear her voice, its cadence. I can hear the delighted infectious laugh that spilled out of her. For almost a year after she died, I kept a recorded message on my answerphone, the last she left, a message of love saying she would ring me in the next few days. Her voice was croaky – she was recovering from a nasty cold. At the end of 2000 I went overseas and put my reliable fax/phone (which I still have) into storage. I had assumed that when I plugged the machine in again, it would have kept its old life and there Lauris would be, still talking to me, but her message had faded away. I still grieve the loss of that last morsel of Lauris alive and active in my life.

She would be 98 this year. I wonder what kind of 98-year-old she would have been? The elderly woman across the Grass Street path made it to 93 and Lauris was determined to follow her example. Never one to admit to frailty, Lauris would undoubtedly still be hauling herself up and down the Grass Street zigzag. If she could no longer manage the hill, I know with an absolute certainty that she would have chosen the same fate as Denis and held her breath until she died.

Being her literary executor means Lauris – embodied in her work – remains a constant in my working life. More than that, there are ways I have chosen to keep her present. I imagine her as an active and crucial part of me, looking after me, watching over me, mothering me. She is often in my dreams, mostly alive though sometimes dead. In a very recent one – on the night after I finished the second draft of this book – she visited me. Suddenly she is in front of me, we are hugging each other, a close affectionate mother/ daughter hug, her cheek warm against mine, her body warm too as I embrace her, turn my head and brush my lips across her very human cheek.

Awareness penetrates that she is invisible but I can feel her substance, hold her in my arms. Friends are with me, including my old friend Kerry, and I ask them if they can see her. No, they say, wondering who I'm talking about. 'Look here, it's Mum,' I say. Kerry puts out a hand, encounters her shoulder, her breathing substance, and as he does so she emerges into visibility, a smiling living presence. Her delight kindles delight in me and we laugh with the pleasure of seeing each other, of being together. As is the way with dreams, that is all; I don't know what happens next, though I wake in the morning with the comforting sense of my mother easing through me.

I live with her still, although as an ethereal rather than material presence. She would love the house I now live in, its view over round, bush-clad hills, the peaceful valley stretching out below the house and its verdant garden. I can hear her voice in my head but, sadly, the words are ones she has already spoken. I listen but there are no new ones, only the possibilities I construct. Yet she is still inevitably, inescapably, unconditionally with me: she is my mother and I love her.

Notes

1. Somewhere you are always going home

1. St Joseph's Māori Girls' College.
2. St Joseph's has a considerable road frontage, so it could be any of a dozen houses. Moreover, in those days houses in rural districts and small towns often had no numbers; they were unnecessary – everyone, including the postie, knew who lived where.
3. Back then it was a male doctor rather than the woman, who delivered the baby: the woman was knocked out so she would not get in the way.
4. Even though my father's mother, Ada, had been a piano teacher, Dad didn't inherit any musical talent; he couldn't even sing in tune.
5. I didn't know this poem before it was offered as a selection for *Night Burns with a White Fire*. It is not included in any of Lauris's published books and has appeared only in *Print Out 11*, a literary magazine that came out in the winter of 1996.
6. I recognise the thinking because it's a piece of mother-to-daughter inheritance, though my own children confronted me with its absurdity and demanded greater rigour in the form of common sense and logic.
7. Barbara Else (ed.), *Grand Stands: New Zealand writers on being grandparents* (Auckland: Vintage, 2000).
8. Lauris went to visit a Czech writer in order to invite him to join the NZSA.
9. Barbara Else (ed.), *Grand Stands*.

2. Hawke's Bay: The Price and Scott families

1. Unlike a neighbouring family who lose a child: Billy remained in the building cleaning the blackboard as a 'first-day monitor' – the painfully confusing mystery of death arriving early in Lauris's life.
2. Her choice was admirably reinforced by economist Brian Easton, who chose this piece for *Night Burns with a White Fire*, writing: 'In her memoirs there is a stunning description by Lauris of her Napier earthquake experience. I used it in an economics book I wrote (to describe the impact of the wool price shock).'
3. Rod Edmond, *Migrations: Journeys in Time and Place* (Wellington: Bridget Williams Books, 2013).

4. Between 1871 and 1891, around 360,000 immigrants arrived in New Zealand, of whom about 154,000 stayed. Over half were English, about 21 percent were Scottish, a similar percentage were Irish, and roughly 10 percent came from continental Europe. Both my families came under Julius Vogel's scheme to develop New Zealand's economy as well as addressing a gross gender imbalance: in 1871, two-thirds of the population of Pākehā New Zealanders over 20 was male.
5. Although now entirely within the boundaries of Greater London, nineteenth-century Middlesex was at least partially rural and, along with London itself, made consistent and regular contributions to New Zealand's increasing population.
6. During most of the nineteenth century, a number of migrants to New Zealand came from northern England, especially Yorkshire and Lancashire.
7. The *Fernglen* carried several thousand British migrants to New Zealand in the 1870s and, like the *Halcione*, made only one trip to Napier.
8. This comes from a booklet Clive wrote in the late 1980s about the family's history. Unless otherwise indicated, all further quotes in this section come from this source.
9. Many of the Price family seem to have acquired this skill, myself included. Clive Price, the only one of Lauris's uncles I can recall meeting, certainly did – he rode competitively.
10. Between the two world wars of the twentieth century, Social Credit ideas of economic democracy – that production should equal consumption (to put it simply) – had reasonably wide currency because they suited the times. The perennial struggle of many writers and artists to make a living led to quite significant support for the policies from diverse literary and artistic individuals, including Charlie Chaplin, William Carlos Williams, Ezra Pound, T.S. Elliot, Aldous Huxley, Sybil Thorndyke, Hilaire Belloc, G.K. Chesterton, to name a few.

3: *Ohakune: Old roads have a life they cannot lose*

1. Dad looks cheerful enough in the photo, though the time would come when he angsted over the thought of having to pay for so many weddings. Fortunately, he didn't have to; I have never married – somewhere along the way I encountered the idea that the role of wife is the last form of slavery, and adopted it as a useful epithet for my determinedly single status. My sisters married, but they were registry office affairs or other unconventional occasions (Stephanie was married in Dad's garden at Greytown), for which he didn't have to fork out vast sums.
2. Lauris pronounced it 'Wong-guy-who'.
3. Lauris and Fanny both suffered the often painful disfigurement of varicose veins.
4. From Victoria University of Wellington, on the history of Ohakune.
5. Tutu (*Coriaria*) contains a lethal neurotoxin.

6. That was not the end of Mollie's story. Not long after her death, Peter Jenkins, our next-door neighbour and a colleague of Dad's, helped Derek Challis, a biology technician from the McGregor Biology Museum at the University of Auckland, dig up the putrefying elephant, cut off her head, take it down to the Mangawhero River and strip it of skin and flesh – 'an awful job', he said. They then packed the head in a crate lined with rimu sawdust, sprinkled bottles of perfume over to mask the stench, sealed it up and freighted it to Auckland to become a teaching exhibit about elephant dentition.
7. This poem by Leigh Hunt (1784–1859) was written in 1834.
8. One summer we had a bird table outside the sitting-room windows and on a particular evening a female possum with a baby on her back climbed up the post on which it was fixed. The scourge that possums are to New Zealand's native bush and fauna was unknown to us in the 1950s and a circle of wide-eyed faces watched fascinated as she delicately picked up bits of bread in her hands and popped them into her mouth. Many a night after that we looked for her but she never came again.
9. A black sheep banished to the colonies, or a younger son who, without an inheritance because of rules of primogeniture, was sent out to 'seek his fortune'.
10. Johnny and Elvis may have been unacceptable, but there was plenty of music that was not. We possessed a record of *My Fair Lady* with Rex Harrison and Julie Andrews in the leading roles, and an album of songs by American folksinger William Clauson, while Camille Saint-Saëns' *Carnival of the Animals* was a special favourite and, like the former two, learned by heart. We had the album *Verses* by Ogden Nash, conducted by André Kostelanetz and read by Noël Coward, which Martin and I would chant along to in our childish New Zealand accents, drowning out Coward's satirical, languid and very chic one. 'Fossils' was a particular favourite, as was 'The Swan', and one of our cats was memorialised from 'Tortoises' – Tortle, daughter of our original cat, Tigger. Much later Lauris's *Carnival of New Zealand Creatures*, set to music by Dorothy Buchanan, was loosely based on – perhaps 'inspired by' is a better phrase – the Saint-Saëns original.
11. How much acting he actually did I have no idea; he may have been involved in *Extrav*, the overtly political Victoria University capping revue of the 1930s and 40s.
12. The Lawns were family friends who, with their two daughters, Barbara and Vicky, lived in Raetihi.
13. Did 'bachelor' as euphemism for homosexual apply to Stan or was he simply a single man? When asked by us curious children why he didn't have a wife he invariably replied, 'I'm waiting for Rachel to grow up.'
14. Even in later years, when money was more reliable, if someone called collect, Trevor would pace the house, demanding that the call be concluded immediately.

4. *Dark days: 1975*

1. Fear no more the heat o' th' sun, / Nor the furious winter's rages, / Thou thy worldly task hast done, / Home art gone and ta'en thy wages. / Golden lads and girls all must, / As chimney-sweepers come to dust. / Fear no more the frown o' th' great, / Thou art past the tyrant's stroke, / Care no more to clothe and eat, / To thee the reed is as the oak: / The sceptre, learning, physic, must / All follow this and come to dust. / Fear no more the lightning-flash. / Nor th' all-dreaded thunder-stone. / Fear not slander, censure rash. / Thou hast finish'd joy and moan. / All lovers young, all lovers must / Consign to thee and come to dust. / No exorciser harm thee! / Nor no witchcraft charm thee! / Ghost unlaid forbear thee! / Nothing ill come near thee! / Quiet consummation have, / And renowned be thy grave!
2. For the earth which drinketh in the rain that cometh oft upon it, and bringeth forth herbs that are meet for them by whom it is dressed, receiveth blessing from God: / But that which beareth thorns and briars is rejected, and is nigh unto cursing; whose end is to be burned. / But, beloved, we are persuaded better things of you, and things that accompany salvation, though we thus speak. / For God is not unrighteous to forget your work and labour of love, which ye have shewed towards his name, in that ye have ministered to the saints and do minister.
3. Changing theatre as we changed the world, challenging traditional notions of what theatre was, who it was for, as well as (we hoped) making fun of the absurdities, lies and cruelties of our political masters. We performed inside and out, in theatres, on beaches, in motor camps, parks and streets, entertaining children and adults alike.

5. *The Edmond family*

1. At that time, ideas about gender roles and equality for women were largely invisible in public debate. After World War II, society was rebuilding itself and women were expected to go home and produce a generation to replace the one that had died on the battlefields of Europe and the Asia/Pacific. With six children, Lauris certainly fulfilled her duty.
2. My family is not unique of course; humorous forgiveness of the foibles of fathers is common, as is the judgement of mothers as controlling, interfering, nagging, manipulative, even cruel.
3. The year Lauris spent in Christchurch at the Speech Clinic, she lived at St Margaret's, a 'Private Educational Establishment for Young Ladies', performing supervision duties in return for free board. As a proper young lady, she learned that to ask for something to be passed at table was vulgar. If you wanted the butter, the ritual was to say to your neighbour, 'Would you like some butter?' The expected response was, 'No, thank you, would you?' 'Yes please.' And the butter would duly be passed. I suppose if someone had the pip with you and felt obstructive, they could make your dining a misery

by ensuring your dinner was butter-less. We were not obliged to perform such absurdities except as an occasional game at the table, but nevertheless, something of those values carried over into family expectations.

4. Of course, this is not just a pattern in our family – moral judgement, untempered by understanding or love, is a persistent thread in Pākehā New Zealand culture, and elsewhere as well.

5. Lauris was awarded the 1981 NZ Post Katherine Mansfield Prize (now known as the Katherine Mansfield Menton Fellowship).

6. As far as I am aware, she didn't write anything more.

6. *Daughter to mother: The wheel turns*

1. Arthur Sewell was Lauris's professor at Waikato University.

7. *Love's green darkness*

1. The poem is 'After a Funeral'.

2. 'The Third Person' has made some interesting journeys beyond New Zealand shores. A number of years after Lauris died, I received a letter from a Ukrainian poet, Hanna Yanovska, who had discovered two of Lauris's poems on the internet – 'On the Te Awamutu Road' and 'The Third Person' – and wrote asking for permission to translate then publish them in *Vseswit*, a long-established Ukrainian journal that specialises in translations of world classics and contemporary works of literature. I didn't ever receive a copy of Hanna's Ukrainian translations so whether or not they were published remains a mystery. I always liked the idea that you could find Lauris anywhere, including a literary journal in Ukraine.

3. Irina, the youngest, longs for Moscow, believing that if only she could get there, all of life's tribulations would disappear.

8. *Laughter and love at the centre*

1. 'Rachel, Baby' … *for Lauris //* I talk with you and you / track my voice back / with a tiny finger I / unhook from my lower lip. / I hold a candle to your / eyes passing it from side / to side. You look past it / to something else, beyond. // You don't notice me until / I light the candle. / The candle guts out almost / drowning until // it begins to glow inside / your eyes inviting me in. / I snuggle down level / seeing eye to eye // with you at last. But / you are not he: nor are / you me holding a candle / irradiating us. // But you are him. And I / am content. I blow out / the candle and it wicks / out smelling strongly // of smoke. I put it aside / blending into your darkness / your softness kissing you / and we're folded together / in love and darkness forever. // Yet I am so unutterably lost / my yearnings deepen: / I light the candle again // I try to be smart alec / and alert to your secret babblings / upsetting you hugely / when I get it all wrong.

2. Bruce visited Lauris in Ohakune, according to her when he was touring *The End of the Golden Weather* with the Community Arts Service, which would make it the early 1960s. The story as Bruce told it to me is that I was a baby, he picked me up, dandled me on his knee, and I responded by peeing on him. It's a good story but the timeframe is not right: by the early 1960s I would have been more than 10 years old, while my youngest sister would still have been a baby. If Lauris had the timeframe wrong and it was me, it certainly wasn't a comment on his abilities as either actor or writer! I saw him perform *End of the Golden Weather* at the James Hay Theatre in Christchurch in 1973, the summer before I attended drama school. It was a consummate piece of live storytelling – engaging, funny, moving and about us. In my years in Wellington, Bruce was playwright, reviewer, actor and pianist. In 1975 I saw him in the Downstage Christmas production of *You're a Good Man Charlie Brown*, playing (naturally) Schroeder, in Bruce's hands a languid, elegant creature. He was a fine playwright and his work should be seen much more often on our stages.
3. Bruce had recently recorded a number of his solo theatre pieces.
4. The Settlement was a café and art gallery on Willis Street.
5. Dad started consistent drinking in Huntly; there was a hard drinking culture around PPTA politics and in Rotary. By the time they moved to Heretaunga he was drinking heavily. I don't believe it was caused by Lauris but by Dad himself and who he was. He struggled with the 'authority' of being a headmaster and dealing with those beneath him who challenged him.
6. It was Beeb.
7. Fleur Adcock, review of *Night Burns with a White Fire*, eds Frances Edmond & Sue Fitchett (Wellington: Steele Roberts, 2017) in *New Zealand Books 119*, Spring 2017.

9. Wellington!

1. Fanny's commitment to the Social Credit Party didn't waver, though. As a teenager, after the 1966 election, when Vern Cracknell finally won a seat in the House (on his third attempt), I asked my grandmother why she voted Social Credit. 'Because Vern Cracknell has a nice face,' she replied. At 16 I found such levity – if that's what it was – incomprehensible; as an already committed 'communist' myself, I harboured a (fortunately unexpressed) contempt for my grandmother's blatantly girlish whimsy.
2. Anne taught speech and drama at the NZDS.
3. First Nancy Coory, the mother of Claudia, my best friend at Kuranui College; subsequently Phyllis Torpy in Hamilton, who had an affinity with both dramatic presentation and the gin bottle, though at the time I was too young and innocent to know about that. Many years later, I realised the tinkling of glass and the gurgle of liquid behind the curtain in the corner of Miss Torpy's teaching studio was Phyllis taking a sustaining gin to get her through the tedious hours of Friday night teaching. No doubt the flattened

New Zealand vowels and the agonised and awkward delivery by the young
of Hamilton and Huntly were enough to drive her to drink!
4. On Lauris's first trip overseas she visited Virginia and her husband in Kenya.
5. Private update from Bridget Williams Books, 26 March 2000.
6. The defence of 'battered women's syndrome' was first used in New Zealand
   – unsuccessfully – in 1994 in the defence of Gay Oakes, a Christchurch
   woman who murdered her husband and buried him in the back yard. She
   was convicted but released eight years later, when the Parole Board finally
   ruled her defence acceptable.
7. *Being Here* was directed by Paul Gittins and performed by Catherine
   Wilkin, Fiona Samuel and Madeleine Hyland.

10. Here and elsewhere

1. Blerta (Bruno Lawrence's Electric Revelation and Travelling Apparition) was
   a New Zealand musical and theatrical co-operative, active from 1971 until
   1975. They travelled around New Zealand in a bus.
2. Red Mole was an avant-garde New Zealand theatre company founded in
   1974 by Alan Brunton and Sally Rodwell. Known for its rough, political and
   experimental style, its productions often combined a low-life New Zealand-
   style humour and sentiment with high-art European Modernism.
3. Another visit to the Soviet Union was a lingering dream for Lauris – she
   wrote to Fleur of the possibility of their going together – but it didn't ever
   eventuate.
4. From the Department of English, Justus-Liebig-Universität, Gießen,
   Germany.
5. From the University of Wuppertal, Germany.

11. Willows and catkins

1. The new collection was *Salt from the North* (Wellington: Oxford University
   Press, 1980).

12. Becoming a writer

1. Two of his paintings graced the walls of her houses: *Tiger in a Tropical
   Storm* and *The Sleeping Gypsy*.

13. Writing her life

1. Paula Green, *Wild Honey: Reading New Zealand women's poetry*
   (Auckland: Massey University Press, 2019), p. 14.
2. Virginia Woolf tellingly wrote, 'For most of history Anonymous was a
   woman.' Only a generation before Lauris, Iris Wilkinson had chosen to

publish under the androgynous pseudonym Robin Hyde. By Lauris's time, however, women were publishing under their own names.
3. C.K. Stead, *Kin of Place: Essays on New Zealand writers* (Auckland: Auckland University Press, 2002); Harry Ricketts and Paula Green, *99 Ways into New Zealand Poetry* (Auckland: Vintage, 2010).

14. The shadow world

1. I remember guilt, too: Rachel and I had met in Cuba Street late one afternoon, a week or so before she died. She dawdled, I was impatient, snapped irritably at her. There is no atonement, no forgiveness, no way back or forward: my inhumanity in that moment will stand forever, the last personal interaction between us.
2. First appearing in *Seven* – a handmade book of seven poems, with linocuts by Jim Gorman and published by Wayzgoose Press in 1980 – this poem didn't make it into any of her other anthologies until it was chosen for *Night Burns with a White Fire.*

15. 28 January 2000

1. Did I have a sense of her going? Not consciously. Did my unconscious, the intuitive essence of me know something my conscious mind didn't? I don't think so. There have been numerous instances in my life when I have simply 'known' something, but at 10.30 that Friday morning, my conscious mind was not tuned to my intuitive one.

Ancestry and descendants of Lauris and Frances Edmond

The paternal family names adopted by wives and children until the mid twentieth century are shown in bold font. Only the first two given names of any individual are shown. Non-Edmond parents of Lauris's grandchildren are absent, as are her great grandchildren, all of whom were born after her death in 2000. *Compiled by Peter Wills.*

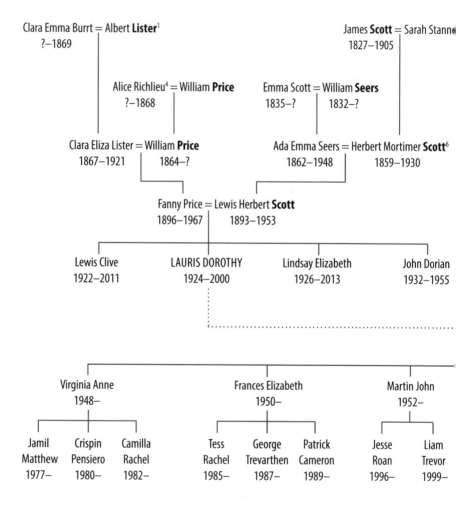

NOTES
1 Came to Aotearoa in 1874 aboard the *Halcione*
2 Given names uncertain: emigrated to Tasmania in 1857 aboard the *Prompt*
3 Landed at Port Nicholson (Wellington) in 1840 aboard the *Bolton*
4 Came to Aotearoa with second husband in 1877 aboard the *Fernglen*

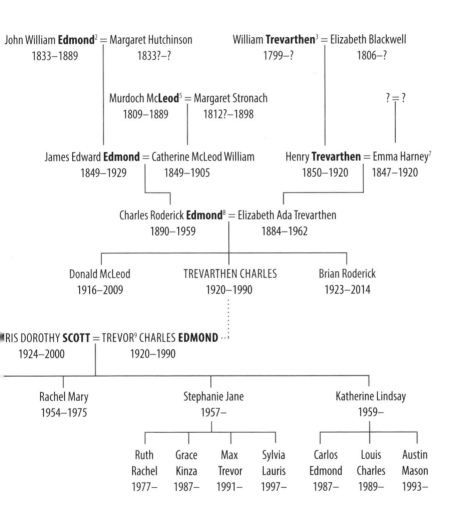

John William **Edmond**[2] = Margaret Hutchinson
1833–1889   1833?–?

William **Trevarthen**[3] = Elizabeth Blackwell
1799–?   1806–?

Murdoch Mc**Leod**[5] = Margaret Stronach
1809–1889   1812?–1898

? = ?

James Edward **Edmond** = Catherine McLeod William
1849–1929   1849–1905

Henry **Trevarthen** = Emma Harney[7]
1850–1920   1847–1920

Charles Roderick **Edmond**[8] = Elizabeth Ada Trevarthen
1890–1959   1884–1962

Donald McLeod
1916–2009

TREVARTHEN CHARLES
1920–1990

Brian Roderick
1923–2014

RIS DOROTHY **SCOTT** = TREVOR[9] **CHARLES EDMOND**
1924–2000   1920–1990

Rachel Mary
1954–1975

Stephanie Jane
1957–

Katherine Lindsay
1959–

Ruth
Rachel
1977–

Grace
Kinza
1987–

Max
Trevor
1991–

Sylvia
Lauris
1997–

Carlos
Edmond
1987–

Louis
Charles
1989–

Austin
Mason
1993–

5 Forcibly shipped to Tasmania 1853–54 aboard the *Sir Allan McNab*
6 Came to Aotearoa in 1885; Ada's mother and Herbert's father were brother and sister
7 Arrived in Aotearoa in 1863 aboard the *Gertrude*
8 Came to live in Auckland with his eldest sister, Margaret, in 1905
9 Trevor's legal given name was Trevarthen

Published by Otago University Press
Te Whare Tā o Te Wānanga o Ōtākou
533 Castle Street
Dunedin, New Zealand
university.press@otago.ac.nz
www.otago.ac.nz/press

First published 2022
Copyright © Frances Edmond
The moral rights of the author have been asserted.

ISBN 978-1-99-004843-2

Editor: Rachel Scott

Printed in China through Asia Pacific Offset.